Winner of the Jules and Frances Landry Award for 2010

CONFLICTING WORLDS

NEW DIMENSIONS OF THE AMERICAN CIVIL WAR

T. Michael Parrish, *Series Editor*

JOE B. FULTON

THE RECONSTRUCTION
OF MARK TWAIN

HOW A CONFEDERATE
BUSHWHACKER
BECAME THE
LINCOLN
OF OUR LITERATURE

LOUISIANA STATE UNIVERSITY PRESS
BATON ROUGE

Published by Louisiana State University Press
Copyright © 2010 by Louisiana State University Press
All rights reserved
Manufactured in the United States of America
FIRST PRINTING

DESIGNER: Mandy McDonald Scallan
TYPEFACE: Whitman
PRINTER: McNaughton & Gunn, Inc
BINDER: John Dekker and Sons

Library of Congress Cataloging-in-Publication Data

Fulton, Joe B., 1962–
 The reconstruction of Mark Twain : how a Confederate
bushwhacker became the Lincoln of our literature / Joe
B. Fulton.
   p. cm. — (Conflicting worlds : new dimensions of
the American Civil War)
 Includes bibliographical references and index.
 ISBN 978-0-8071-3691-1 (cloth : alk. paper) 1. Twain,
Mark, 1835–1910—Political and social views. 2. Literature and society—United States—History—19th
century. I. Title.
 PS1342.S58F853 2010
 818'.409—dc22
                                    2010004082

The paper in this book meets the guidelines for perma-
nence and durability of the Committee on Production
Guidelines for Book Longevity of the Council on Library
Resources. ∞

For Hallie
and Our Children
Rory, Felicity, Alder, and Fiona

Ab urbe condita

CONTENTS

PREFACE

"A House divided against itself cannot stand." I believe this government cannot endure, permanently half *slave* and half *free*. I do not expect the Union to be *dissolved*—I do not expect the house to *fall*—but I *do* expect it will cease to be divided. It will become *all* one thing, or *all* the other.

—ABRAHAM LINCOLN, June 16, 1858

Out West there was a good deal of confusion in men's minds during the first months of the great trouble—a good deal of unsettledness, of leaning first this way, then that, then the other way. It was hard for us to get our bearings.

—MARK TWAIN, December 1885

Nowhere was Abraham Lincoln's "House Divided" speech so apt as in Missouri, separated from the free soil of Illinois by the permeable barrier of the Mississippi River. Samuel Langhorne Clemens was born in 1835 in that border state of Missouri, a state that played a central role in antebellum politics. Debate over the legislation that brought Missouri into the Union, the Missouri Compromise (1820–1821), was so divisive that former President Thomas Jefferson wrote that it rang a warning "like a fire-bell in the night." Geography, political and natural, placed Missouri at the center of the national slavery debate with such legislation as the Wilmot Proviso (1846), the Fugitive Slave Act (1850), and the Kansas–Nebraska Act (1854). Even the Supreme Court decision in *Dred Scott v. Sandford* (1857) hinged on the question of citizenship, with Chief Justice Roger B. Taney writing for the majority that "Dred Scott was not a citizen of Missouri within the meaning of the Constitution of the United States." The house was truly divided against itself in Missouri, the northernmost frontier of American slavery.[1]

"United we stand, divided we fall" was engraved on the state seal and emblazoned on the state flag, but to some it seemed a perverse choice. Sam Clemens called it "a misleading motto altogether." Missourians like Clemens lived amid all the contradictions of slavery in a country that proclaimed in its Declaration of Independence, "We hold these truths to be self-evident; that all men are created equal." As citizens of a border state, Missourians were confronted always by the contradiction, and so the divisiveness was more than sectional; it was social and psychological. Bounded by free states (Illinois and Iowa) and the contested territory of Kansas, Missouri exemplified the "House Divided," its very existence as a state the result of a divided House of Representatives. Little wonder that when the war came, as Sam Clemens wrote, "there was a good deal of confusion in men's minds during the first months of the great trouble—a good deal of unsettledness, of leaning first this way, then that, then the other way." Sam Clemens wavered, too. He later became famous as the writer Mark Twain, author of such classics as *The Adventures of Tom Sawyer* (1876) and *Adventures of Huckleberry Finn* (1885), the latter book telling the inspirational story of Huck Finn, a young boy who heroically defied social mores to help the runaway slave Jim escape to freedom. In part because of this work, when Clemens died in 1910, the American *littérateur* William Dean Howells crowned him the "Lincoln of our literature." That was in the future, however, for while Sam Clemens was growing up in a slaveholding family in a slaveholding borderland, he detested Yankees, free African Americans, and abolitionists with equal vehemence. Like the slaveholding South he was raised in, Sam Clemens experienced a postwar reconstruction. What Mark Twain became, we partly know, but mystery has long shrouded what he was before and how he arrived at a personal reconstruction. Soon after the Civil War erupted, Clemens enlisted in the Confederate irregulars and experienced "two weeks' service in the field" before deserting. His actions and attitudes before the war gave no hint that decades later our foremost literary arbiter would laud him as the "Lincoln of our literature."[2]

Clemens was very much a part of southern slave culture and for some time made common cause with the Confederacy. Most scholars and biographers have whitewashed those biographical facts, suggesting the author's devotion to the Confederacy had always been lukewarm or even nonexistent. Scholarship has thus accelerated Clemens's reconstruction, effacing the process in a rush to confer the mantle of the "Lincoln of our literature." The hasty assertion that all was well with Twain smacks of the indecent haste with which in 1876 America also maintained that all was well in the southern states, thus ending Reconstruction long before its work was completed. With Twain scholarship, too, there has been a pronounced effort to reassure the world that America's favorite writer was at heart all along really a Democrat—or, more historically accurate in the context of the Civil War and Reconstruction, a Republican. Certainly, by the time Clemens wrote *Adventures of Huckleberry Finn,* a satire of the Missouri Compromise, the Fugitive Slave Act, and the *Dred Scott* decision, or *The Tragedy of Pudd'nhead Wilson* (1894), a satire of Jim Crow laws and the notion that "one drop" of "black blood" made one legally a black, he was indeed on the right side of history. Others have put the date far earlier, even as early as mid-1861, when Sam Clemens was suddenly, magically reconstructed. The reconstruction of the South was a process rather than an event, and so it was with Sam Clemens. That process, far from being brief and painless, spanned decades and was quite traumatic, as apostasy to the gods of one's youth must always be. The present study is not biography per se, but an analysis of the writing Clemens produced during the years leading up to the Civil War, the war years themselves, and Reconstruction. These works reveal the reconstruction of Mark Twain, a personal reconstruction that paralleled and responded to what transpired on American battlefields and in American politics. Sam Clemens traveled an arduous path from secession to union, from proslavery Confederate bushwhacker to Mark Twain, the "Lincoln of our literature." This is the story of that journey.

Before that trek progresses any further, however, I wish to thank those who have helped me along the way, both professionally and personally. A great many of the texts discussed in this book have never been collected and republished. Some exist in archives, some are located in files of newspapers at libraries, and still others survive only as fragments. Sam Clemens burned copies of his western writings on several occasions in an effort to hide his juvenilia, both authorial and political. Consequently, Twain's reconstruction is also a reconstruction of texts he wrote during and after the Civil War. Finding them has truly been the work of many hands, of Twain scholars of the past who accomplished pioneering work, figures such as Edgar M. Branch, Henry Nash Smith, and Dixon Wecter, to the more recent electronic scholarship of Barbara Schmidt, who has done much to make many newspaper sources truly available. The assistance of archivists has been especially important for this study. I would like to thank Anita Tufts at the Confederate Research Center of the Texas History Museum at Hill College in Hillsboro, Texas, who aided in the research of many figures from Mark Twain's band of Confederate irregulars in Missouri. A research visit to Hannibal, Missouri, was valuable as well, and I would like to express my gratitude to Curator Henry Sweets, for his cordial reception of a fellow Twainian. For her excellent research and kind assistance with Twain's writings during Reconstruction, I am most grateful to M'Lissa Y. Kesterman, reference librarian at the Cincinnati Historical Society Library. Likewise, I am deeply appreciative for the help of Dean M. Rogers, special collections assistant at the Vassar College Library. Neda Salem of the Mark Twain Project at the University of California at Berkeley has assisted with numerous requests, both during a research visit to the Bancroft Library and also many times via long distance. A research visit to Reno, Carson City, and Virginia City, Nevada, was most illuminating. The staff at the Nevada State Library and Archives was very helpful and have my gratitude, as does State Archivist Guy Louis Rocha.

Closer to home, I owe a tremendous debt of gratitude to Dr. T. Michael Parrish, the Linden G. Bowers Professor of American History at Baylor University, who encouraged me to look beyond the series of articles I had envisioned and reconstruct the concept as a book. He was absolutely correct, and I am grateful for the suggestion. Were it not for the professionalism and good humor of our departmental secretaries Mrs. Lois Avey and Mrs. Julie Sherrod, the days would seem twice as long and would be half as productive. I would also like to express my gratitude to Dr. Dianna Vitanza, chair of the Department of English; to Dr. Larry Lyon, dean of the Graduate School; and to Dr. Lee Nordt, dean of the College of Arts and Sciences, for travel funding, leave time, and moral support. Graduate research assistants Alisha Barker and Mandy Nydegger performed countless hours of library research, tracking down obscure references, locating and ordering microfilm, and performing a myriad of other details too numerous to mention; they have my heartfelt appreciation. Rita Patteson of Baylor's Armstrong Browning Library provided the illustrations from original copies of Twain's *Following the Equator* and "The Private History of a Campaign that Failed." Digital images of these illustrations are provided courtesy of the Baylor University libraries. Baylor University and the Lilly Foundation provided release time, travel assistance, and material support. I am especially grateful for the Baylor Horizons grant that funded a research trip to the Mark Twain Papers at the University of California at Berkeley; a University Research Council grant that funded a research trip to Hannibal, Missouri; and the Centennial Professorship that provided funding for a research trip to Nevada. This study has benefited from my several visits to the Center for Mark Twain Studies at Elmira College, and I am most grateful to my friends Gretchen Sharlow, Barbara Snedecor, Michael Kiskis, and Mark Woodhouse for their hospitality.

Among Mark Twain scholars, I would especially like to thank Alan Gribben, J. R. LeMaster, Michael Kiskis, and the late Hamlin Hill for their support and encouragement. I am always happy to have the chance to acknowledge my mentor Leland S. Person, whose delight in American literature still inspires me. Civil War buff, fellow Twainian, and childhood friend State Representative Matthew Lehman (Republican, Indiana) also had a hand in this study from the very beginning. Many years ago, he commented that it was odd that William Dean Howells referred to Twain as the "Lincoln of our literature," since the writer had actually written very little about Lincoln. His comment stuck with me, needling me to comprehend in what ways Howells's comment might have been apropos.

"In the South," Mark Twain observed in *Life on the Mississippi*, "the war is what A. D. is elsewhere: they date from it." Everything is "since the waw; or du'in' the waw; or befo' the waw; or right aftah the waw; or 'bout two yeahs or five yeahs or ten yeahs befo' the waw or aftah the waw."[3] With the Romans, the founding of the city of Rome was the time from which everything was dated. Instead of "befo' the waw" or even A.D., they used the expression *ab urbe condita*, from the founding of the city. It is to those who have been there from the very beginning that I now thank: my siblings, Susan, John, Jane, and Jim; my parents, Blaine and Phyllis Fulton; and to my own branch of the family, "the Tribe of Joseph," as we are sometimes called. I seem to have known my wife, Hallie, from the very beginning, recognizing in her a true friend from our first meeting. Our children, Rory, Felicity, Alder, and Fiona, have brought great joy into our lives. As I reflect on my own parents and siblings and their importance in my life, I hope, too, that one day my children will look back and think of their parents and siblings as having been present *ab urbe condita*, from the very beginning— and along every step of the way.

THE RECONSTRUCTION OF MARK TWAIN

"THE KILLING OF STRANGERS"

Mark Twain's Missouri and the Civil War, 1835–1861

And it seemed an epitome of war; that all war must be just that—the killing of
strangers against whom you feel no personal animosity.
—MARK TWAIN, December 1885

Civil war! Dey ain' no sich war. De idear!—people dat's good en kind en polite en
b'long to de church a-marchin' out en slashin' en choppin' en cussin' en shootin' one
another—lan', I knowed dey warn't no sich thing.
—MARK TWAIN C. 1897

[H]e was the most desouthernized southerner I ever met.
—WILLIAM DEAN HOWELLS, 1910

GUIDING A FLATBOAT OF HOGS between the sandbars and
grassy islands of the Sangamon River, Abraham Lincoln, the future
sixteenth president of the United States of America, watched first
for the confluence with the Illinois River and then for the dramatic
moment when that tributary rushes into the mighty Mississippi
River. Arriving downriver in New Orleans in May 1831, Lincoln was struck
for the first time by slavery as something other than the political abstrac-
tions of constitutional law and states' rights. Instead of hearing politicians
parsing the theoretical grammar of slavery, here the stark reality of the
slave markets shocked Lincoln with revelatory force. In New Orleans,
Lincoln witnessed, as his cousin John Hanks recalled, "negroes chained,

maltreated, whipped, and scourged . . . I can say, knowing it, that it was on this trip that he formed his opinion of slavery. It run its iron in him then and there, May, 1831. I have heard him say so often."[1]

Four years after Lincoln's journey into the heart of the slaveholding South, Samuel Langhorne Clemens, the future Mark Twain, was born. In later years, many would compare Clemens and Lincoln: westerners from border states, they were masters of the American dialectal style and champions of human liberty. In 1897, Charles Miner Thompson noted the "kinship" between the politician and the author: "But in spite of the lack of polish Lincoln was great: may not Mark Twain, the writer, in spite of his crude literary manners, be great, also?" T. M. Parrott compared Clemens to both Lincoln and Ulysses S. Grant: "And like these great Americans— both it may be noted, representatives of his own section—Mark Twain has devoted his great powers to the service of the right." In 1910, the comic writer George Ade discussed how Americans "cherished a private affection" for Clemens and so called him "Mark" or "Sam," just as "Abraham Lincoln was simply 'Abe' to every soldier boy." For leading author and influential editor of the *Atlantic Monthly* (1871–1881) and *Harper's Monthly Magazine* (1900–1920) William Dean Howells, it was partly the writer's language, his use of the "Abraham Lincolnian word," that justified the comparison. But it was more than that. Most memorably, in 1910, Howells eulogized his friend as "the most desouthernized Southerner I ever knew. No man more perfectly sensed, and more entirely abhorred, slavery." Howells proceeded to his famous conclusion:

> Next I saw him dead, lying in his coffin amidst those flowers with which we garland our despair in that pitiless hour. After the voice of his old friend Twichell had been lifted in the prayer, which it wailed through in broken-hearted supplication, I looked a moment at the face I knew so well; and it was patient with the patience I had so often seen in it: something of a puzzle, a great silent dignity, an as- sent to what must be, from the depths of a nature whose tragical seriousness broke in the laughter which the unwise took for the whole of him. Emerson, Longfellow, Lowell, Holmes—I knew them all and all the rest of our sages, poets, seers, critics, humorists; they were like one another and like other literary men; but Clemens was sole, incomparable, the Lincoln of our literature.

The connection writers like Howells, Parrot, Ade, and Thompson claimed between Clemens and Lincoln, while "fantastical enough," as Thompson confessed, made sense in many respects. Rough, unpolished, larger than life figures, they were liberators, each in his own way. Both were born in slave states and grew up in humble, at times straitened, circumstances. Historian Orville Vernon Burton has observed that some early Republicans distrusted Lincoln because of his southern heritage, citing the example of Senator Benjamin Wade, a leading figure from the party's Ohio delegation. Wade derided Lincoln's southern background and even referred to the future president as "born of 'poor white trash.'" Both Lincoln and Twain became reconstructed southerners. Lincoln touched the American soul with his rough-hewn eloquence drawn straight from the folk and freed the slaves; Clemens liberated American prose from its staid demeanor and stuffy language, even as he championed freedom in society by attacking the country's vestigial racism. As Howells put it in 1901, Clemens wielded "a comic force . . . united with as potent an ethic sense of the duties, public and private, which no man denies in himself without being false to other men." Clemens, as Mark Twain, became a public figure who called society to live up to the ideals of Lincoln. That was not where he began, however. Before he became the "Lincoln of our literature," Sam Clemens had to liberate himself from much of his early training.[2]

Like Lincoln, Sam Clemens embarked on a trip that reveals much about his later career, but it was a trip that complicates any simple comparison between the two men. On August 19, 1853, at the age of seventeen, Clemens left Missouri for New York City, concealing the fact from his mother. He was going to the metropolis to experience the Crystal Palace Exhibition and the World's Fair. "I arrived in New York," he recalled in later years, "with two or three dollars in pocket change and a ten-dollar bank bill concealed in the lining of my coat." His accommodations were "villainous," and he dismissed the event itself as "a little World's Fair" His reaction at the time was yet more negative. The fair exhibited such delights as a hall of flags from many nations, an exhibition of new machinery, and the Latting Observatory, located next to the fairgrounds. While Clemens found the Crystal Palace "a perfect fairy palace—beautiful beyond description," what struck the young man most was a horrifying vision of racial intermingling. Sam Clemens went to the city for spectacle in the Crystal Palace but found the spectacle on the streets. He wrote with revulsion of strolling the avenues and seeing "Niggers, mulattoes, quadroons, Chinese, and some the Lord no doubt originally intended to be white, but the dirt on whose faces leaves one uncertain as to that fact." Collectively, they were "human vermin."[3]

These attitudes were drawn from the aristocratic, slaveholding South, particularly Virginia. The inhabitants of Hannibal, Missouri, as Clemens recorded, "had come from slave States and still had the institution of slavery with them in their new home." Even his mother, a famously kind-hearted woman, "was not conscious that slavery was a bald, grotesque and unwarrantable usurpation." Neither did his father suffer qualms. "At first my father owned slaves," Clemens admitted in his autobiography, "but by and by he sold them and hired others by the year from the farmers." Judge John Marshall Clemens sold one of those slaves in January 1842, when Sam was six years old, for "ten barrels of tar." Sam's uncle, John Quarles, at whose farm he spent many happy times, possessed numerous slaves. Sam's contact with them was comfortable, informal, and—so it seemed to him—friendly. The citizens of Hannibal "had never heard it [slavery] assailed in any pulpit, but had heard it defended and sanctified in a thousand." Clemens summed up the attitudes in his little town on the Mississippi by stating that "slavery was right, righteous, sacred."[4]

Such attitudes were deeply ingrained, making Twain's reconstruction a protracted one. It was not a "desouthernization," as Howells asserted, but rather an embracing of racial justice that went contrary to his upbringing. As literary scholar Hal Bush has rightly stated, Clemens experienced "a fairly radical 'conversion' regarding relations with black Americans." That conversion was likewise an apostasy, and began in earnest as Sam Clemens saw the "right, righteous, sacred" beliefs of white supremacy assailed by the Civil War. The destruction of those most revered beliefs was a cataclysm that instilled in the writer a skepticism toward *all* of the grand ideas advocated by later preachers and politicians. The experience of defeat creates an inherent duality in one's perception of the meaning of history and its unfolding in contemporary events. Discussing the condition of being vanquished, historian Reinhart Koselleck has claimed that figures such as Thucydides, Polybius, and Augustine derived their views of the world from political and social defeat: "The skeptical attitude that forced itself upon them became a method." Koselleck's own awareness stemmed from the perspective of German defeat in the World Wars and his own role as a participant in that defeat. What happens when a society's beliefs, such as National Socialism (Nazism), are shown by history not to have been "right, righteous, sacred," but to have been wrong, immoral, and profane? The reconstruction of Mark Twain involved the defeat of southern ideology and the abolition of its "right, righteous, sacred" beliefs, among them, slavery. Forever after, Clemens viewed politics cynically, as the experience of defeat exacerbated the inherent skepticism of the "Show Me State." Reflecting from the perspective of years, Clemens was disturbed to find childhood memories marred by an awareness of the gulf separating him from his slave playmates in Hannibal and on the nearby Quarles Farm: "We were comrades and yet not comrades; color and condition interposed a subtle line which both parties were conscious of and which rendered complete fusion impossible." It is sometimes claimed that contact with African Americans changed Clemens's attitudes. Perhaps that was true in later years, as Clemens and former slaves shared a history. Contact with slaves during childhood, however, indoctrinated Sam every day into the values of white supremacy. Such contact did nothing to change his racist ideas, but did everything to form and reinforce them.[5]

Neither did the contact with free blacks in the North awaken Sam to the possibilities of a more democratic society. He traveled by steamboat and rail, but landed in the North as one would on an alien world. In his first letter home, dated August 24, 1853, Sam wrote of seeing the courthouse in Syracuse, New York: "The trip, however, was a very pleasant one. Rochester, famous on account of the 'Spirit Rappings' was of course interesting; and when I saw the Court House in Syracuse, it called to mind the time when it was surrounded with chains and companies of soldiers, to prevent the rescue of McReynolds' nigger, by the infernal abolitionists. I reckon I had better black my face, for in these Eastern States niggers are considerably better than white people." Clemens had something of a personal interest in this case that tested the Fugitive Slave Act, for it was a case that demonstrated again the centrality of Missouri to antebellum politics. Just as the *Dred Scott* decision was based on Missouri law, the McReynolds referred to was a Hannibal, Missouri landowner whose slave, Jerry, had escaped slave territory to freedom in Syracuse, New York. Adopting the name Henry, he lived and worked in Syracuse for the better part of a decade before being recognized by a Missourian, who then informed John McReynolds of the fact. Henry's former owner dispatched agents to Syracuse to recapture the escaped slave, calling on local law enforcement for assistance. Henry was taken into custody, but outraged citizens stormed the courthouse and freed the man. The case became a cause célèbre and an early test of the Fugitive Slave Act.[6]

Passed by Congress in 1850, the Fugitive Slave Act strengthened the Fugitive Slave Laws of 1793, which had been weakened by the Supreme Court case of *Prigg v. Pennsylvania* (1842). That case had interpreted the 1793 laws as directing *only* federal authorities to assist in the capture and return of fugitive slaves, while concluding that state officials "may, if they choose, exercise that authority, unless prohibited by state legislation." The Fugitive Slave Act of 1850, by contrast, *required* public officials as well as private individuals in the North to assist in the capture of fugitive slaves. Those harboring an escaped slave could be fined $1,000, held liable for damages of $1,000 per slave, and were subject to imprisonment for six months. Federal authorities targeted Boston and Syracuse as test cases, for the cities were home to notable figures in the abolition movement— Samuel J. May and Gerrit Smith in the former and Wendell Phillips and William Lloyd Garrison in the latter. Frederick Douglass derided the visits to Syracuse by Secretary of State Daniel Webster and President Millard Fillmore, during which they alternately wheedled and threatened citizens while "preaching the new gospel of slave-catching." Despite such efforts at cajoling and coercing (and in part because of them), the Fugitive Slave Act of 1850 radicalized attitudes in the North. As Ulysses S. Grant wrote in his memoirs, northerners had been indifferent to the issue of slavery until the new laws took effect, but "they were not willing to play the rôle of police for the South in the protection of this particular institution." Even those who usually eschewed politics became radicals. "The last year has forced us all into politics," proclaimed Ralph Waldo Emerson to the citizens of Concord. Exhorting the audience, he declared that the law "must be disobeyed." As historian Walter A. McDougall has rightly noted, the Fugitive Slave Act might have "passed into history as the great Compromise of 1850 that appeased advocates of states' rights, extinguished the burning issues of the day, and gave the republic a new lease on life," but in reality "it *assaulted* states' rights, and it *fanned* the flames of disunion." In the North, abolitionism, prior to the Fugitive Slave Act of 1850, involved a tiny minority of zealots; afterward, its influence increased dramatically when such eminent figures as Emerson publicly embraced it.[7]

The northernmost slave state, Missouri shared long borders with Iowa; Kansas, which entered the Union as a free state in 1861; and Illinois, with which it shared the permeable barrier of the Mississippi River. "By design," as journalist Terrell Dempsey has succinctly phrased it, "Missouri was a peninsula of slavery in free territory." Political geography forced Missourians into politics long before the passage of the Fugitive Slave Act of 1850. Suspicions abounded that abolitionists were slipping into the state and ferrying slaves across the river to freedom. "It is our opinion," wrote one Hannibal journalist, "that the emissaries of negro-stealing societies are prowling about the country, exciting the slave population to insubordination, and enticing them away from their masters . . . Several stampedes among the negroes have taken place recently in this vicinity." Slaves being a property like cattle, owners feared such "stampedes," but they had other fears, too. Losing a valuable slave was one thing, but facing possible violence was another. In the article, "Abolitionist Incendiaries," the *Missouri Courier* told of an incident in which an "abolitionist peddler" attempted to convince a slave to commit "some outrage." The paper failed to specify the outrage, but it noted ominously the occurrence of "many revolting barbarities committed by negros of late." Hannibal papers of the 1840s and early 1850s included sensational reports of bands of escaped slaves traveling with knives and guns committing rape and murder. In his recollections of childhood, "Villagers of 1840–3," Clemens recalled the case of a slave known as "Glasscock's Ned," who was arrested for having "raped and murdered a girl of 13 in the woods. He confessed to forcing 3 young women in Va, and was brought away in a feather bed to save his life—which was a valuable property." The slave, that is, had escaped punishment for the earlier rapes in Virginia because the owner, not wanting to lose the slave's value, smuggled him into Missouri. The slave was hanged on January 11, 1850. Scholar Dixon Wecter has noted that the slave's "confession at the foot of the gallows was printed as a pamphlet" by Joseph Ament, publisher of the *Missouri Courier*, where Sam Clemens, then fourteen, worked as a typesetter. Young Sam may himself have set the type for the confession. The same paper chronicled the lynchings that typically followed charges of rape or murder by slaves, including one example when the accused slave, "a demon in human shape," was caught up by a lynch mob and "*burned at the stake.*"[8]

For those in Missouri, abolitionists were subversive traitors of the most dangerous sort. "[A]ll you had to do was to slip up behind a man and say Ablitionist," Clemens wryly commented, "if you wanted to see him jump, and see the cold sweat come." His father, Judge Clemens, sat on the jury that sent three such "ablitionists" to the state penitentiary for twelve-year sentences. The great weapon against such militant northern extremists, as southerners viewed them, was the Fugitive Slave Act, which would force northerners to honor the rights of slave owners or be punished for failing to do so. The legislation was, quite simply, the law of the land that attempted to coerce northerners to acknowledge the property rights seen by southerners as guaranteed by the Constitution. When Sam Clemens recalled the courthouse in Syracuse "surrounded with chains and companies of soldiers, to prevent the rescue of McReynolds' nigger, by the infernal abolitionists," he voiced the popular outrage in Missouri that federal law was not protecting their rights, even while foreshadowing Huck's fear in *Adventures of Huckleberry Finn* (1885) that he might be labeled "a low-down ablitionist" for not handing over Jim, Miss Watson's escaped slave. In issues of the Hannibal papers of the time, some of which Sam Clemens himself may have set the type for, the very titles hectored readers: "Another Abolition Riot— Rights of a Missourian Outraged," "Mob at Syracuse," and "The Syracuse Outrage." In white-hot prose, the paper recounted how the Syracuse mob, which shattered the windows of the courthouse before breaking down the doors, was not hindered by city officials. Citizens, law enforcement, and local government in the North had defied the new laws governing fugitive slaves. "Slaveholders may now set it down as an established fact," the paper complained bitterly, "that their chance of recovering a fugitive slave is almost as good in Canada, a foreign country, as in the Northern states of this Union." From the opposite side of the issue, Frederick Douglass agreed, asserting that "the rescue of Jerry did most to bring the fugitive slave bill into contempt and to defeat its execution everywhere." The house was so divided that the North seemed an alien land to Clemens, a feeling evident as well in works written long after the author's reconstruction.[9]

Clemens's letter criticizing the "infernal abolitionists" for their rescue of "McReynolds' nigger" was written ostensibly to his mother, but his brother Orion published it in the *Hannibal Journal*. Sam likely knew the letter would be published, for the tone fit other letters he had written for publication. It resembled his 1854 letter to the *Muscatine Journal*, in which he reported a visit to Washington and lamented that the Senate Chamber had fallen from its earlier days. "Its glory hath departed. Its halls no longer echo the words of a Clay, or Webster, or Calhoun." Henry Clay and John C. Calhoun were southerners, while Daniel Webster was a senator from Massachusetts and secretary of state in the Fillmore administration. Together, the three had been involved in most of the great debates over slavery from the Missouri Compromise to the debates leading up to the Fugitive Slave Act. Calhoun died on March 31, 1850; Clay died on June 27, 1852; and Webster died on October 25, 1852. The "glory" that vanished with the death of these three senators involved the commitment to secure the Union by guaranteeing the states' rights coveted by the South. Webster devoted his entire influence and reputation to passing the Fugitive Slave Act, an astonishing *volte-face* that infuriated northerners. "At last, at a fatal hour," lamented Ralph Waldo Emerson, Webster "crossed the line, and became the head of the slavery party in this country." In the South, Webster occupied a prominent place in a pantheon of statesmen that included Clay and Calhoun. By contrast, Clemens disparaged Senator Stephen A. Douglas, who looked "like a lawyer's clerk," and as for the hated abolitionist Senator William H. Seward, it looked "like a respectable wind would blow him out of the country." Many in Missouri wished for such a wind. By contrast, the senator from Missouri, Thomas Hart Benton, repined "silent and gloomy in the midst of the din, like a lion imprisoned in a cage of monkeys, who, feeling his superiority, disdains to notice their chattering." These letters were prototypes of the *Alta California* letters Clemens wrote on his trips to New York, Nicaragua, Europe, and the Holy Land in 1866–1867 as well as his letters written as a Washington correspondent during the Reconstruction and Impeachment crises of 1867–1868. The few scholars who have commented on the racist attitudes reflected in the letter from his 1853 visit have dismissed them, suggesting that the writer's attitudes changed rapidly, practically overnight. "The attitude Clemens exhibits here—hardly unusual for a seventeen-year-old white Southerner on his first visit to the North—would change radically by 1861," scholar Edgar Branch has contended. The true process was considerably more complex. Later, in 1867, with his personal reconstruction well underway, Clemens wrote again from New York City: "I have seen negroes sitting stuck up comfortably in a car, and lovely young white ladies standing up before them, block after block, clinging to the leather supports that depended from the roof. And then I wanted a contraband for breakfast." A "contraband" referred to a slave who had escaped behind Union lines and so was declared "contraband of war." As Secretary of War Edwin M. Stanton put it in his 1861 directive, former masters disloyal to the Union had "no claim" on their property. By using the term "contraband," Clemens suggested that the blacks sitting on the streetcars really did not belong in the North, but rather back "home" on southern plantations. Clemens's attitudes toward race relations did not change overnight.[10]

While Abraham Lincoln's trip to New Orleans looms large in American history as a conversion moment in the life of the future president, Sam Clemens's trip to New York City makes one wonder precisely when the future Mark Twain became the "Lincoln of our literature." It certainly was not on that 1853 trip to America's most diverse city. That Clemens underwent such a reconstruction is not in doubt; rather, the nature and timing of the conversion are open questions. Given his political opinions prior to the Civil War, his racist views of immigrants, and his belief that "slavery was right, righteous, sacred," there can be no doubt where his sympathies lay in the years leading up to the war. After his 1831 trip to New Orleans, Lincoln went on to become a lawyer, a volunteer in the Blackhawk War, and a local and state politico. He played an important role in the founding of the Republican Party, opposed the westward spread of slavery, and as president preserved the Union and freed the slaves. Meanwhile, Sam Clemens retreated from what he had seen in New York and embraced reactionary politics. Indeed, throughout the 1850s, he flirted with nativism and the Know-Nothing Party. When Fort Sumter was fired on, thousands of patriotic southerners enlisted in the Confederate cause. Sam Clemens was one of them.[11]

Samuel Langhorne Clemens, like most people living in border states like Missouri, had mixed feelings about secession, slavery, and the Civil War. During the war's first month in the spring of 1861, the border states Virginia, Tennessee, North Carolina, and neighboring Arkansas voted to secede. A bill of secession promoted by Missouri Governor Claiborne Jackson prior to the shelling of Fort Sumter had failed, but that hardly indicated support for the Washington government's policy. With wide popular support, Governor Jackson refused Washington's request for four thousand soldiers, instead demanding that the state's neutrality be honored. "As long as there was a sectional fence to straddle prior to 1861," historian Michael Fellman has stated, "most Missourians kept their perch on it." After Fort Sumter, that precarious perch became a target, and the situation in Missouri remained unstable throughout the war. As many southerners rushed to enlist in the Confederate Army, Sam Clemens vacillated. Events pressured him to decide. In April 1861, the Union Navy established a blockade at the city of

Memphis for the purpose of establishing military control of river traffic. The reason was clear. "Who held the Mississippi would hold the country by the heart," as General John C. Frémont put it. In April 1861, Sam was a pilot serving under Captain David De Haven, an ardent secessionist. Rather than go north from New Orleans, De Haven piloted his boat the *Alonzo Child* to Memphis. In later years, Sam wrote of seeing the "bars put up at Memphis" blocking river traffic. His telegraphic notebook entry captured the excitement of experiencing the historic moment on the decks of the *Alonzo Child:* "Heard of firing on Fort Sumter April 18—at Vicksburg on way down (the day after it happened.) We hoisted stars & bars & played Dixie."

On December 10, 1889, Sam's childhood friend Will Bowen, memorialized in *The Adventures of Tom Sawyer* (1876) as Joe Harper, reminded Sam of this event. What sparked Will's memory and the letter was the death four days before of Jefferson Davis, president of the Confederate States of America.

> He was a Union man—from clearheadedness & sense of right & with his great Patriot heart—named as President to secure his service & brains & thus swept into the mighty tide of political revolution— of which none know better than yourself, for with your own eyes you saw it all. Do you recall the first gun of the war directed *at you* from Vicksburg Fort, expecting to capture the boat that had Floyd's Pittsburg armament, going to Baton Rouge. You were on watch on the "Alonzo Child"—Do you know she was afterward the Arkansas that ran through Farragut's fleet? But lord old fellow too little time now for those old memories. Tomorrow—we all assemble in as fine a Representative Hall as America affords—in memorial service. The whole South mourns Jeff Davis today.

Will's brother Sam Bowen had been in the Marion Rangers with Sam Clemens. All three had become pilots on the river before the war. This firsthand account of Sam's childhood friend confirms something long suspected of the future Mark Twain: that he believed in the Union, but not in the North. Before the war, he often chastised those who voiced anti-Union sentiments, yet he sided with the South in the great conflict. Like Jefferson Davis, according to Will Bowen, Sam had been "swept into the mighty tide of political revolution."[12]

Will Bowen recounted how Federals had fired on the *Alonzo Child*, but the captain Sam served under told a different, less reliable story. The *Alonzo Child*, according to Captain De Haven's 1876 testimony to the Senate Committee on Naval Affairs, was attacked by "one of the confederate batteries" in Memphis and subsequently confiscated. In 1862, Federals captured the steamboat near Yazoo City. In his deposition, De Haven testified to his loyalty and pursued a claim against the government, disguising the fact that he had continued to serve as captain of his craft after the alleged "confiscation" by the Rebel fleet. In all, the Confederate government had paid De Haven $101,023.46 for the use of his steamboat and for his services. Much of his 1876 testimony was perjured, but the committee voted to compensate De Haven $50,000 for the loss of the steamer. The boondoggle recalls some of Clemens's later Civil War–inspired stories such as "The Facts in the Case of the Great Beef Contract" (1870), in which an October 1861 contract to "furnish to General Sherman the sum total of thirty barrels of beef" grew into a progressively more complicated entanglement that finally can only be unwound by "the Circumlocution Office of Washington." De Haven realized outrageous profits from the two warring governments, especially considering his craft had been appraised at a mere $35,000. Sam Clemens avoided some of this drama by shifting from the *Alonzo Child* to the steamboat *Nebraska*. Other adventures awaited him there. On May 21, 1861, the *Nebraska* arrived in St. Louis, Union officials having decided to allow it to pass through the blockade. It was the last steamboat to pass from South to North before the noose was tightened. In the years between his trip to New York City and the start of the Civil War, Clemens had become a steamboat pilot. Now that the war was shutting down commercial traffic and both sides craved military pilots, history was forcing a decision.[13]

It is curious that Clemens bothered to travel north at all. Assuming Clemens possessed strong southern sympathies, he might have remained in the South and enlisted in the regular Confederate Army, or more likely still, the Confederate River Fleet. Or, if his northern sympathies predominated, he could have enlisted in the Union River Fleet. In *Life on the Mississippi* (1883), Clemens noted a couple of interesting facts. "We were approaching Memphis, in front of which city, and witnessed by its people, was fought the most famous of the river battles of the Civil War. Two men whom I had served under, in my river days, took part in that fight: Mr. Bixby, head pilot of the Union fleet, and Montgomery, Commodore of the Confederate fleet."

In April 1861, both sides were clamoring for experienced pilots, and Sam enjoyed important connections to both of them. Either fleet would have welcomed him. Clemens chose not to choose.[14]

Instead, Sam hid among relatives in St. Louis, hardly leaving the home of the Websters, his cousins. According to the recollections of Annie Moffett, his niece, Uncle Sam was on the lam:

> In the spring of 1861, when I was eight years old, Uncle Sam returned home to St. Louis, his occupation of pilot lost forever. He came on the last boat from New Orleans to get through the Union lines. He was obsessed with the fear that he might be arrested by government agents and forced to act as pilot on a government gunboat while a man stood by with a pistol ready to shoot him if he showed the least sign of a false move . . . One day a man called and gave the name Smith. Grandma went to the parlor and recognized him as a friend of Uncle Sam's. He had come with the wild project of forming a company to join General Price. Uncle Sam accepted at once, and so began his three weeks' experience as a confederate soldier, which he describes in one of his sketches.

Some critics have questioned the reliability of the memories of the then-eight-year-old niece, but one should not dismiss them out of hand. After the war, Colonel Thomas L. Snead, an aide-de-camp to the pro-secessionist governor of Missouri, Claiborne Jackson, explained the northern strategy. The actions of Francis P. Blair, Captain Nathaniel Lyon, and other pro-Union leaders were designed to "make it impossible for Missouri to secede, or out of her great resources to contribute liberally of men and material to the South." Over the course of May and June 1861, Lyon secured control of federal arsenals and Camp Jackson near St. Louis; On May 21, 1861, he quelled mobs when his soldiers (intentionally or not—there is some dispute on this point) fired on civilians, killing dozens during the time Clemens would have been hiding out in St. Louis. That action, while securing the arsenal at Camp Jackson for the federal government, was, in the words of historian William E. Parrish, "a colossal blunder" that urged many toward secession and the Confederacy.[15]

If Clemens contemplated joining General Sterling Price's Confederate Volunteers, Lyon's strategy would have rendered it exceedingly difficult.

Colonel Snead summed up the implications of the Union actions in May and June 1861 this way:

> It was also the most brilliant achievement of Lyon's well-conceived campaign. The capture of Camp Jackson had disarmed the State, and completed the conquest of St. Louis and all the adjacent counties. The advance upon Jefferson City had put the State government to flight and taken away from the Governor the prestige which sustains established and acknowledged authority. The dispersion of the volunteers that were flocking to Boonville to fight under Price for Missouri and the South extended Lyon's conquest at once to the borders of Iowa, closed all the avenues by which the Southern men of North Missouri could get to Price and Jackson, made the Missouri River a Federal highway from its source to its mouth, and put an end to Price's hope of holding the rich and friendly counties in the vicinity of Lexington till the Confederacy could send an army to his support, and arms and supplies for the men whom he was concentrating there.

Sam Clemens had landed in a volatile and dangerous part of Missouri. Critics have wondered why Sam, if he actually was desirous of fighting against the Union, failed to go south and join the Confederate Army. Colonel Snead identified a major reason: the success of Captain Lyon's plan. The "Southern men of North Missouri" referred to the fact that General Price was separated from the counties above St. Louis. The slave population in Missouri was greatest in a band from east to west in the central part of the state as well as in those counties along the Mississippi River. Culturally and economically, the most "southern" counties in Missouri were located along the Missouri River, that is, geographically toward the central and northern part of the state. Marion County, Sam's county, was a slave county surrounded by counties with few slaves, a condition analogous to the geopolitical position of the state of Missouri within the larger Union. The significance of this became apparent when Lyon, now a general, cleaved those counties from General Sterling Price in the south. By driving General Price farther south, Lyon imposed between him and potential volunteers a band of Union forces stretching across the state. Sam Clemens was one of the "Southern men of North Missouri" who was prevented from joining General Price's army in the southern part of the state.[16]

It is unclear how serious Sam may have been about joining General Price's army then forming in southern Missouri; what is clear, is that after successfully dodging the authorities, he returned home to Hannibal. According to Absolom Grimes, one of Sam's Hannibal friends, the future Mark Twain evaded Federal authorities yet again. In "Campaigning with Mark Twain," the first chapter of *Absalom Grimes, Confederate Mail Runner* (1926), Grimes claimed that in May 1861, all pilots were required to sign a loyalty oath to renew their licenses. Hearing this, "I walked out, followed by Sam Bowen and Samuel L. Clemens." The three were then accosted by a "Federal lieutenant and four privates," who informed them of their orders "from General John B. Grey, commander of the District of St. Louis, to escort you three gentlemen to headquarters." The general impressed them into service, but the three fled when he received visitors, "leaving General Grey to enjoy his tête-à-tête with the ladies." Some analysts have doubted Grimes's account, noting that many of the details seem to come straight from Clemens's own published accounts. Other details unique to Grimes's account have been discounted because they differ from Clemens's account. It bears pointing out that the veracity of every firsthand account of Sam Clemens's activities prior to leaving for the Nevada Territory has been called into question, most especially the comments of the author himself. After the escape from the Federals, Grimes's story went, Sam enlisted in the Marion Rangers along with many childhood friends, including Sam Bowen, Absalom Grimes, Ed Stevens, and John Meredith.[17]

Named for Marion County, Missouri, the Marion Rangers was a Confederate militia in a region accustomed to violence carried out by both antislavery and proslavery bushwhackers. Clemens enlisted around the second week of June. He wrote later that "In June I joined the Confederates in Ralls County, Missouri, as a second lieutenant under General Tom Harris and came near having the distinction of being captured by Colonel Ulysses S. Grant. I resigned after two weeks' service in the field, explaining that I was 'incapacitated by fatigue' through persistent retreating." Scholar Fred Lorch has reported that attitudes in northern Missouri, while certainly still fluid, had begun to shift against secession: "At mid-June, when Clemens arrived, three companies of Union Home Guards were in complete control." Aggressive and competent, General Lyon had authorized the formation of the Missouri Home Guard to assist in maintaining federal control over the state. In June 1861, the Marion County Battalion Home Guard Infantry began patrolling the streets of Hannibal, paying particular attention to local stores and the railroad. Given that sentiment in his state, in his family, and in his own mind was divided, but that the political winds in both his home and his family were shifting toward Union, how did Sam Clemens, the writer who would become the "Lincoln of our literature," choose for rebellion? In later years, Clemens attributed his decision to non-ideological concerns. They were more social than political, but this hardly meant that the decision was not heartfelt. Culturally, Sam Clemens looked to the South for everything. He became a pilot on the Mississippi River, plying the southern route to New Orleans. Unlike Abraham Lincoln, Sam seemed untroubled by the human trafficking he must have witnessed in the Crescent City. Furthermore, Sam's job setting type for newspapers in the slaveholding South surely instilled in him a deep awareness of the political issues of the day—as demonstrated by his letters, however racist, from New York City. As the distinguished Twainian Louis J. Budd has observed, "Though it is unrealistic to conclude that he took no time for girls and practical jokes and studied every letter by subscribers who signed as 'Junius' or 'Vox Populi,' his term as Orion's unpaid assistant gave him an early glimpse of what goes on behind the façade of campaign oratory." At the age of twenty-six, having dropped piece after piece of antimony slugs into place to spell out political speeches and news about Missouri bushwhackers in "Bleeding Kansas" next door, having engaged in "Great rejoicing" when Louisiana went out of the Union on January 26, 1861, Sam Clemens joined the Marion Rangers with an awareness of what he was doing: that he was enlisting as a bushwhacker. "Harmless enough for the moment," scholar J. Stanley Mattson has concluded, "they were potentially dangerous. For it was of just such stuff that terror-bent vandals like Quantrill's Raiders had been made." William C. Quantrill, it will be remembered, ordered his Missouri bushwhackers to cross the border into Kansas and "[k]ill every man big enough to carry a gun" during the notorious raid on Lawrence in August 1863.[18]

It was in 1885 that Clemens penned his most extensive statement on the war, "The Private History of a Campaign That Failed." In his sketch, loosely based on his experiences during June 1861, Clemens captured the sense of divided loyalties in the border state of Missouri. "It was hard for us to get our bearings," he observed, using a piloting metaphor suggesting the feeling of being at sea on the big river. In part, Clemens's decision to side with the South was haphazard and contingent on outside events, for it owed something to the proclamation in which that southern-leaning governor

Claiborne Jackson called for "fifty thousand militia to repel the invader," the Union forces that had occupied the largest cities and military facilities. This led directly to Sam joining the "herd of cattle" known as the Marion Rangers. As he discovered years later, the Union commander in charge of the northern Missouri theater of operations was none other than Ulysses S. Grant himself. In later years, Clemens exaggerated this connection, writing in 1885, "To-day talked with General Grant about his & my first Missouri campaign in 1861 (June or July.) He surprised an empty camp near Florida, Mo., on Salt river, which I had been occupying a day or two before. How near he came to playing the devil with his future publisher!" Clemens and Grant had been close during that "first Missouri campaign," but not quite that close. Scholar John C. Gerber, in his study of the chronology of Clemens's experiences, has commented that the author "cannot be criticized too harshly for stretching the facts by a few miles and by two or three weeks." As Grant pushed into Missouri, Sam went west with his brother Orion, who had been appointed by President Lincoln to serve as Nevada territorial secretary. Nevertheless, Clemens considered calling his article "My Campaign against Grant."[19]

Most discussion about Clemens's Civil War experiences has focused on that single article, which he retitled, "The Private History of a Campaign That Failed." Published in the same year that Ulysses S. Grant's *Memoirs* appeared, this highly fictionalized account of Sam's experiences with the Marion Rangers was originally part of the *Century Magazine*'s "Civil War Series." Appearing in installments from November 1884 through November 1887, the series extolled the virtues of the Union and Confederate warriors who provided eyewitness accounts of "the heroic deeds of which they were a part." Editors strived to publish vivid, compelling, and authoritative accounts. Some accusations of bias did take place, and one of the editors, Robert Underwood Johnson, was even challenged to a duel by a former Confederate who disagreed with one of the articles. Other military officers adopted a more pacific approach to disagreement and wrote letters contesting certain points, objections that were sometimes printed in the "Memoranda on the Civil War" section of the journal. In many respects, Clemens's article did not fit with the series, and it is little wonder that the editors chose not to include his article when the rest were collected as the four-volume *Battles and Leaders of the Civil War* (1887). Historian Timothy P. Caron has identified one reason for the exclusion: Clemens's piece opposed "the sentimental narratives of sectional reunion and harmony." Such opposition must have been problematic for the editors; historian Gaines M. Foster has invoked the *Century Magazine* series as one manifestation of the impulse to sectional reunion. "The articles in the two-year series, therefore, ignored or soft-pedaled divisive issues and instead emphasized the experience of battle itself." Foster has even cited the articles as the "single most important series in the new journalistic homage to the South." While not sectionally divisive in his article, Clemens certainly did not highlight the importance of the experience of battle itself. Rather, he took aim at the central tenet of the series: the nobility of the war.[20]

Clemens's article was replaced by Colonel Thomas L. Snead's "The First Year of the War in Missouri." The illustration of the "Raw Recruit" (Figure 1) used on the first page of "The Private History of a Campaign That Failed," featuring a country bumpkin dressed in butternut carrying a squirrel rifle, was somewhat inappropriately tacked onto the beginning of Snead's article. The comic illustration must have stuck out the way Clemens's article had from the others. An even less flattering illustration accompanied Clemens's description in *Following the Equator* (1897) of his two weeks as "a military man." Clemens joked that his strategy was "to tire the enemy" by running. Dan Beard's illustration (Figure 2) presented a callow Sam lost in an oversized uniform, trailing a sword and epaulets as if playing dress up, fleeing Grant's army. The writer Rodman Gilder discussed the illustration with Beard in 1940, a year before the artist's death: "Dan informed me that he drew a fanciful picture of Twain and a dozen other boys as they were being chased by cavalry headed by General Grant." The illustration provided a humorous accompaniment to the text, just as the "Raw Recruit" had with the 1885 version of the story. Neither matched the heroic story and figures of the military authors in the *Century* series, however. Indeed, Clemens, a deserter from a disorganized militia, made poor company for the other writers, among whom marched such luminaries as Generals P. G. T. Beauregard, Ulysses S. Grant, John Bell Hood, Joseph Johnston, James Longstreet, George B. McClellan, George Meade, William Rosecrans, and William T. Sherman. These writers, and many more besides, wrote first-person narratives about their experiences in particular battles of the Civil War. Clemens's contribution, as Tom Z. Parrish has phrased it, "is a good example of how a creative writer can exploit an experience that the ordinary person would want to forget."[21]

FIGURE 1. Illustration of the "Raw Recruit" from the first edition of "The Private History of a Campaign That Failed." Courtesy Baylor University's Armstrong Browning Library.

FIGURE 2. Dan Beard's *Following the Equator* illustration of Mark Twain
fleeing General Grant's army. Courtesy Baylor University's Armstrong
Browning Library.

Clemens's experiences as part of a Rebel militia, whatever those experiences really were, did not necessarily disqualify him from participation in
the series. It was not what he did or did not do in April 1861 that made his
article an irritant; rather, it was what Neil Schmitz has called the writer's
"reconstructive humor" that put him beyond the pale. Consider the issue
of maps, for example, which were extensively used in the series. Excluding
tables, charts, and illustrations, *Battles and Leaders of the Civil War* contains
nearly two hundred maps. "Work in all the maps you can," exhorted Robert

Johnson, when negotiating with Clemens for his contribution. Johnson was the archetypic editor, advising his author as to the quantity of maps and the type of material to include even while demanding the article "as p. d. q. as this weather will permit." Finally, he cautioned Clemens: "Have mercy on us as to space." Among all these demands, Johnson's request for maps was noteworthy. The maps provided a crucial element of the collection's appeal, as they formally imposed meaning on the irrationality of war. The much vaunted fog of war dissipated as the maps authoritatively asserted that all was comprehensible. Particularly from a border state perspective, where even allegiances were clouded and it was hard to "get our bearings," having a map that stated *this* is where the lines were drawn at such and such a time made a powerful statement about war. The series was an exercise in orienteering in a situation where people were disoriented, the maps arguing that one can make sense of war, albeit many years later.[22]

Johnson hardly needed to encourage Clemens to use maps in what the editor referred to as "that little article on your experiences in the Rebel army." Clemens frequently poked fun at the reliance on maps. In 1865, while in California, he had created a burlesque report of a geological expert, one "Professor G.," complete with a map of "the Great Vide Poche Company on Mount Olympus." The map for the "Empty Pocket" mining company featured such comic details such as a "Jackass Rabbit in rapid motion, coming down the road, apparently from Robinson's Ferry." The map proper, while containing all the usual elements of a map, was flawed. "By reference to the Map, it will be seen that the course of the principal lode or vein is apparently uncertain & irregular, & has the general direction of a streak of lightning. The map is not absolutely correct in this matter, the vein being really almost straight, but at the time the Prof was drawing it, seated upon a log, he was persistently besieged by piss-ants, & the acute angles in the course of the vein demonstrate with singular fidelity the extraordinary suddenness & fury of their assaults." Clemens burlesqued the popular faith in maps, for here the professor charted each detail as precisely as he could while "besieged by piss-ants," even while missing the overall truth of the scene: the mine had no gold. The "pocket," both in the general sense of one's pockets as well as the mining term that Clemens defined in his autobiography as "a concentration of gold dust in one little spot on the mountainside," was empty. Later, in 1870, Clemens published his burlesque "Map of the Fortifications of Paris." This map, a crudely drawn block print of Paris with many labels printed in mirror image, showed the Seine River running through the city, but also featured such comic additions to *La Ville-Lumière* as the Rhine River and the Erie Canal. Clemens claimed that he published the map due to public demand: "General Grant's outspoken commendation originated this demand, and General Sherman's fervent endorsement added fuel to it." Clemens foregrounded the military nature of the map, beginning by invoking the two greatest Union generals. Moreover, this map detailed the fortifications of Paris, and was an example of a military map for the "suffering soldiers of our land," as he put it. He appended "OFFICIAL COMMENDATIONS," the first of which purported to be from Grant himself: "It is the only map of the kind I ever saw." Sherman, too, stated that "It is but fair to say that in some respects it is a truly remarkable map."[23]

In "The Private History of a Campaign That Failed," Clemens also poked fun at the reliance on maps. He titled his first map "The Seat of War." A crudely drawn map of the Mississippi River with Marion, Monroe, Ralls, and Pike counties roughly delineated and labeled (Figure 3), the map could be called "a truly remarkable map." To understand Twain's use of the maps, one should compare them to those used in Ulysses S. Grant's *Memoirs*. General Grant contributed articles to the *Century* series covering four campaigns: Shiloh, Vicksburg, Chattanooga, and The Wilderness. Clemens was intimately familiar with Grant's work because he had become publisher to the general and former president after learning that he was all but destitute following the defalcations of a business associate. Owner of the Charles Webster Publishing Company, Clemens was in a unique position to market the general's book throughout the North. He assured Grant that marketing the book by subscription would yield much more money than what other publishers had offered him. Clemens was right. A year after Grant's death, Clemens presented his widow Julia with a check for more than $200,000, the largest royalty check ever written. Clemens recalled that ultimately the firm's publication of Grant's *Memoirs* "paid Mrs. Grant something like half a million dollars."[24]

Serving as Grant's publisher surely influenced how Clemens wrote "The Private History of a Campaign That Failed." During the time that Clemens was writing his own account of his scant two weeks in the Marion Rangers, he frequently visited Grant, who was fighting the last battle of his life: completing his *Memoirs* before dying of throat cancer. Grant finished his writing

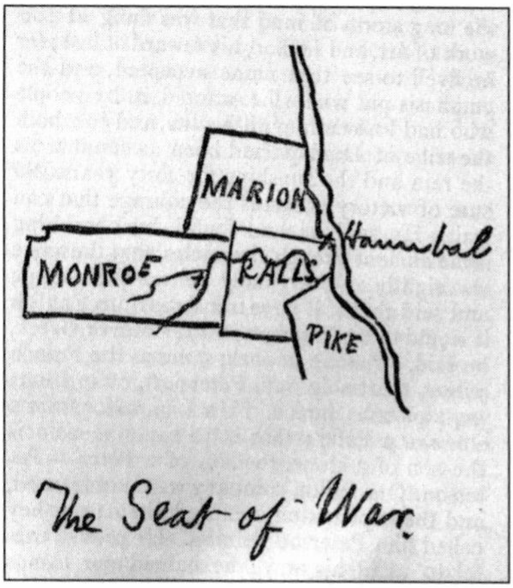

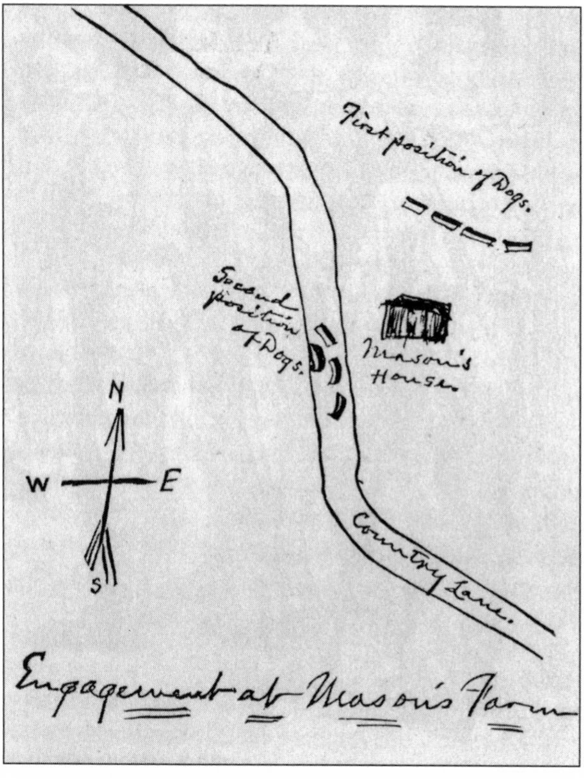

The Seat of War.

Engagement at Mason's Farm.

FIGURE 3. Mark Twain's hand-drawn maps for "The Private History of a Campaign That Failed." Courtesy Baylor University's Armstrong Browning Library.

on July 19 and died four days later, on the morning of July 23, staying alive, as biographer John Simon has rightly said, "by sheer will until he had completed his task." Clemens visited him frequently during his final months, and was in contact in other ways, too. "Whenever galley proofs or revises went to General Grant," Clemens wrote in his autobiography, "a set came also to me." As the general's publisher, Clemens may have been directly responding to what he had seen in Grant's book, in particular the general's "Map of the SEAT OF WAR 1861–1865," which depicted more than half of the United States. Thus, while he was certainly responding generically to all such military maps, Clemens was doubtless influenced by Grant's use of them. Maps showing the "seat" of war, meaning the region in which the war took place, usually focused on the macrocosmic aspects of the conflict. Grant's map conveyed not only the stolid belief in the comprehensibility of war, but also limned its vast scope and significance. The map identified individual towns and cities, rivers and streams, and tagged railroads and mountain chains. All this and more Grant's map did. Clemens, by contrast, tagged his hometown of Hannibal and the four contiguous counties, but included the Mississippi and other rivers without labeling them at all. The differences underscored the point that, while Grant gave his memoirs the title *Personal Memoirs of U. S. Grant*, Clemens chose "Private" memoirs, and focused on the *very* small bit of the war he had actually participated in. Icons of the war, Clemens's maps asserted one of the themes of his story: that all war stories are, at their core, local and individual. From its inception, the *Century* series was supposed to serve as "an intimate and authentic record," and Clemens's maps, for all their humor, did serve the former purpose, if less so the latter.[25]

In the other map in Figure 3 Clemens endeavored to illustrate, as he put it, "what was perhaps the most mortifying spectacle of the civil war." Bearing the title "Engagement at Mason's Farm," the map set out in humorous detail the attack on the Marion Rangers by Farmer Mason's dogs. With its "First position of Dogs." and the icons of small rectangular boxes arranged in a slight semicircle and the "Second position of Dogs." closer to the soldiers' position on the "Country Lane.," the map echoed efforts by military maps in Grant's *Memoirs* and the *Century Magazine* to arrest a moment in battle even while capturing the dynamic movement over time of opposing forces. Clemens used small, unfilled rectangular boxes to represent the dogs, like those Ulysses S. Grant in his *Memoirs* and other generals in the *Century* articles employed to denote Union troops. Of course, in this presentation, such icons contributed to the joke. The boys' lively retreat was provoked by the farm dogs that chased them, teeth bared to attack their rear guard. Clemens's maps, like many Civil War battle maps, labeled areas by family farm name. Hence, in Beaureguard's "Topographical Map of the Bull Run Battle-Field," labels like "The Carter Farm" and "Sudley Farm" featured prominently. On Clemens's map, the farm was "Mason's Farm." When the Marion Rangers arrived there, the "mortifying spectacle" led Farmer Mason to deride them as "a curious breed of soldiers" and interrogate them about their knowledge of tactics. While the boys' comprehension was limited and their maneuvering haphazard, Mason's dogs seemed more disciplined. Upon the arrival of the Marion Rangers, Mason's dogs offered a warm welcome, as "each of them took a soldier by the slack of his trousers and began to back away with him." Now here was the "Seat of War" with a vengeance!

Clemens's maps in the "The Private History of a Campaign That Failed" recalled his "Map of the Fortifications of Paris," for in both he lampooned a military situation, even appending spurious endorsements by military authorities such as Grant and Sherman. Scholar Bruce Michelson has suggested that Clemens drew the Paris map to make light of the fact that "Bismarck's armies were plowing toward the French capital to topple the Second Empire." To Clemens, the European conflict "seemed trivial, especially so soon after the Civil War." Likewise, Clemens did not intend his maps to argue that everything made sense. Quite the opposite. They visually expressed the confusion of the young men of mixed loyalties living in a state of border confusion. Historian David W. Blight has termed the Century's attempt to heal the wounds of war by focusing on the shared experience of battle a "reconciliationist strategy." Similarly, Peter Messent's discussion of Clemens's sketch is compelling, but he has argued that the narrative "undermines the whole brand of heroic thinking" while not "undermining the accompanying reunionist message." Clemens's reconstructionist strategy, however, opposed such a glowing reunion. The war did not make sense, and embracing former foes hardly did anything other than to heighten the absurdity. The Civil War maps provided Clemens with a way to laugh at the grotesque situation he found himself in as he attempted to "get his bearings" and as the country tried to get its bearings in the 1880s. The maps that editor Robert Johnson had requested were supposed to make sense of reality and then turn around and assert the idea that war and the current political reality made sense. By design, Clemens's maps failed to do this. Implicitly, his maps ridiculed the very idea that the experience of war was reducible to explanation. Twain scholar John Bird, in his illuminating study of Clemens's use of metaphors, has connected the confusion of directions on the maps with the confusion of allegiances in the story. Bird has concluded that "the confusion of direction, the metaphor that underlies everything, shows that all war is insane." Clemens's maps visually "reconstructed" the Civil War, highlighting the confusion of the historical moment and questioning the high-minded purpose of foregrounding "the heroic deeds" in the *Century Magazine* series without addressing larger questions, such as, "What did it all mean?"[26]

Sam needed more than a map to get his bearings in June 1861. Consider, for example, the oath he took as part of the Marion Rangers. Colonel John Ralls, a hero of the Mexican War, conducted the ceremony inducting Sam Clemens and his friends into the Confederate irregulars.

> Afterwards he took us to a distant meadow, and there in the shade of a tree we listened to an old-fashioned speech from him, full of gunpowder and glory, full of that adjective-piling, mixed metaphor, and windy declamation which was regarded as eloquence in that ancient time and that remote region; and then he swore us on the Bible to be faithful to the State of Missouri and drive all invaders from her soil, no matter whence they might come or under what flag they might march. This mixed us considerably, and we could not make out just what service we were embarked in; but Colonel Ralls, the practiced politician and phrase-juggler, was not similarly in doubt; he knew quite clearly that he had invested us in the cause of the Southern Confederacy.

Colonel Ralls obviously suffered from the "Sir Walter Disease," as Clemens termed it, symptoms of which included "inflated speech." Confusion engendered by the oath of allegiance was general, and many members of the Missouri Guard resisted leaving the state to fight against the Union Army. After all, they had enlisted to defend the state against all invaders, not to become an offensive army of invaders. In Clemens's 1877 speech "My Military History," delivered to the "Putnam Phalanx Dinner for the Ancient and Honorable Artillery Company of Massachusetts, Hartford," he recalled the induction ceremony. Colonel Ralls "made us swear to uphold the flag and Constitution of the United States, and to destroy every other military organization that we caught doing the same thing, which, being interpreted, means that we were to repel invasion." Funny, yes, but the joke was really on the soldiers for whom the orders had to be "interpreted." Even after the Civil War, the questions of states' rights, limits of federal power, and the authority of the Constitution have remained unsolved, matters of constant, often vitriolic, debate. In Will Bowen's letter to Sam lamenting the death of Jefferson Davis, he invoked the president of the Confederacy as a champion of states' rights and thus "the Apostle of Liberty to Americans" just as President Lincoln was "the Apostle of Freedom to Slaves."[27]

Clemens exhibited his pride in his home state in a letter to William H. Clagett, February 28, 1862, from Carson City in the Nevada Territory:

Well, Billy, tell Tom Smith that they've been and gone and done it. Old Curtis, you know. He has thrashed our Missourians like everything. But by the Lord, they didn't do it on the Sacred Soil, my boy. They had to chase 'em clear down into Arkansas before they could whip them. There's consolation in *that*. If they had remained on the Soil, Curtis couldn't have done it. It's all in the Soil, you know. Take a Missourian on his own soil, and he is invincible. Now, when I was on the soil, I used to be as terrible as an army with banners; but out here on this quartz foundation, you see, I don't amount to a Damn. That's what's the matter with *me*. And they have taken Fort Henry, and Fort Donelson, and the half of Tennessee—and the stars and stripes wave over the Capitol at Nashville.

They have taken Fort Henry, and Fort Donelson, and the half of Tennessee. Twain's glibness might almost mask the pronouns he selected to denominate the Union forces as "they." The passage may indicate why Sam had been interested in returning to Missouri to enlist in the Marion Rangers. However difficult it was to "get our bearings," the idea that one might resist both secession and invasion from the North did not seem at all contradictory to many who lived in the border states. Confederate General Sterling Price had served as governor of Missouri and had opposed secession, but when the "sacred soil" of Missouri was "invaded" by Federal troops, like Sam Clemens, he sided with the Confederacy.[28]

In "The Private History of a Campaign That Failed," Clemens likewise undermined the heroism of the deeds, as many Twain scholars have argued. Edgar M. Branch has described the experiences as "a farcical two weeks as a Confederate irregular." Similarly, Paul Fatout has labeled the Marion Rangers "a homespun Southern military unit—military only by a great stretch of the imagination." Clemens described how pro-southern farmers donated extra mules and horses to the cause, but the "town boys" could never seem to manage them. Sam's mule, Paint-Brush, threw him off consistently, adding insult to injury by braying in victory each time. "[N]ot entirely destitute of military resources," Sam managed to deal with his recalcitrant mule. Other less than heroic experiences included losing several guns and their only keg of gunpowder in a brook and wounding each other in a fight in a corncrib by hurling ears of corn that "were half as heavy as bricks."[29]

This stultifying lack of heroism was the most notable feature of Clemens's contribution to the *Century* series. At the same time, however, he emphasized the danger. When the Marion Rangers fled, they did so because they were pursued by the Union forces who hoped to hang as many Rebels as possible. As Clemens wrote in "The Private History of a Campaign That Failed," reports had reached the small band that "a detachment of Union soldiers was on its way from Hannibal with orders to capture and hang any bands like ours which it could find." The "raw recruits," fearing that "the halter might end us before we were a day older," fled. Huddling pathetically in a thunderstorm, they found that the "romance" had been drowned out of their campaign. Neither Sam, nor any of the other soldiers, ever doubted "that so barbarous an order had been given."[30]

There was good reason not to doubt it. Looking back from the vantage point of 1885, Clemens certainly knew that those belonging to militias were often summarily executed. He was aware, for example, of the "Palmyra Massacre," the October 1862 execution of "ten Confederate guerillas, already in custody." Sam knew one of the Rebels slated for execution, Dr. James W. Frazer, who had been saved only because of the fact that, as biographer Dixon Wecter has reported, "at the last moment a young soldier, unmarried, heroically volunteered to take his place, and did so." Dr. Frazer was saved only because he was married; his wife happened to be Sam's childhood sweetheart, Laura Hawkins, the model for Becky Thatcher in *The Adventures of Tom Sawyer* (1876). Clemens was also certainly aware of General John C. Frémont's declaration of martial law, which stated that "men bearing arms without authority of the Union government were to be executed." Attorney General Edward Bates, the Missouri Republican who wrangled Sam's brother Orion his government post in Nevada, advised Federals in his home state not to arrest guerillas, but to shoot them: "They should be *summarily shot by thousands.*" In Marion County, Sam's "Seat of the War," General John Pope ordered the confiscation of property belonging to those who failed to surrender such irregulars as the Marion Rangers. Presumably, then, Sam could have lost his life, and his family could have lost their property. While one may quibble over many details of Clemens's claims about his war experiences, given the situation in Missouri at the time one can hardly contest the emotional content of his war experiences or his reconstruction of them. As he wrote to an unidentified correspondent, "I confine myself to life with which I am familiar when pretending to portray life. But I confined myself to the *boy*-life out on the Mississippi because that had a peculiar charm for me, and not because I was not familiar with other phases of life. I was a *soldier* two weeks once in the beginning of the war, and was hunted like a rat the whole time. Familiar? My splendid Kipling himself hasn't a more burnt-in, hard-baked, and unforgettable familiarity with that death-on-the-pale-horse-with-hell-following-after, which is a raw soldier's first fortnight in the field—and which, without any doubt, is the most tremendous fortnight and the vividest he is ever going to see." Clemens may have experienced a bare fortnight of the war, but it was enough to grasp the fear of the raw recruit. Moreover, labeling the actions by Union officers toward the militias in Missouri "barbarous" can hardly be called a "reconciliationist" strategy.[31]

Clemens's battle plan for his sketch involved undermining the stated purpose of the series of illuminating the "heroic deeds" of the war. He achieved this most notably in his depiction of General Thomas Harris, who commanded—or tried to command—the irregulars in northern Missouri. In "The Private History of a Campaign That Failed," Clemens noted the disparity between the now "Brigadier-General Thomas H. Harris," who had been "the sole and modest-salaried operator in our telegraph office." The Hannibal boys he tried to command simply mocked him: "Oh, now, what'll you take to *don't,* Tom Harris!" Confederate General Richard Taylor fumed in his memoirs about these soldiers of the frontier where "distinctions of rank were unknown." General Taylor complained that "Officers and men addressed each other as Tom, Dick, or Harry, and had no more conception of military gradations than of the celestial hierarchy of the poets." Clemens, who had read Taylor's *Destruction and Reconstruction* (1879), likely had this particular passage in mind when he wrote that these boys "did not know what it meant to be ordered around by Tom, Dick, and Harry, whom they had known familiarly all their lives." As Clemens wrote in "My Military History," the volunteers "did not seem to have any correct idea of military discipline." As an example, Sam told of one recruit who responded to direct orders with the retort, "Who was your nigger last year?" Such lack of discipline was common in Missouri, but Clemens offered no adult reflection on the great variance between his attitudes toward Tom Harris in 1861 and his retrospective attitudes in 1885, when he should have known that General Harris had earned a bit more respect. Ulysses S. Grant, in a letter to Jesse Grant written on July 13, 1861, referred to Clemens's supposedly inoffensive Harris as "the notorious Tom Harris with his 1200 secessionists." In a letter to his wife Julia, written the same day, Grant returned to the subject: "There will also be a Regt. & a half over at Mexico on the North Missouri road and all of us together will try and surround the notorious Tom Harris and his band."[32]

Grant's comments on the "notorious" telegraph operator came not a month after Sam's enlistment. Clemens did note that "there were those among us who afterward learned the grim trade; learned to obey like machines; became valuable soldiers; fought all through the war, and came out at the end with excellent records." Tom Harris was one of these. What Clemens failed to mention about Harris is significant. It bears pointing out, too, that Clemens referred to General Harris as Thomas H. Harris rather than Thomas A. Harris. The mistake was quite possibly unintentional, but it certainly fit with his systematic deheroicizing of Harris who, after all, was one of the Hannibal boys who had *not* deserted his post. Clemens may have felt some pangs at having left the field where a generation of soldiers proved their manhood. In his autobiography, Clemens described standing next to General William Tecumseh Sherman during public events at which, inevitably, a band would strike up "Marching through Georgia." Sherman would "rage and swear" at the song he had grown to hate. "I think I suffered a shade more than the legitimate hero does," Clemens philosophized, "he being privileged to soften his misery with the reflection that his glory was at any rate golden and reproachless in its origin, whereas I had no such privilege, there being no possible way to make mine respectable." Scholar

Elmo Howell has suggested that in deserting, Clemens "had in his own mind betrayed himself by giving in to a weakness in character that was to lead on to the doubt and despair of his old age."[33]

If demeaning Harris was a psychological tactic, it certainly involved conscious artistic decisions about how to write the sketch. Clemens left out many details about Harris's career, for instance, that he had been publisher of the *Missouri Courier* in the 1850s, a paper where Sam had apprenticed to Joseph P. Ament before leaving in January 1851 to work for his brother Orion's rival paper. More to the military point, Clemens failed to mention that Harris had attended the U.S. Military Academy for two years, and had served in the Missouri Mormon War (1838); the Iowa War (1839), a boundary dispute sometimes referred to as the "Honey War"; and the Mexican War (1846–1848). Some of these military experiences presaged his later taking charge of militias in Missouri during the early days of the Civil War. Missouri, it is well to remember, had a long history of irregular militias and military actions. As a border state and a slave state, Missouri eagerly provided the bushwhackers that made "Bleeding Kansas" bleed. Harris was part of such irregular military actions throughout his youth. His obituary in the *Daily Globe-Democrat* (St. Louis) for April 10, 1895, included these high points of his career: "Gen. Harris distinguished himself while a boy and a resident of Missouri. He lived with his parents near Hannibal, Mo., when the Mormons were routed out of Illinois. When the citizens of Missouri rose up against Joseph Smith and his followers, Harris, who was then but 16 years old, got together a regiment from Hannibal, and led it against Smith and his followers. Under his leadership the regiment defeated a detachment of Smith's men and set them on their march out of Missouri." His obituary in the April 11, 1895 edition of the *Palmyra Spectator* (Missouri) referred to him as "a resident of Hannibal and one of its most prominent and picturesque citizens." During the 1850s, he seemed even to have been a soldier of fortune or freebooter in Cuba, Venezuela, and Nicaragua. Clemens's omission of these activities was particularly important because they illustrate that, far from being merely "the sole and modest-salaried operator in our telegraph office," Thomas Harris had racked up quite a record of organizing and directing guerilla warfare.[34]

In other respects, too, Harris was an important figure in the history of Missouri. A Democrat, he was elected to the Missouri state legislature. After the war came, Harris was elected to the Confederate Congress, serving from 1861 to 1864. Although Missouri did not secede, it was claimed by the Confederate government as part of the Confederacy, in part because the governor at the time of secession, Claiborne Jackson, supported secession after the "invasion" of Missouri by Union forces. Harris held an important position on the Committee on Military Affairs while serving in the Confederate Congress and championed bills both to raise more troops in Missouri and to care for disabled veterans and their families. He corresponded with George W. Randolph, secretary of war in the Jefferson Davis administration, concerning the Union Army's executions without trial of members of the Missouri State Guard who were fighting for the Confederacy. Notable among his resolutions was "That the Committee on Military Affairs be instructed to inquire into the expediency of providing by law for the payment, regulating the military status, and other relief of officers of men who have been irregularly organized and sworn into the military service of the Confederate States and performed actual service in the field." This resolution was agreed to, and included such groups as the Marion Rangers. Harris is best remembered for having played a pivotal role in the Siege of Lexington, Missouri, on September 18–20, 1861.[35]

In sum, Harris was far—very far—from the mild-mannered telegraph clerk that Clemens described. It is doubtful that Sam Clemens in 1861 thought of him that way. Certainly, writing retrospectively in 1885, the same year Grant's *Personal Memoirs* appeared, Clemens knew better. He knew better because he had learned of Harris's reputation—if he had not known it before—when reading that Union general's manuscript, where he wrote of his first campaign as commander of his own troops: "to move against Colonel Thomas Harris." Grant, in fact, used Harris as the example of the Confederate leader who tested his mettle. He invokes Harris at the start of his *Memoirs* and two chapters before the end, hundreds of pages later. For Grant, having the "moral courage" to lead his troops against Harris, symbolized his coming of age as a commander. Yet Clemens persisted in his characterization of Harris as something less than a hero. Why? While doing so may have served psychological ends, it certainly served artistic ones, for it helped undermine the heroism of war. Clemens needed Harris to be just a neighbor whom circumstances turned into a soldier. In "The Private History of a Campaign That Failed," Clemens seized for his theme the absurdity of war, in particular, the madness of a Civil War in a border state, where allegiances shifted and no one on the Confederate side, not even General Tom Harris, yet wore a uniform. Against this backdrop, Clemens focused on the confusion of the young recruits and their panic-stricken retreat from a Union colonel later revealed to be Ulysses S. Grant.

In the much-discussed climax of his story, Clemens described the shooting of an unarmed stranger who wore no uniform—not necessarily a sign of civilian status. According to the text, Sam was one of the six members of the militia to fire on the man. "And right away a figure approached in the forest path; it could have been made of smoke, its mass had so little sharpness of outline. It was a man on horseback; and it seemed to me that there were others behind him. I got hold of a gun in the dark, and pushed it through a crack between the logs, hardly knowing what I was doing, I was so dazed with fright. Somebody said 'Fire!' I pulled the trigger." Sam listened as the unarmed man in civilian clothes "muttered and mumbled like a dreamer in his sleep, about his wife and child" and then died. Many scholars have dismissed the story as untrue. In *Mark Twain at West Point,* for example, Twain scholar Philip Leon has labeled Clemens's claim that he killed a man "almost certainly a complete fabrication." John Gerber, too, has cautioned readers that the work is "primarily a literary rather than an historical document," comparing the Marion Rangers to "Tom Sawyer's gang." Clemens left himself a note in his writing journal that indicated he had considered writing a much more obviously fictional account: "Put Huck & Tom & Jim through my Mo. Campaign & give a chapter to the Century. Union officer accosts Tom & says his name is US Grant." One cannot know for certain what Sam's experiences were during his brief service to the Confederacy, or what he might have become had he not deserted. Still, it is profoundly naïve to dismiss the Missouri militias that formed around Hannibal as enjoying "a little camping-out expedition and a good time," as Albert B. Paine, Clemens's biographer, once did. After all, Clemens recalled that his boyhood friend John Meredith had been "a meek and bashful boy" before the war but "became the cruelest of bushwhacker-leaders in the war-time." Of his old friend, Sam wrote, "when the Civil War broke out he became a sort of guerrilla chief on the Confederate side." He showed no quarter to any Unionists, be they old pals, neighbors, or even noncombatants, and "he was remorseless in his devastations and sheddings of blood." Likewise, one should not dismiss out of hand the situation on the ground in Missouri at that time. As General John C. Frémont described the situation when he arrived in Missouri in July 1861, "the whole State of Missouri was a battle-field." It was nothing new to the state, which was formed by the Missouri Compromise and contributed its share of partisan fighters to "Bleeding

Kansas" after the Kansas–Nebraska Act. As David Potter has argued, "Missourians were first openly to invoke the use of force" to establish Kansas as a slave state in the 1850s. In a real sense, Congress and the Supreme Court made Missouri and its environs the battleground leading up to the Civil War. That was very much a part of the divisive background in the area. "It would scarcely stretch the truth," as James McPherson has expressed it, "to say that the Civil War began along the Missouri–Kansas border in 1854 and lasted there eleven years instead of four."[36]

The Civil War continued on the printed page after the collapse of the Confederacy. Multiple purposes motivated the soldiers who contributed to *Battles and Leaders of the Civil War.* Certainly, there were attempts at the objective "non-political discussion" the series editors strived for, but a recurrent theme pervaded many of the articles: justification. Many, perhaps most, of the articles in the *Century* series strained at the dictum to be "non-political." Frequently, those writing about their experiences, while usually not taking partisan sides in terms of Union versus Confederate, did engage in political disputes regarding criticisms of actions they took or failed to take during military campaigns. Ironically, the writers most often directed their Parthian shots toward those on their own side. General John C. Frémont, for example, justified actions he took during the Missouri campaign such as the "establishment of martial law," for which he was criticized and then removed by President Lincoln, by arguing that they proved in time to be necessary. Clemens, too, may have been trying to assuage some guilt at having deserted and missed the war, as some have contended. In that sense, Clemens's contribution to the *Century* series resembled many other articles that contained extensive justifications of their authors' war records.[37]

Clemens further connected his sketch with the series by putting his retreat into the context of the earliest months of the Civil War, "making it as far as possible, characteristic of the state of things in Missouri early in the War," just as editor Robert Johnson had requested of him. The first issue in the series printed by the *Century Magazine* was General Beauregard's article "The Battle of Bull Run" that appeared in the November 1884 issue of the magazine. Clemens referred to that battle in his own last paragraph. "There was more Bull Run material," he wrote, "scattered through the early camps of this country than exhibited itself at Bull Run. And yet it learned its trade presently, and helped to fight the great battles later." This "Bull Run material," as Clemens termed it, consisted of the undisciplined actions of raw recruits whose efforts were frequently misdirected by poor leaders, producing an entire history of accusations, explanations, and justifications that infused the series *Battles and Leaders of the Civil War*. As for Sam Clemens, he deserted, despite the fact that General Harris, the former telegraph operator, exhorted the troops to stay. "Harris ordered us back; but we told him there was a Union colonel coming with a whole regiment in his wake, and it looked as if there was going to be a disturbance; so we had concluded to go home. He raged a little, but it was of no use; our minds were made up. We had done our share; had killed one man, exterminated one army, such as it was; let him go and kill the rest, and that would end the war. I did not see that brisk young general again until last year; then he was wearing white hair and whiskers." Clemens always made his desertion into a joke. In his autobiography, too, he wrote, "I resigned after two weeks' service in the field, explaining that I was 'incapacitated by fatigue' through persistent retreating." His comic justifications twisted a grotesque gibe out of his war experiences—and out of everyone else's.[38]

Clemens aimed at a much greater target than such a limited "private" history and good-natured tomfoolery. His description of failure revealed a great deal about what changes he had undergone between June 1861 and the summer of 1885, when he wrote the article. Whether any of the details of "The Private History of a Campaign That Failed" were literally true is, in this sense, beside the point. What is significant, is that in 1885, Clemens depicted himself as having been a confused young man in a border state reaching a profound conclusion about the nature of war. Describing the aftermath of the shooting, he philosophized that "I could not drive it away, the taking of that unoffending life seemed such a wanton thing. And it seemed an epitome of war; that all war must be just that—the killing of strangers against whom you feel no personal animosity; strangers whom, in other circumstances, you would help if you found them in trouble, and who would help you if you needed it." In his May 11, 1885 letter to Mark Twain, *Century Magazine*'s Robert Johnson had invited the author to "join the ranks" with the other generals, but with his "The Private History of a Campaign That Failed," Clemens broke ranks, became a rogue, and fired at both sides in the Civil War. Writing his article for inclusion in the *Century* series, Clemens offered a singular antiwar burlesque that undermined his editor's fundamental assumptions about the purposes and nobility of warfare. In *Ghosts of the Confederacy: Defeat, The Lost Cause, and the Emergence of the New South, 1865 to 1913*, historian Gaines M. Foster has argued that the "rapid healing of national divisions" after the Civil War meant that neither the North nor the South gained the insight or wisdom the tragic conflict offered. Southerners, especially, suffered from the lack of perspective patient reflection would have afforded. "Southerners participated in the celebration, even though they had lost the war. Surprisingly, they never questioned whether defeat implied something was wrong with the cause or their society. Their cause had been just and the failure the result only of overwhelming numbers, they concluded. Conceivably, defeat might have impelled them to question the morality of slavery and, in the process, of southern race relations. It might have led southerners to be more skeptical of their nation's sense of innocence and omnipotence. But it did not. Late nineteenth-century southerners gained little wisdom and developed no special perspective from contemplating defeat." Foster's claim may hold true for some of nineteenth-century southern society, but there were many exceptions. Southerners learned lessons from the war, but not always the lessons northerners hoped to teach. Confederate-soldier-turned-politician John Warwick Daniel delivered a speech bearing the evocative title "Conquered Nations" in 1877. Daniel exhorted his constituents at the University of Virginia this way:

> But still in the broad vista of successive ages certain distinct truths appear: that conquest has been often the most instructive educator of mankind; that it has often elevated the conquered and prostrated the conqueror, sometimes elevated both; that the little nations have been conquerors because they possessed some element of manifest superiority over their greater rivals; that where a nation was unfit for the missions of conquest, its victories have been transitory and evanescent; and that where the conquered was worthy to live and rule and make and enjoy freedom, he has never failed to re-assert his independence and supremacy; that ideas govern the world, and that the best types of mankind, with the best ideas as their guides and guardians, are the conquerors in the long run.

The speech was quite remarkable and Daniel analyzed very precisely the potential lessons of defeat. No one can insist that Daniel was unreflective, but the lessons he learned were of might, power, and how to conduct a war on new grounds. His war was for white supremacy in the United States and for American imperialism abroad. Who can say the lessons he learned were without influence after the Civil War? Clemens and his fellow-writer and fellow ex-Confederate George Washington Cable became critics of American society, northern and southern, after having experienced defeat. Both learned lessons from the war about might, power, and how to conduct a new, rhetorical war. "The Private History of a Campaign That Failed" was one of many of writings in which Clemens demonstrated both skepticism and a new perspective, not just on the South but also on larger American culture. What Clemens achieved in "The Private History of a Campaign That Failed" illustrates historian Koselleck's claim that "Historical change feeds upon the vanquished. Should they survive, they create the irreplaceable primary experience of all histories: that histories take another course than that intended by those involved." Clemens survived to write a history for the victors that did not place the laurel on the brow of the victors. War was just killing the neighbors. It may have been the "barbarous order" Clemens criticized that would have executed without trial Ab Grimes, Sam Bowen, and even Sam Clemens. Or it may have been the Marion Rangers killing an unarmed man who may have been a civilian. For Clemens, it was murder, whoever did the killing. "The Private History of a Campaign That Failed" paralleled that Civil War-in-miniature published in the same year, the Grangerford–Shepherdson feud in *Adventures of Huckleberry Finn* (1885), or the later work *Tom Sawyer's Conspiracy* (1897–1900). The slave Jim protested in the latter book, "*Civil* war! Dey ain' no sich war. De idear!—people dat's good en kind en polite en b'long to de church a-marchin' out en slashin' en choppin' en cussin' en shootin' one another—lan', *I* knowed dey warn't no sich thing." Clemens, with his border state background, understood that war was inherently *uncivil*.[39]

Equally important was the "reconstructed southerner" persona that Clemens created to make this larger point. Reconstruction refers to the years from 1865 to 1877 when the defeated states of the Confederacy were reorganized prior to allowing them to reassume full statehood. It involved, at different times, such requirements as acknowledging the primacy of the Constitution, passing laws that affirmed the rights of freed male slaves to vote, and the establishing of "free constitutions." President Lincoln, in his fourth annual message, delivered on December 6, 1864, noted that "Important movements have also occurred during the year to the effect of molding society for durability in the Union. Although short of complete success, it is much in the right direction that 12,000 citizens in each of the States of Arkansas and Louisiana have organized loyal State governments, with free constitutions, and are earnestly struggling to maintain and administer them. The movements in the same direction, more extensive though less definite, in Missouri, Kentucky, and Tennessee should not be overlooked." The idea of "molding society for durability in the Union" was central to the concept of Reconstruction. The "molding" of individuals for "durability in the Union," at least for those who had taken up arms against federal authority, involved also taking the 1867 loyalty oath.

> I, _____, do solemnly swear (or affirm), in presence of Almighty God, that I will henceforth faithfully support, protect, and defend the Constitution of the United States and the Union of the States thereunder, and that I will in like manner abide by and faithfully support all laws and proclamations which have been made during the existing rebellion with reference to the emancipation of slaves. So help me God.

There is no evidence that Clemens ever took the loyalty oath, although it is possible that he did. Had he remained in Missouri, he certainly would have been faced with the necessity, for it was a requirement for voting and many other civic functions from early 1862 through 1870. Reconstruction meant administering loyalty oaths and creating laws and institutions that mirrored what a "free" society would produce in the belief that the people would, eventually, be molded by those same institutions.[40]

The loyalty oath, like the Reconstruction Acts imposed on the South, attempted to coerce behavior but also aimed at reaching the minds and hearts of the defeated forced by circumstances to recite the words. Needless to say, attempting to control thoughts and attitudes legislatively or militarily has a poor performance record. As James Russell Lowell wrote in the *Biglow Papers* (1867), likening southerners to wolves who have forsworn eating sheep,

> Ez for their oaths they wun't be wuth a button,
> Long 'z you don't cure 'em o' their taste for mutton;
> The' ain't but one solid way, howe'er you puzzle:
> Tell they're converted, let 'em wear a muzzle.

For many years, neither the loyalty oath nor the Reconstruction Acts themselves were able to compel speech or behavior, let alone assure former

Rebels were "converted" in their hearts. Union officer and writer John W. De Forest, famous for his great Civil War novel *Miss Ravenel's Conversion from Secession to Loyalty* (1867), served after the war in South Carolina as part of the occupation. In 1868, De Forest reflected on the difficulties facing a military occupation: "I so interpreted my orders as to believe that my first and great duty lay in raising the blacks and restoring the whites of my district to a confidence in civil law, and thus fitting both as rapidly as possible to assume the duties of citizenship. If the military power were to rule them forever—if it were to settle all their difficulties without demanding of them any exercise of judgment or self-control, how could they ever be, in any profound and lasting sense, 'reconstructed?'" Reconstruction, in De Forest's interpretation of his orders, involved "molding" both blacks and whites "for durability in the Union." The larger Reconstruction of the South required the reconstruction of individual minds.[41]

The idea of molding or policing thought was fraught with difficulties. It probably was "a fool's errand," as Union officer Albion Tourgeé suggested by the title of *A Fool's Errand* (1879). Tourgeé expressed his opinions freely in his autobiographical novel about life as a carpetbagger in the South during Reconstruction: "The South has been changed only in so far as the overwhelming power of the conqueror has rendered change imperative." Power subdued disloyal activity to some degree, but even power had limits. It could not compel thought; therefore, the "molding" envisioned by President Lincoln was consistently thwarted. "The people of the South have surrendered in the war what the war has conquered; but they cannot be expected to give up what was not involved in the war," declared that unreconstructed Rebel Edward Pollard in *The Lost Cause: A New Southern History of the War of the Confederates* (1868). "The Southern people stand by their principles," he warned in implicit challenge. Those principles expressed themselves in a variety of ways, most frequently in the myriad of positive expressions one sees in a people rebuilding their homes, cities, and lives. Yet throughout the Johnson, Grant, and Hayes administrations, secret terroristic organizations such as the nascent Ku Klux Klan flouted the loyalty oaths and the Reconstruction Acts. Ideally, "molding society for durability in the Union," as President Lincoln described it, would have meant re-creating society along lines of the free institutions of the northern states. What actually happened, in many instances, was an aggressive, violent assertion of southern identity.[42]

Many commentators have seen in Clemens's postwar career, in particular his friendship with Ulysses S. Grant, his many speeches at West Point, and the plethora of addresses to primarily Union veteran groups a capitulation of sorts, even a second desertion. Some detractors have accused him of crass opportunism. While labeling the author's shift in loyalties a "conversion" and a "reconstruction," scholar Arthur G. Pettit has viewed it as "carefully calculated" and not altogether honest. "When loyalty to the Confederacy proved a handicap in the face of shifting Western opinion," Pettit has opined, Clemens simply changed sides. "[I]t did not take him long to decide that dropping the Confederate South was indeed a small price to pay." Similarly, for Twain scholar Hal Bush, Clemens's "conversion" from a "southern sympathizer to northern acolyte" may have been heartfelt, but also seemed a betrayal of his origins. "After the Civil War," humorist Roy Blount Jr. has argued, "Twain moved . . . to purge himself of the stigma of Southernness." Clemens's friend William Dean Howells, of course, famously asseverated that Clemens "was the most desouthernized southerner I ever met."[43]

For Samuel Langhorne Clemens, reconstruction meant neither a desouthernization nor a northernization. Far from it. Clemens's reconstruction involved a simultaneous embracing of the principles codified in the loyalty oath and an exaggerated assertion of his southern identity. Like the Rebels described by De Forest and Tourgeé, defeat did not cause Sam Clemens to reject his southern identity; rather, like Edward Pollard, whose *The Lost Cause* (1868) was neither a *mea culpa* nor an *apologia* so much as a call to arms in a new campaign, Clemens asserted his southernness in an aggressive way, as the grounds on which he would fight a battle to reconstruct larger American culture. This is not to say that Clemens was unreconstructed in the way that Pollard was, but rather that the experience of defeat molded him in unexpected ways. The persona of a "reconstructed southerner," that is, as a former Rebel who embraced the principles of Union and Emancipation, allowed him to attack the very Yankees who, with their "uncivil war," had crippled the South and destroyed all Clemens had known in his youth as "right, righteous, sacred." And it launched the assault on the Union's own ground, something the Confederate armies were rarely able to do. "The Private History of a Campaign That Failed," with its indictment of the Civil War and war generally, was one important example. Scholar Forrest G. Robinson has suggested that the "failure" of the title "may appear as the record of a victory, albeit a somewhat inadvertent victory, over the palpable madness of war." Hamlin Hill, too, has argued that, in contrast to the other articles in the *Century* series, "Twain's Civil War was chaotic, disorganized, unpredictable, and unjustly homicidal." Defeat became a moral victory for one who had learned the cost of aggression and was forced to see both sides of the issue. To understand the complex persona Clemens created as a reconstructed southerner, consider the example of Thucydides, who wrote *The Peloponnesian Wars*, the history of the Greek civil war, from a perspective that recalls Clemens's work. "As commander," Koselleck has observed in *The Practice of Conceptual History*, "Thucydides came a few hours too late to liberate Amphipolis, which was allied with Athens. For this, he was banished for twenty years because he 'was on both sides,' as he added laconically. After the unique surprise that things worked out differently than intended, a perspective was imposed which allowed him to reconstruct the war from a distance, from the standpoint of both parties." Sam Clemens was born seeing both sides, was born into the border mentality with all its conflicted loyalties. He expressed the sense of seeing both sides to sectional conflict in many of his autobiographical works. In "Villagers of 1840–3," his notebooks and journals, and *Life on the Mississippi* (1883), the writer recalled friends who joined the Union or the Confederate war effort. As mentioned earlier, in *Life on the Mississippi*, Clemens reported that his old mentor Horace Bixby became commander of the Union River Fleet on the Mississippi, while Commodore Montgomery, another captain Sam had served under, led the Confederate River Fleet. Sam Clemens was divided, was on both sides, and remained so even as he became Mark Twain. It was part of his border state heritage, but it also inhered in his identity as a pilot. "Living both North and South as they did," Albert Paine, Clemens's official biographer posited, "they saw various phases of the question and divided their sympathy." Pilots truly saw both—or all—sides, for as they traveled up and down the Mississippi and its navigable tributaries, they experienced every shading of political opinion.[44]

Clemens's feelings mixed in *Life on the Mississippi* like the muddy waters of the Mississippi and the blue waters of the Ohio at their confluence in Cairo, Illinois. His divided sensibilities were visible well down the river. In April and May 1882, Sam Clemens returned to the river to freshen his memories as he expanded a series of articles he had published in the *Atlantic Monthly* in 1875. Those original articles, collected as "Old Times on the

Mississippi," swelled into the much longer version, *Life on the Mississippi*. In this expanded version, Clemens moved beyond his childhood memories to encompass the politics of Reconstruction as he tracked the effects of the Civil War on the South he had known. Clemens found that, while the war may have been over, it was still everywhere, even in how people conceived of reality. "In the South," he reported, "the war is what A. D. is elsewhere: they date from it." Everything is "since the waw; or du'in' the waw; or befo' the waw; or right aftah the waw; or 'bout two yeahs or five yeahs or ten yeahs befo' the waw or aftah the waw." So it was with Sam Clemens. As he witnessed the degraded present and conjured the "dead and pathetic past," all arising from the "invasion" and defeat of the southern land that had formed his identity, he took for his central theme the concept of historical change. Historian Reinhart Koselleck has argued that in history written by the defeated, "change itself became the great theme of history," as it certainly did with Clemens; the experience of defeat in the Civil War made the theme of historical change the central preoccupation of Clemens's life. Clemens was not alone in this. Senator John Warwick Daniel spoke to this in "Conquered Nations" when he asserted that "my theme comprehends universal history—all nations are conquered nations." Clemens duly recorded the battles on the river: Vicksburg, Belmont, and Fort Pillow, among others. He noted changes in the once-familiar towns, lamenting the "decayed, neglected look" of the once gleaming antebellum plantation homes and the general "blight of the war" visible on every steamboat, in every town, and on many faces. Returning to his childhood home, he found that "I could not clearly recognize the place. This seemed odd to me, for when I retired from the rebel army in '61 I retired upon Louisiana [Missouri] in good order." Making his way to Hannibal, Sam inquired about childhood friends and received the oft-repeated response, intoned like the tolling of a bell: "Killed in the war."[45]

Life on the Mississippi is best known for the writer's criticism of southern culture. "Sir Walter Scott," Clemens insisted, "had so large a hand in making Southern character, as it existed before the war, that he is in great measure responsible for the war." From Scott, southern culture gained its "sham grandeurs, sham gauds, and sham chivalries." Such criticism notwithstanding, one can say that while *Life on the Mississippi* reflects Sam's changed politics, it also reveals a heart that was still way down South in Dixie, for it beat in the pathos of every line as he revisited the lost world of the antebellum South. His explicit endorsements of southern culture ranged from the slight, such as his praise of the "pleasant custom—long ago fallen into decay in the North—of frequently employing the respectful 'Sir.'" Clemens's criticism of Unionist politics and Reconstruction, however, went beyond such (perhaps picayune) social niceties. One instance occurred when a pilot who detected the writer's attempt to travel incognito joshed him about the government monopoly on alligators: "You cut down a live-oak, and the Government fines you fifty dollars; you kill an alligator, and up you go for misprision of treason—lucky duck if they don't hang you, too. And they will, if you're a Democrat." The pilot was joking, of course, but he distilled a serious criticism of postwar arithmetic: Democrat = Disloyal. The situation Clemens discovered in the reconstructed South was one in which the molding of "society for durability in the Union" called for by President Lincoln was demonstrably incomplete—as regards to both sides and the author himself. In his writing journal from the trip, too, Clemens commented on the political situation. "While here on the ground one does not see the bloody shirt waved nor hear of outrages of a political nature. Everybody seems so humane and decent and orderly that one is not conscious of being out of his own country or in anything of a strange land. The fire-eater may exist, but one does not run across him." Here, Clemens contrasted the real situation "on the ground" in Louisiana with what Republican politicians charged when symbolically "waving the bloody shirt" of Lincoln and all other Union martyrs. Sam felt at home—not "out of his own country"—as perhaps, with his drawl and his secessionist background, he felt in the North even in the 1880s.[46]

Second Lieutenant Sam Clemens mustered in and blustered out of the war early, but he used those experiences throughout his writing career to craft a reconstructed persona. This persona championed southern culture and values while at the same time assuring society that "we no longer regret the result," as Clemens affirmed in his 1901 speech on the anniversary of Lincoln's birth.

> We of the South were not ashamed of the part we took. We believed in those days we were fighting for the right—and it was a noble fight, for we were fighting for our sweethearts, our homes, and our lives. Today we no longer regret the result, today we are glad that it came out as it did, but we of the South are not ashamed that we made an

endeavor. And you, too, are proud of the record we made . . . The old wounds are healed, and you of the North and we of the South are brothers yet. We consider it to be an honor to be of the soldiers who fought for the Lost Cause, and now we consider it a high privilege to be here tonight and assist in laying our humble homage at the feet of Abraham Lincoln.

Clemens created a persona of the southernized reconstructed southerner, not of a desouthernized or northernized southerner. He accentuated his "southernness." In so doing, he created an image of the reconstructed southerner who experienced the panorama of history from a cosmic vantage point. Clemens's speech did not partake of "the language of forgetfulness and fraternalism" that historian David Blight has identified as being part of the rush to reconcile North and South. In the typical reunion speech, Blight has argued, something was always absent: "In this vision of the terms of the Blue-Gray reunion, slavery was everyone's and no one's responsibility. America's bloody racial history was to be banished from consciousness." Clemens's 1901 Lincoln speech emphasized reunion, true, but not by denying the benefits for human liberty of the southern defeat. Most such events did not even broach the idea that the Confederate cause might have been wrong.[47]

Similarly, in a myriad of later works, Clemens invoked his identity as a reconstructed southerner specifically for the utility of criticizing both the South and the North. Scholar Louis J. Budd has recorded how frequently Clemens, in his public lectures, "imitated a simple rural upbringing" without using "the pose of the Unreconstructed rebel." At the same time, Clemens exploited some "sectional aggression," as Budd has aptly called it, citing as an example his speech, "Plymouth Rock and the Pilgrims" (1881). Here, Clemens summoned the whole history of the Pilgrims, commenting on their slaughter of the Indians, banishing of the Quakers, and the cruelty to the slaves "brought into New England out of Africa." Here, one witnesses the truth of what scholar Neil Schmitz has observed, that Clemens was "Northern in his detestation of Southern moral turpitude, Southern in his contempt for the moral rectitude of the hypocritical Northeast." Clemens based his criticisms on his own identity, telling the audience, "I am a border ruffian from the state of Missouri." The expression "border ruffian" referred to the bushwhackers Missouri sent into Kansas before and during the Civil

War. Clemens fashioned this pose to deride the pretensions of the Yankees, these "pious buccaneers." Implicitly, Clemens asked his audience, with his exaggerated drawl, in what way, other than winning the Civil War, were these "Plymouth rocks" better than Sam's father, who once sold a slave for ten barrels of tar?[48]

In *The Gilded Age* (1873), Clemens, along with Charles Dudley Warner, a neighbor in the Nook Farm community of Hartford, Connecticut, penned these words: "The eight years in America from 1860 to 1868 uprooted institutions that were centuries old, changed the politics of a people, transformed the social life of half the country, and wrought so profoundly upon the entire national character that the influence cannot be measured short of two or three generations." Many of those changes struck Sam as negative. In the novel, Clemens named the age—the Gilded Age. He criticized the increase in graft, the double-dealings in social and political life, and the rule of the dollar. The satire demonstrated that Clemens's reconstruction had at its core an aggressive social criticism of postbellum American life. Most notably, he wrote his work "Battle Hymn of the Republic (Brought Down to Date)" (c. 1901), a parody of Julia Ward Howe's prophetic hymn, with its imagery drawn from the biblical book of Revelation. Clemens pointedly did not bring the hymn "up" to date, but "down" to date, to fit a depraved world that sings, "As Christ died to make men holy, let men die to make us rich." By parodying this particular song, with all its storied connections to the Union cause, Clemens associated the triumph of the Federal forces with all the excesses wrought by the energy and capital unleashed by the war. His particular target was American involvement in the Philippines, and he thus linked nascent American imperialism with the successes and excesses of Federal power. Likewise, in "To the Person Sitting in Darkness" (1901), Clemens criticized American imperialism in Cuba, China, and the Philippines (among other places) by invoking the "Trinity of our national gods." This trinity consisted of "Washington, the Sword of the Liberator; Lincoln, the Slave's Broken Chains; the Master, the Chains Repaired." This critique of American power centered on reforging chains Lincoln had sundered. Seeing all of his own southern deities uncrowned created in Clemens a deep skepticism toward patriotism generally. In his essay, "As Regards Patriotism" (1901), Clemens did not criticize the South for misplaced patriotism in the war, but pointed out that "[b]efore the Civil War it [patriotism] made the North indifferent to slavery and friendly to the slave interest," but after secession it caused those same people to go "raging South." Clearly, the experience of defeat had taught lessons unintended by the victors, for Clemens implied that northern hypocrisy, as much as northern arms, had won the war.[49]

In "The United States of Lyncherdom" (1901), Clemens himself went "raging South," exhibiting all the ardor of the convert, the reconstructed southerner, irate at the failure of the supposedly reconstructed country, North and South, to live up to its ideals. To write this anti-lynching editorial, he adopted the mantle of the prophet, calling America to account for its sins, political and general. Clemens began by stating, "And so Missouri has fallen, that great state!" References to biblical passages were many. Judging by his use of the word "great" as a qualifier following the identification of the place that has fallen, he seemed to be referring to Revelation 14:8, "And there followed another angel, saying, Babylon is fallen, is fallen, that great city." Clemens began the second section with a formal prophetic invocation, "O, Missouri!" that, again, had many possible biblical sources, recalling most obviously Jeremiah 4:14, "O Jerusalem, wash thine heart from wickedness, that thou mayest be saved" (see also Jeremiah 22:29 and Matthew 23:37). While "O, Missouri" had the ring of burlesque to it, as did the title "The United States of Lyncherdom," Clemens was dead serious. He criticized a country founded on principles of democracy, that fought a tremendous war over slavery, and that prided itself on the rule of law only to turn away from this grand inheritance.[50]

In this work, Clemens preached to the South based on religious principles. As he argued, "in my time religion was more general, more pervasive, in the South than it was in the North, and more virile and earnest, too, I think. I have some reason to believe that this is still the case" Always there was the paradox, however, that in this "region of churches" the citizens "rose, lynched three negroes—two of them very aged ones—burned out five negro households, and drove thirty negro families into the woods." Clemens went raging North as well, and exhibited the anger of the southerner at the reputation his home state had received. The "world," he remonstrated, "will not stop and think—it never does, it is not its way; its way is to generalize from a single sample." The generalization will be that "The Missourians are lynchers." In the second section, Clemens pointed out that the "lynching mania" has "reached Colorado, it has reached California, it has reached Indiana—and now Missouri! I may live to see a negro burned in Union

Square, New York, with fifty thousand people present, and not a sheriff visible, not a governor, not a constable, not a colonel, not a clergyman, not a law-and-order representative of any kind." The example of a lynching in Union Square was to identify lynching as a human problem, not a specifically southern problem, and his examples from the West and Midwest, like his hypothetical example from the East, generalized that point. "The people in the South are made like the people in the North," he asserted. The criticism of Missouri and the South became a much wider critique of American culture. After all, where were the *Federal* troops, the ones who had won the war, when such outrages occurred? No, the Missourians were not lynchers. Americans were. For his title, he did not choose the "Confederate" states of lyncherdom, but "The United States of Lyncherdom."[51]

Clemens concluded his anti-lynching masterpiece with an apocalyptic scene right out of the most vivid passages from the books of Ezekiel and Revelation. Discussing the number of lynchings in the United States, he suggested the country should

> place the 203 in a row, allowing 600 feet of space for each human torch, so that there may be viewing room around it for 5,000 Christian American men, women, and children, youths and maidens; make it night, for grim effect; have the show in a gradually rising plain, and let the course of the stakes be uphill; the eye can then take in the whole line of twenty-four miles of blood-and-flesh bonfires unbroken, whereas if it occupied level ground the ends of the line would bend down and be hidden from view by the curvature of the earth. All being ready, now, and the darkness opaque, the stillness impressive—for there should be no sound but the soft moaning of the night wind and the muffled sobbing of the sacrifices—let all the far stretch of kerosened pyres be touched off simultaneously and the glare and the shrieks and the agonies burst heavenward to the Throne.

Clemens elaborated a nightmare reminiscent of biblical descriptions of the Babylonian captivity, defeat of the Israelites by enemy powers, and the destruction of Jerusalem. Here, however, no exogenous enemy imposed apocalypse, but an enemy within the United States and within American souls. The rhetoric of human torches was extreme, but the lynching crisis encouraged such extreme rhetoric. Such works should have given Howells second thoughts about calling Clemens "desouthernized." Nor was he "a Southern writer in Unionist discourse," as scholar Neil Schmitz has suggested, for Clemens exploited his southern identity to call the entire country to account—but not quite in the way the Unionists would have wanted. After all, by attacking the failures of Reconstruction, the rise of American imperialism, or the lack of rights for black citizens, Clemens was not attacking the South, but the American government that had defeated the South. Heretical to both the Union and the Confederacy, the reconstructed Twain refused to participate in the "language of forgetfulness and fraternalism" that historian David Blight has noted as part of the reconciliationist impulse after the Civil War. By imagining the American landscape illumined by burning bodies of lynched African Americans and having no civil authority, say, the White House, putting a stop to it, Clemens fought for justice even as he attacked the hypocrisy of the very Union that had destroyed the "right, righteous, sacred" values of his southern childhood. "The United States of Lyncherdom" was the zenith of Clemens's use of the reconstructed southerner persona to attack larger American culture.[52]

For many southerners, the Reconstruction Acts and a loyalty oath were the main sources of pressure to "reconstruct." "White organizations" such as the Ku Klux Klan and more general social factors in many parts of the South rewarded those who remained "unreconstructed." For Clemens, however, who deserted and went west very early in the war, other factors promoted Reconstruction. Among these were the divisive and devastating nature of war in the border states, his anger at being labeled "secesh" while in the West, and his growing desire for literary success. Biographers have noted, too, the influence of his abolitionist in-laws, the Langdons. More than any other factor, however, the fact of defeat, of having witnessed the "right, righteous, sacred" beliefs of his childhood revealed as wrong, wicked, and sacrilegious imposed upon Clemens a profound skepticism toward high-sounding words. Defeat awakened Sam Clemens to the fact that elevated words—whether spoken by a Sir Walter Scott, by a Colonel Ralls, or by preachers and politicians, North and South—hid sordid truths. Having seen both sides, or all sides, of the Civil War, Sam Clemens went on to write works like "The War Prayer" (1905), a stunning sketch in which a prophet of God strode into a church during wartime to put into words what people were really praying for when they asked for their arms to be blessed:

O Lord, our God, help us to tear their soldiers to bloody shreds with our shells; help us to cover their smiling fields with the pale forms of their patriot dead; help us to drown the thunder of the guns with the shrieks of their wounded, writhing in pain; help us to lay waste their humble homes with a hurricane of fire; help us to wring the hearts of their unoffending widows with unavailing grief; help us to turn them out roofless with their little children to wander unfriended the wastes of their desolated land in rags and hunger and thirst . . . imploring Thee for the refuge of the grave and denied it—for our sakes who adore Thee, Lord, blast their hopes, blight their lives, protract their bitter pilgrimage, make heavy their steps, water their way with their tears, stain the white snow with the blood of their wounded feet!

Clemens, having seen the triumph of the North and the concomitant destruction of the South, understood that war was just "the killing of strangers," or here, praying "a curse upon a neighbor." His own history taught him to look for both sides of the prayer and also to see both sides to the conflict. Unlike many of Clemens's later works, "The War Prayer" made no direct mention of the Civil War, but every line was imbrued with that bloody, fratricidal history.[53]

Desertion did not end Sam Clemens's war; rather, it marked the beginning of a war fought to defend his background and actions and to understand them for himself. His defeat created no truckling subservience. Rather, this defensive, rear-guard action became an offensive frontal charge, one in which Clemens created and exploited the identity of the reconstructed southerner. Such an identity gave him the credibility to address the southern situation both as one who knew it intimately and as a loyal citizen. Moreover, it provided him with the ground to dissent from the reunited country's hypocritical orthodoxies of triumphalism, and to criticize America—*North and South*—after the war. With his reconstructed persona, Samuel Clemens became Mark Twain and emerged as one of America's preeminent advocates for social justice and racial equality. He would rightly be called the "Lincoln of our literature."

CHAPTER 2

"I NATURALLY LOVE A YANKEE"

Twain's Civil War in Nevada, 1861–1864

Fellow-citizens, *we* can not escape history.
—ABRAHAM LINCOLN, December 1, 1862

[I]t is about the d——est country in the world for
things to happen in. *My* calculations never come out right.
—MARK TWAIN, March 8, 1862

T HE OVERLAND STAGECOACH, overburdened by bulging sacks of government mail, a Webster's *Unabridged Dictionary,* and the two brothers, Sam and Orion Clemens, rolled "day and night, through sagebrush, over sand and alkali plains" for nearly two thousand miles before arriving in Carson City, Nevada Territory, on August 14, 1861. The territory had only been officially designated on March 2, 1861, and Sam accompanied his older brother Orion Clemens, recently appointed by President Lincoln to be secretary to Territorial Governor James W. Nye. His brother's appointment provided Sam with an expedient way to escape Federals who wanted him for a Union pilot; to abandon the Marion Rangers he had joined, perhaps half-heartedly; and to escape history. As Sam lamented in a letter home, however, "It is about the d——est country in the world for things to happen in. *My* calculations never come out right." History has a way of catching up with people, and so it was in the Nevada Territory, where Confederate Second Lieutenant Sam Clemens found himself immersed in the politics of the Civil War.[1]

Sam Clemens expected to strike it rich in the West, but like most of his plans in Nevada, this one failed to pan out, unless one counts the ten days he and his mining partner Calvin Higbie were millionaires before their claim was jumped because they neglected to record it properly. That lost mine was one of many claims Sam did not back up after deserting from the Marion Rangers, for it was in this remarkable land that Sam Clemens became Mark Twain, first using the pen name in early 1863. While in Nevada, writing for the Virginia City *Territorial Enterprise,* Clemens wrote such hoaxes as "Petrified Man" (1862), "A Bloody Massacre Near Carson" (1863), "How Is It?—How It Is" (1864), and other fake news items designed to satirically reveal deeper truths. Washoe, as the territory was familiarly known, was both a desolate place "in the midst of a desert of the purest—most unadulterated, and uncompromising *sand,*" as Sam informed his mother, and a place effervescing with vibrant, violent life and all the stock in trade of a dime western novel: "The country is fabulously rich in gold, silver, copper, lead, coal, iron, quicksilver, marble, granite, chalk, plaster of Paris, (gypsum,) thieves, murderers, desperadoes, ladies, children, lawyers, Christians, Indians, Chinamen, Spaniards, gamblers, sharpers, cuyotès (pronounced ki-yo-ties), poets, preachers, and jackass rabbits." Politically, the volatile environment of wealth and absence of social cohesion produced what historian Kenneth Owens has called a "disruptive, confused, intensely combative, and highly-personal form of politics that can best be described as chaotic factionalism." Likewise, the risks and potential rewards of mining in the area created, as historian Gunther Peck has remarked, "a pervasive ethos of risk-taking in Virginia City." The very landscape contributed its share. Even today, life in Virginia City and Carson City seems tenuous indeed. Gazing at endless miles of desolation dotted by occasional evidence of mining operations, one thinks, "Yes, I could strike it rich out here; I could also die out here." Yet the lifestyle and landscape inspired a bemused affection and a burlesquing creativity. As Joseph Goodman, the editor who hired Sam Clemens away from the mining camps to write for the Virginia City *Territorial Enterprise,* wrote in his poem, "Virginia City,"

> In youth, when I did love, did love
> (To quote the sexton's homely ditty),
> I lived six thousand feet above
> Sea-level, in Virginia City;

The site was bleak, the houses small,
　　The narrow streets unpaved and slanting,
But now it seems to me of all
　　The spots on earth the most enchanting.

The politics, possibility, and danger of such a raw place contributed to the outlook and the style of newspapers. Writers attacked politicians and each other with vigor and regularity. Great liberties were taken with the news, with isolation sparking a devil-may-care creativity. Even the newspaper titles in Nevada were fresh: Virginia City's *Daily Old Piute* and Austin's *Reese River Reveille,* among others. The Carson *Appeal* even created a fictional rival, the Waubuska *Mangler,* which many mistook for a real paper.[2]

While today people chuckle over the hoaxes Clemens pulled about the discovery of a petrified man near Carson City, these overtly political sketches were often viewed less indulgently in the Nevada Territory. In his autobiography, Clemens wryly commented that the "government of the new Territory of Nevada was an interesting menagerie." Clemens greatly enjoyed poking sticks at the beasts in that menagerie, and it was not unusual for the bipeds among them to charge into the offices of the Virginia City *Territorial Enterprise,* blood on their minds. William M. Stewart, who later became the first senator from the newly formed state of Nevada, was one of these. Stewart complained bitterly about an article Clemens had written that "had not the slightest foundation in fact." Stewart was scandalized rather than mollified when the reporter admitted the charge, flatly stating that he had written it "because it was humorous." Although Stewart depicted himself as storming into the offices to defend someone else's reputation, he himself may have been the target. In his "Letter from Mark Twain" of May 16, 1863, Clemens lampooned Stewart's methods as a lawyer: "But Bill Stewart— thunder! Now, you just take that Ophir suit that's coming off in Virginia, for instance—why, God bless you, Bill Stewart'll worry the witnesses, and bullyrag the Judge, and buy up the jury and pay for 'em; and he'll prove things that never existed—hell! what won't he prove!" Little wonder that Stewart referred to Clemens's employment at the *Enterprise* as tarnishing what was "otherwise a very reputable paper." On his stagecoach journey to the Nevada Territory, somewhere near Fort Laramie, Clemens witnessed the first of many shooting deaths he would see in the West. He realized that westerners "plainly had little respect for a man who would deliver offensive opinions of people and then be so simple as to come into their presence unprepared to 'back his judgment'" by force of arms. It was a lesson he should have learned, for it would have saved him grief later.[3]

Clemens's infamous hoax, "A Bloody Massacre Near Carson" (1863), told the gory tale of Philip Hopkins, who murdered seven of his nine children and his wife, whose "scalpless corpse . . . lay across the threshold." Clemens's fake news article blamed the man's rampage on an article in the San Francisco *Bulletin*, which led Hopkins to switch his investments from Nevada mines that were allegedly "cooking dividends in order to bolster up our stocks." When he subsequently lost his investment, Hopkins went berserk. In the "article," Hopkins lost money by way of the misrepresentations of a California company guilty of the same practice. Clemens's purpose, as scholar Richard Lillard has observed, "was to slap back at the San Francisco *Bulletin*" for failing to report on the unethical business practices of California companies. The hoax had a political bite to it, as Clemens chastised California papers for driving down the value of mining stocks in the Nevada Territory. Clemens called the piece "my fine satire upon the financial expedient of 'cooking dividends,' a thing which became shamefully frequent on the Pacific coast for awhile." Regrettably, as the author recalled in 1870, "I made the horrible details so carefully and conscientiously interesting that the public simply devoured *them* greedily, and wholly overlooked . . . the guide-boards I had set up to warn him that the whole thing was a fraud." Such "guide-boards" included referring to Hopkins as a husband, a father, *and* a bachelor. Clemens also planted a "great pine forest" in the hoax, even though the region "looks something like a singed cat, owing to the scarcity of shrubbery," as the writer described it in "Washoe.—'Information Wanted'" (1864). Clemens intended for his hoax to be so obviously satirical "that even a one-eyed potato could see it." Yet, many papers reprinted the article, and the outraged cries of their duped editors echoed for years.[4]

Clemens's "Petrified Man" hoax achieved even wider circulation. Clemens adhered to the style of a news article, relating in dead-pan reportorial prose the discovery of a petrified man near the mining camps. Certain details should have given pause to careful readers. "The body was in a sitting posture, and leaning against a huge mass of croppings; the attitude was pensive, the right thumb resting against the side of the nose; the left thumb partially supported the chin, the fore-finger pressing the inner corner of the left eye and drawing it partly open; the right eye was closed, and the fingers of the right hand spread apart." Winking and thumbing his nose at the reader with this description, Clemens provided plenty of cues that the "article" was a hoax. Nevertheless, it was picked up by the wire service and traveled as far as the august pages of the scientific journal, the *London Lancet*. Clemens had aimed the hoax at a more local target. He wrote to his brother that the story was "an unmitigated lie, made from whole cloth. I got it up to worry Sewall." Scholar Louis Budd notes that Judge G. T. Sewall, in addition to serving as Humboldt County judge, "had been a partner in the Silver City *Washoe Times* and had quarreled with Orion Clemens in November 1861 over their contract to print the journals and laws of the first territorial legislature." Bad blood seems to have contributed to the sketch, which tells of "Justice Sewell or Sowell, of Humboldt City" who, in a ridiculous turn of events, conducted an inquest on the petrified man to determine the manner of his death. The nub of the sketch had people clamoring "to bury the poor unfortunate," which would require removing him from the rocky ledge with dynamite. Judge Sewall, however, "refused to allow the charitable citizens to blast him from his position." An appointed judge, Sewall was doubtless sensitive to the unclear pronoun reference that rendered it impossible to tell if the petrified man or the sitting judge required blasting from his position. Clemens delighted in angering the judge, though he claimed to not understand the man's enmity. In an earlier letter to William Clagett, he had written: "I have heard from several reliable sources that Sewall will be here shortly, and has sworn to whip me on sight. Now what would you advise a fellow to do?—take a thrashing from the son-of-a-bitch, or bind him over to keep the peace? I don't see why he should dislike me. He is a yankee,—and I naturally love a yankee."

While details are scarce, it seems that Sewall, an appointed judge and staunch Unionist, considered Clemens a southern sympathizer, or Copperhead. That term emerged in mid-1861, when Republicans began using it to refer to the "Peace Democrats" who leaned toward the South and opposed the war. With "Petrified Man," Clemens at least gave Sewall more specific reasons to dislike him. Clemens continued to do so. In a July 12, 1863 news item, one of his occasional letters from the territory to the San Francisco *Morning Call*, he reported that a coach "rolled down a slight precipice, and was smashed to pieces," injuring Sewall. As a service to his readers who might have forgotten the man's name, Clemens continued: "Mr. Sewall is the profound Justice of the Peace who held an inquest last Fall at Gravelly

Ford, on the Humboldt River, on a petrified man, who had been sitting there, cemented to the bed-rock, for the last three or four hundred years. The citizens wished to blast him out and bury him, but Judge S. refused to allow the sacrilege to be committed." Clemens obviously delighted in tormenting the judge. He recalled the events in "A Couple of Sad Experiences" (1870) and claimed that "for about eleven months, as nearly as I can remember, Mr. Sewall's daily mail contained along in the neighborhood of half a bushel of newspapers hailing from many climes with the Petrified Man in them, marked around with a prominent belt of ink . . . I hated Sewall in those days, and these things pacified me and pleased me. I could not have gotten more real comfort out of him without killing him."[5]

Readers found Clemens's writings so humorous, they often missed the underlying political satire, however. That is true of some professors, too, who have seen in the writer's jokes nothing at all serious. Paul J. Carter's argument is just one of many that one might cite: "Washoe journalism . . . molded Twain's mental attitudes and habits until he became comparatively insensitive, almost indifferent, to serious problems. His tendency to emphasize the trivial or fanciful at the expense of the vital or rational is dramatically evident in his seeming ignorance of the implications of such a political, social, and moral crisis as the Civil War." Clemens's writings in the Nevada Territory, or "Washoe" as people called it back then, were often overtly political, and it bears pointing out that while generically, these two works, "A Bloody Massacre Near Carson" and "Petrified Man," were both technically hoaxes, they were also satires. Clemens named them so in his comments about them, terming them examples of "reformatory satire." Risking a comparison to a "one-eyed potato," contemporary readers often missed this aspect of these works, and it bears noting the insistence with which Clemens employed the term "satire." Of "Petrified Man," he concluded that "it was altogether too delicate, for nobody ever perceived the satire part of it." Similarly, the author's "pleasant financial satire" about a distraught shareholder attacking his family with knife and axe tricked newspapers—even neighboring newspapers that should have known better—into reprinting the article. One of these newspapers, the *Daily News* from nearby Gold Hill, Nevada Territory, reprinted the hoax with this preface:

HORRIBLE—The most sickening tale of horror that we have read for years, is told in the Enterprise of this morning; and were it not for the respectable source from which our contemporary received it, we should refuse to give it any credence.

Give it credence, they did, with the result that Samuel L. Clemens as Mark Twain became a favorite whipping boy for the Gold Hill *Daily News* and many other papers. "Mr. Mark Twain is not content to let the memory of his late silly imposition upon the public pass from the minds of men . . . We took exceptions to being made the dupe of his nonsense, and a medium for its dissemination." The following month, after reporting in "An Asylum Needed" about an actual instance of "butchery" by one Jerry Davis that sounded like Clemens's fictional account of the Hopkins family massacre, the Gold Hill *Daily News* included this small footnote: "*Look out for old Hopkins, Mark Twain and Jerry Davis." Clemens's satires eventually found their targets, but only after the vehicle for satire, the details, had rendered the works infamous. It was a pattern he would repeat. Mark Twain became a popular name on the *Enterprise* by aggravating those in power, often through the satirical thrusts of hoaxes, burlesques, and satires. Those works helped Sam Clemens become the Mark Twain we know. They would also prove his undoing in the Nevada Territory.[6]

The idea that Clemens was blind to political and social problems is obviously untrue, but what of Carter's assertion that the writer was unconcerned with the "political, social, and moral crisis" of the Civil War? Scholar Henry Nash Smith, too, has claimed that "[t]hroughout his stay in Nevada he avoided public reference to the War or to the issue of loyalists versus Copperheads." Quite the contrary. During the debate about changing the name of "Lake Bigler" to "Lake Tahoe," Clemens vented his dissenting opinion in the article "Bigler vs. Tahoe" (1863), lambasting the latter name as a "spoony, slobbering, summer-complaint of a name. Why, if I had a grudge against a half-price nigger, I wouldn't be mean enough to call him by such an epithet as that." It is easy, but misleading, to ascribe this comment merely to racism, for Clemens's comment is not gratuitous, but central to his argument in the piece. Critic Joseph Coulombe, for example, has ignored the political dispute underlying "Bigler vs. Tahoe" in his analysis, suggesting only that it "exposed how his [Twain's] racial animosity (even when intended as a joke) was sometimes a cover for his insecurity." But "Bigler vs. Tahoe" had at its heart territorial politics. The comment's explicit racism and implicit reference to slavery related to John Bigler's political allegiances. A former governor of California, the pro-southern Democrat was considered a Copperhead and traduced as John "Bigliar." Rather than allow the lake to be "poisoned by Copperheadism," the name was changed. Clemens's "Bigler vs. Tahoe" was quickly countered by "Tahoe vs. Bigler" in the neighboring Gold Hill *Daily News.* The paper praised the name Tahoe, which had been "substituted for that of the copperhead Ex-Governor Bigler." Clemens's defense of the name Lake Bigler and his reference to slavery with the "half-price nigger" comment invited charges of southern or "secesh" sympathies.[7]

Similarly, in his hilarious "Unfortunate Blunder" (1863), Clemens recounted how a drunken Irishman reeled into the First Presbyterian Church under the impression that it was a meeting of the "Union League," an organization promoting loyalty to the Union among Republicans and Democrats. These organizations, as historian Walter A. McDougall has noted, sometimes degenerated into "paramilitary auxiliaries that rallied Republicans and bullied critics of the war." Clemens would not be bullied, however. "The fo'man o' Th' Pride o' the West has dis-dis-ch-(hic!)-*airged* me," the Irishman blustered, "bekase I'm a bloody d——d Blaick Republikin!" A "Black Republican" belonged to the radical wing of the party that favored abolition and the vote for former slaves. The term was an epithet used by Democrats, especially those from the South. Interestingly, the Irish, unlike the drunken example in the sketch, were not known for their support of the Republican Party, or Union Party, as it was called during the president's bid for reelection; "Union" tried to bring in Democrats into the "bigger tent," as might be said today. Such efforts were necessary. According to historian Frank L. Klement, in the election of 1860, an astonishing "ninety-eight percent of the Irish-Americans voted the Democratic ticket and distrusted Lincoln." In Clemens's sketch, the drunk is apparently part of the 2 percent minority. Reeling into the meeting, he hailed Colonel John Collins, staid member of both the Union League and the First Presbyterian Church, embarrassing this pillar of the community with his familiarity. The humor here was not disloyal, that is to say, it was not anti-Union, but it was certainly not pro-Republican, as Clemens jabbed at the odd political bedfellows one found in the party that included obviously recent immigrants as well as the settled and staid. The sketch derided Radical Republicanism and those adherents like Colonel Collins whose discomfort with their political allies showed them to be far less egalitarian in practice than in their preaching.[8]

Clemens created the persona Mark Twain in an environment of tremendous political ferment, with the Nevada Territory pursuing statehood at a time when many inhabitants sympathized with the Confederacy or at least with the southern views of race and slavery. Many southerners settled the region. Virginia City was named after one of them, "Old Virginny" Finny, a fugitive from California justice who named the spot after accidentally breaking a bottle of whiskey against a rock. He jokingly christened the spot after himself to justify having spilled the whiskey. While there were notable exceptions, most Nevadans were for the Union, but most were certainly not for abolition. As John W. De Forest wrote about his southern heroine Lillie in the great Civil War novel *Miss Ravenel's Conversion from Secession to Loyalty* (1867), "She was slightly unionized, but not in the least abolitionized." Clemens's biases, too, remained with southern culture, and perhaps even with the Confederacy in the early years. If in his public writings he conveyed these attitudes under the protective coloration of burlesque, in his private correspondence he was more explicit. Recalling the cantankerous yellow mule he had ridden during his brief stint as a Confederate with the Marion Rangers, Sam wrote to his sister-in-law Mary "Mollie" Clemens in January 1862: "'Paint-Brush' in the hands of the enemy! God forgive me! this is the first time I have felt melancholy since I left the United States." The lamented Paint-Brush had been captured by the Union. However jokingly, when Clemens said, "if he [the mule] has gone over to the enemy, let him go," the Union remained "the enemy."[9]

Similarly, in February 28, 1862, Clemens wrote again to William Clagett: "He has thrashed our Missourians like everything. But by the Lord, they didn't do it on the Sacred Soil, my boy. They had to chase 'em clear down into Arkansas before they would whip them. There's consolation in *that*. If they had remained on the Soil, Curtis couldn't have done it . . . Now, when I was on the soil, I used to be as terrible as an army with banners; but out here on this quartz foundation, you see, I don't amount to a Damn. That's what's the matter with *me*. And they have taken Fort Henry, and Fort Donelson, and the half of Tennessee—and the stars and stripes wave over the Capital at Nashville." The battle Sam referred to was the beginning of the Pea Ridge Campaign. General Sterling Price, the Confederate leader whose troops Sam may have been attempting to join prior to his taking the oath with the Marion Rangers, was driven out of Springfield, Missouri, on February 11, 1862. The Union commander, General Samuel R. Curtis, forced them into Arkansas, where from March 6 to 8, 1862, the battle, "the bloodiest of the war on the western border, and one of the most decisive," raged. Twain scholar Henry Nash Smith has cited this letter as evidence of the author's shifting attitude toward the Union. Clemens, he argued, "ridicules" the Missourians. The letter's tone, while comical, seems more of a lament than otherwise, and it is prudent to recall that Clagett shared Sam's occupation as a newspaperman *and* his reputation as a Copperhead. Billy Clagett's "reconstruction" paralleled Sam's in several respects. Spurred on by his apparently disloyal editorials, a mob of soldiers attacked his father's newspaper, the Keokuk *Constitution*. Clagett's press was cast into the Mississippi River because the *Constitution* was part of the pro-southern Copperhead press. In Nevada, Clagett threaded a delicate course, but engaged actively in Union (as opposed to Republican) politics. He raised the ire of some in Republican circles when he marred the July 4th festivities, as one columnist complained, by quoting "Private Miles O'Reilley's song. A reference to the 'nigger,' and the raising of the question as to whether our people are 'for' or 'against' that individual, was uncalled for." The editorialist bristled at Clagett's performance, saying that it "looks very much like straining at effort to please a certain element whose loyalty to the Government is not to be depended upon a great deal." The song contained these popular lines:

> To the tenets of Douglas we tenderly cling,
> Warm hearts to the cause of our country we bring;
> To the flag we are pledged—all its foes we abhor—
> And we ain't for the "nigger" but we are for the war.

Written by Charles G. Halpine using the persona of an Irish Union private "Miles O'Reilly," these lines quoted by Clagett infuriated Republicans but expressed the attitude of many in Virginia City. By 1864, Clagett was campaigning for William Stewart in his bid to become Republican senator from Nevada. Clagett was himself elected as a state representative on the Union ticket, but even then, his candidacy was suspect. The Virginia City Daily *Union*, for example, withheld its endorsement, castigating Clagett for having opposed resolutions that he deemed "too strong in the language used to

denounce the rebels, and their traitorous sympathisers in the loyal states."
"No half-way loyalty will answer in this contest," concluded the editorialist. Clagett continued to support the Republican Party half-heartedly. Just
as in the 1884 presidential election Sam Clemens became a Mugwump (a
Republican who supported the Democratic presidential candidate), Clagett
parted with Republicans frequently in the postwar decades, even denouncing them as "money-changers" in his pro-silver pamphlet *Money, Banks,
Panics, and Prosperity* (1898).[10]

Critical commentary of Clemens's years in the West has ignored the
political context, Clemens's associations, and even the writer's work. Little
wonder, then, that what few studies have been written have asserted contradictory ideas. On the one hand, some have suggested that Sam Clemens,
having escaped from the Civil War, quickly became a committed Republican
and a staunch Unionist. On the other hand, many scholars have asserted
that Clemens was simply indifferent to politics, that having been burned by
his involvement in the politics of the Civil War, he simply avoided politics
entirely. Neither is accurate. Henry Nash Smith in *Mark Twain of the Enterprise,* for example, has written, "Nor was Mark Twain interested in national
politics, despite the fact that the momentous issues of the Civil War filled
the Nevada newspapers and lay just beneath the surface of everyday life in
the Territory." In this, scholars have been misled by the author himself, who
immersed himself in local and national politics while claiming otherwise.
One suspects intentional irony when Clemens agreed to take charge of
the Virginia City *Territorial Enterprise* during Joseph Goodman's absence:
"I stipulated . . . that I should never be expected to write editorials about
politics or eastern news. I take no sort of interest in those matters."[11]

In fact, while Clemens disliked writing straight editorials, he delighted
in lampooning politics, local and national, throughout his Nevada years.
With Orion installed as secretary to the governor of a territory that hoped
to ratify a state constitution and join the Union, it could hardly have been
otherwise. Even before Clemens began working for the *Territorial Enterprise,*
back in the silver mining camp of Aurora, he wrote his first letters for the
paper, signing them "Josh." As might be expected from such a pseudonym,
they were burlesques, or "joshes," but they were of an overtly political nature. For example, he famously imitated the inflated oratory of a politician
who subjected the mining camps to a fulsome, fussy, and effusive Fourth
of July harangue. Similarly, after he became a professional newspaperman,

Clemens penned "The Great Prize Fight, The Only True and Reliable Account of the Great Prize Fight for $100,000 at Seal Rock Point, On Sunday Last, Between His Excellency Gov. Stanford and Hon F.F. Low, Governor-Elect of California" (1863). In this work Clemens cast the reporting of a political convention into the language of bare-knuckle brawling. He returned the metaphor of "throwing one's hat into the ring" back to its roots as he not-so-subtly suggested the lack of civility in western politics even while ticking off a few local figures, such as Virginia City's "Bullyragging Bill Stewart" who served as an assistant to Governor Leland Stanford. Clemens also invoked national politics, however, for the adversaries sported "Union colors around their waists." Clemens deployed military language throughout the description of this "battle," with even the referee being one General Wright. Indeed, the work satirized the squabbling among Union politicians while the country was embroiled in a civil war, and Clemens was responding directly to the disastrous 1863 California Republican Convention, which saw a floor fight between Governor Stanford, who was not nominated for another term, and his rival, Frederick Ferdinand Low, the man who became California's first governor to serve a four-year term. Consider these lines: "At this stage of the game the battle ground was strewn with a sufficiency of human remains to furnish material for the construction of three or four men of ordinary size, and good sound brains enough to stock a whole county like the one I came from in the noble old state of Missouri." For the adversaries, this was a "game," contrasting with the "battle ground" and the "human remains" one found there. The piece appeared on October 11, 1863; following the bloody July with the Battle of Gettysburg and the ferocious Battle of Chickamauga in September, the description of the political prize fight must have seemed grotesquely hilarious. Clemens described how Stanford "let fly one of his battering rams and caved in the other side of Low's head" so that it resembled "a beet which somebody had trod on." Low responded in kind, however, "and sent one of his ponderous fists crashing through his opponent's ribs and in among his vitals, and instantly afterward he hauled out poor Stanford's left lung and smacked him in the face with it." As Clemens wrote in "A Couple of Sad Experiences," the 1870 article in which he looked back on the misadventures surrounding "Petrified Man" and "A Bloody Massacre Near Carson," people often misread burlesque. "To write a burlesque so wild that its pretended facts will not be accepted in perfect good faith by somebody, is very nearly an impossible thing to do." Many people did accept Clemens's burlesques "in perfect good faith," but on other occasions when they realized the humor of his writing, they simply missed its point. "In other instances," Clemens wrote, "the 'nub' or moral of the burlesque—if its object be to enforce a truth—escapes notice in the superior glare of something in the body of the burlesque itself." A smack in the face with a lung qualified as the sort of "superior glare" that might cause one to miss the political point that in 1863, American politics was an extension of the Civil War in a different arena.[12]

Most significant for dispensing with the notion that Clemens was disinterested in politics was his involvement with the Third House, a carnival or burlesque version of the territorial legislature. In the very letter where he proclaimed his disinterest in politics, Sam proudly noted his status as "his Excellency Gov. Mark Twain, of the Third House." The Third House, presided over by newspapermen, met after the evening adjournment of the actual territorial legislature. The Third House consisted primarily of legislators and newspaper reporters, and it was bawdy, raucous, and satirical. The title "Third House" referred to the territorial government that initially had two houses, but the term also echoed the Fourth Estate—Journalism—the estate that has kept politicians honest, or has tried to, when it has kept itself honest. Descriptions of its meetings make one envy the very flies on the walls privileged to witness them. Sessions took place in venues as diverse as saloons and Carson City's First Presbyterian Church. As befit a burlesque legislature, a certain license was exercised, with both politicos and their characteristic lingo the butt of the jokes.[13]

Burlesque is oppositional, not only in form, but also in content. The Third House was inherently an anti-legislature, with the oath taken by the members for the Third House patterned closely after the actual one.

The oath from the Nevada State Constitution:

I do . . . solemnly swear (or affirm) that I have not fought a duel, nor sent or accepted a challenge to fight a duel, nor been a second to either party, nor in any manner aided or assisted in such duel, nor been knowingly the bearer of such challenge or acceptance, since the adoption of the Constitution of the State of Nevada, and that I will not be so engaged or concerned, directly or indirectly, in or about any such duel, during my continuance in office.

Compare this to Clemens's burlesque in "Nevada State Constitutional Convention; Third House":

> We do solemnly affirm that we have never seen a duel, never been connected with a duel, never heard of a duel, never sent or received a challenge, never fought a duel, and don't want to. Furthermore, we will support, protect and defend this constitution which we are about to frame, until we can't rest, and will take our pay in scrip.

Little wonder that, as Clemens explained in *Roughing It* (1872), "the Territorial legislature was usually spoken of as the 'asylum.'" Contorted legalistic political language begged to be burlesqued, and even for those who had never, ever, *ever* heard of duels, this bylaw from the Nevada Constitution certainly presented an inviting target. The way the Nevada legislators affixed one qualification after another suggested the kind of doublespeak and governmental mumbo jumbo produced by the innumerable committees and subcommittees of what Clemens called "the Circumlocution Office of Washington." The burlesque hinted that, in the context of the wild West that was Washoe, it was probably as difficult as herding cats to keep legislators—or reporters, witness later events with Goodman and Clemens—from dueling.[14]

The "Nevada State Constitutional Convention; Third House" was published in the Virginia City *Territorial Enterprise*, on December 13, 1863. In his previous "Letter from Mark Twain" of December 12, Clemens had promised a "*verbatim* report of its proceedings." Whenever Clemens alleged that he recorded something verbatim, let the reader beware. In this delightful confection, Clemens doubtless improved the flavor of the original. In the sketch, Governor Twain followed the order of business from the prayer, which was "dispensed with, on the ground that it was never listened to by the members of the First House," to the adjournment. The burlesque had a real bite. Because the members of the First House were present at the Third House and drink flowed freely, the humor was rough and pointed. Governor Twain, for example, barked at Samuel Youngs, a delegate to the First House: "You have been sitting there for thirty days, like a bump on a log, and you never rightly understand anything." Clemens mercilessly browbeat a favorite target, William Stewart, a delegate to the convention and later a senator from Nevada. Stewart became known as the "Father of American Mining Law," and one can see why, even in this burlesque. Clemens lampooned Stewart's oft-repeated argument that mines should not be taxed, for "if you tax the mines, you impose a burden upon the people which will be heavier than they can bear. And when you tax the poor miner's shafts, and drifts, and bed-rock tunnels, you are NOT taxing his property; you are NOT taxing his substance; you are NOT taxing his wealth—no, but you are taxing what may become property some day, or may not; you are taxing the shadow from which the substance may eventually issue or may not." Stewart made a good point, but it was a point he made too long and too frequently to be ignored by a satirist. Governor Twain ordered him to sit down, saying, "You and your bed-rock tunnels, and blighted miners' blasted hopes, have gotten to be a sort of nightmare to me, and I won't put up with it any longer. I don't wish to be too hard on your speech, but if you can't add something fresh to it, or say it backwards, or sing it to a new tune, you have simply got to simmer down for awhile."[15]

One delegate after another fell to the sharp fusillade, and finally, in mock desperation, Governor Twain, here presiding as the "President" of the Third House, asserted what the real issues at hand were: "The President—'No, sir! The question is, shall we tolerate religious indifference in this community; or the rights of conscience; or the right of suffrage; or the freedom of the press; or free speech, or free schools, or free niggers.'" Clemens captured in comic form some of the basic issues of Nevada territorial government in 1863, a time when most citizens were pro-Union but did not favor "free niggers." Voters rejected the proposed constitution on the first go-round by a huge plurality, at least in part because it was, as one Copperhead journal termed it, "that free nigger Constitution."[16]

The assembly concluded with Governor Twain berating the politicos, saying, "Gentlemen, your proceedings have been exactly similar to those of the convention which preceded you. You have considered a subject which you knew nothing about; spoken on every subject but the one before the house, and voted without knowing what you were voting for or having any idea what would be the general result of your action." He then enjoined the Chief Page to bring "a spoonful of molasses and a gallon of gin, for the use of the President." One does not believe for a minute that Clemens recorded this meeting of the Third House in shorthand even as he participated in it—that misrepresentation was part of the fun. The comic piece likely approximated the kind of chaff that went on, however. The practice of roasting the delegates, whether in reality during the Third House or figuratively in publishing the account in the *Territorial Enterprise,* was part of the unruly, turbulent, rough and tumble politics of the territory.[17]

Clemens's performance as "His Excellency Gov. Mark Twain, of the Third House" was tremendously important to his evolving public persona. The Third House was born amid the ferment of the territorial aspirations to become a state and all the questions of law and destiny that implied. The political language used by the territorial delegates was itself an imitation of existing political language. The Third House as an institution made light of ponderous ideas and language, but it would be a mistake to assume that the group was apolitical. Satire is inherently political and often seemingly disloyal as it savages those who humorlessly see themselves as answering the higher calling of politics and public service. Hal Clayton preceded Clemens as governor of the Third House, though in one instance he adopted the persona of "Captain Jim, Chief of the Washoes, and Governor (de facto) of Nevada." In November 1862, Clayton penned an infamous burlesque of Governor James Warren Nye's annual message and circulated it as a broadside. The document bristled with many barbs that certainly could have caused him trouble, not the least of which was this pointed prose:

> Your Executive would without the least hesitation, evasion, or compunctions of conscience, have resorted to the last great war emergency, in the first place, by the immediate issuance of his proclamation, to take effect instanter, instead of *in futuro,* enslaving the millions of free born whites on this continent, and freeing the millions of enslaved blacks; rearing, in lieu of our present form of government, handed down to us by our revolutionary forefathers as a bequest to be transmitted to your and my posterity untarnished, a negro oligarchy, to become the supreme rulers of the benighted, ignorant and downcast people, who have neither the will or capacity to govern and control themselves, and thereby would have forever placed a quietus upon our existing difficulties.

Horseplay with bombastic, legalistic language amused readers, but the harsh edge to the "Annual Message" was sharpened by territorial politics. Governor Nye had a reputation for quashing political debate and justifying it, as President Lincoln did, on the exigencies of the Civil War. Dictatorial in style, Nye's demeanor and politics rubbed many in Washoe the wrong way. For good reason was the region jokingly referred to as the "Nye-vada Territory" by the New York *Leader*. Most notable in this satirical raillery were the needling references to "negro oligarchy" and the Copperhead canard that abolition would lead to black supremacy. Clayton then called on Clemens's brother Orion, Nye's secretary, to serve as the doorkeeper of the newly refurbished asylum "for the keeping and confinement of the members of the two lower branches of the legislature." Clayton's broadside was a tamer version of David Croly's pamphlet *Miscegenation* that would appear the following year and contribute to Clemens's hasty exodus from Nevada. Clayton's burlesque ran little risk of people missing the point, as people often did with Clemens's (usually) more subtle political burlesques. The following summer, Clayton was arrested by Lieutenant Mathewson and incarcerated at Fort Churchill, as Clemens wrote in one of his occasional letters to the San Francisco *Morning Call*. Clayton had been charged with "persisting in the uttering of disloyal sentiments, notwithstanding the repeated warnings which he had previously received." Despite this setback, Clayton served as president of the Third House again in 1864 as well as several times after the war. Clemens's involvement in the Third House necessarily immersed him in politics, regional and national. On December 17, 1862, the Third House actually met while the First House was in session. They gathered in the street around bonfires, attempting to influence the Corporation vote. The vote did go their way, and the event revealed that even the mock legislature cherished certain political agendas.[18]

What was Clemens's political agenda during this time? Involvement in a travesty government required knowledge about the issues and procedures of the actual government. Clemens was immersed in both. In fact, his very presence at the Third House was due to his reporting on the Constitutional Convention then taking place. His extensive reporting on the first Constitutional Convention from November 2 to December 11, 1863 and on the still longer second Constitutional Convention that spanned forty days in January and February 1864 (reporting with a colleague), gave full play to both his humor and his engagement with underlying political issues, such as his parody of Stewart's speeches against the mining tax. Clemens even lobbied on behalf of a bill to require notary publics for the certification of official documents. His deep involvement with politics and politicians should make readers suspicious of claims that he had no knowledge of or interest in politics. Indeed, awareness of Sam Clemens's work as a political reporter should influence how we read his works of this and later eras. His office as a humorist and as a reporter coincided—even in those works with a more literary bent.

Claiming a lack of interest in politics served Clemens as a kind of strategic political cover. While enjoying the respect of many individuals, he remained vulnerable to criticism as disloyal in an environment where the Territorial Governor Nye referred to him as "a damned Secessionist." Nye's judgment was doubtless exaggerated by his own office, for as governor of the Nevada Territory, he had the delicate task of overseeing the transition to statehood at a time when other states were attempting to secede. This surely colored his view of Sam Clemens. Local and regional politics were national politics in Nevada. Not only did Sam's position as a reporter not protect him, his constant involvement in politics and even in those convivial after-hour meetings of the Third House contributed to his reputation as disloyal. During those years in Nevada, he was frequently denounced as disloyal, "secesh," and a Copperhead. Even the *Enterprise* itself, a decidedly pro-Union newspaper, was at times accused of disloyalty. The *Aurora Daily Times*, published in Esmaralda County, Nevada Territory, so denounced the *Enterprise* in an 1863 article entitled "The Virginia Press": "The Enterprise is guilty of 'copperish' language in saying that 'we do not believe Abraham Lincoln to be a great General or that he is the ablest statesman in the country.'" Mild criticism smacked of high treason during the territory's attempt to join the Union during a time of disunion. Nevada's slogan "Battle Born" applied to Mark Twain as well.[19]

Clemens responded to such charges by mocking and taunting as a means of turning criticism back to its source. In the April 1, 1864 issue of the *Enterprise*, for example, he derided those who exaggerated hints of disloyalty. For the April Fool's Day issue, he lampooned Thomas Fitch, who had been the editor of the *Union*, the rival newspaper that caused Clemens a great deal of trouble while in Nevada. Fitch had also engaged in a duel in 1863 with Joseph Goodman, Sam's editor at the *Enterprise*, but it is unclear to what degree Clemens considered him an enemy. In his article about the first attempt at the duel, "A Duel Prevented" in the August 2, 1863 *Enterprise*, and in later autobiographical reminiscences about the actual duel in which Goodman wounded Fitch, Clemens expressed no *personal* dislike of Fitch. He wrote of him frequently, often using him as the butt of jokes, but he did that with friend and foe alike. Clemens and Dan De Quille benefited from Mrs. Fitch's cooking, yet both laughed about stealing the couple's firewood during the winter. Decades later, Clemens still joked about Fitch, then an old man, saying that in the West when he is recognized "friendly people slap him on the shoulder and call him—well, never mind what they call him; it might offend your ears, but it does Fitch's heart good." One supposes they greeted him with some variant of "Well, Tom Fitch, you old son-of-a-bitch!" Clemens's use of Fitch in the April 1 burlesque probably had something to do with the political position the editor occupied as a Republican lawyer, orator, and arbiter in the California patronage dispute of 1861, when Fitch was selected to meet with President Lincoln to determine how official positions would be awarded after the election. The Lincoln administration considered Fitch one of the leading Republicans in the West. In Nevada, Fitch served as a member of the 1863 Constitutional Convention, and after statehood, this "silver-tongued orator," as Clemens dubbed him, was elected congressman. Clemens depicted Fitch at times as a demagogue, calling his oratory "a regular masked battery. He lulls you into a treacherous repose, with a few mild and graceful sentences, and then suddenly explodes in your midst with a bombshell of eloquence which shakes you to your very foundations." Clemens used Fitch in his April Fool's Day piece, "Another Traitor—Hang Him!" as the prototype of the Radical Republican secesh-hunter. In the burlesque, Fitch accused one W. F. Myers of arguing that "negroes were inferior to white men . . . and that by said slanderous language the colored race aforesaid were greatly scandalized, and the Government of the United States brought into disrepute and the Southern Confederacy encouraged, and Uncle Abe greatly maligned and traitors benefited." Clemens's burlesque of judicial language provided the vehicle for him to scoff at a political climate that exaggerated the dangers posed by the legitimate exercise of free speech. The racist opinions that landed the unfortunate Myers before the judge were frankly widely held, a fact that strengthened the burlesque, particularly since the article recommended the "defendant be punished either by hanging . . . and that he also be compelled to take the oath of allegiance." The satire "Another Traitor—Hang Him!" was more than an April Fool's Day joke, and it revealed the irony of a Unionist politics that avowed freedom for all races but not freedom of speech as guaranteed by the Constitution.[20]

The sketches that precipitated Clemens's second "desertion" were those involving the Sanitary Commission. Founded by private doctors as a charity, the Sanitary Commission was recognized on June 9, 1861, by order of the Secretary of War Edwin M. Stanton. The Sanitary Commission raised money through direct pleas, fundraisers such as balls, and large-scale events like "Sanitary Fairs." The commission used the money to purchase medical supplies and warehouses and to fund transportation. The largest single disbursement was nearly $2 million for supplies such as bandages, medicine, and fresh fruits and vegetables. The West played a key role in the founding and funding of the Sanitary Commission. The first check from California, for example, contributed $100,000 and arrived on September 19, 1862. This, according to the leaders of the fund, "was the making and saving of the United States Sanitary Commission." Like the Union Club, the group also served an important social function, particularly in the Nevada Territory, where participation and contributions functioned as the outward signs of inward loyalty to the Union cause. The organization was patriotic, high minded, and occasionally parochial in its outlook, but it did remarkable work during the war and was later reorganized as the American Red Cross. In an 1867 notebook entry, Clemens wrote, "'Israel is smitten before the Philistines!' (Heavy news) 'There hath been a great slaughter & 30,000 of our men have perished, & lo there is no Sanitary Commission.'" Even in an era of similarly "great slaughter" on the fields of Antietam, Gettysburg, and—closer to home—Wilson's Creek, the Battle of Lexington, and the Pea Ridge Campaign, Clemens could joke about it.[21]

Before Clemens's fateful gibe at the expense of the Sanitary Fund, he had already in his dealings with the ladies of Washoe stepped on more than a few toes. For example, in his January 12, 1864 "Letter from Mark Twain, Miss Clapp's School," the writer tweaked two ladies who featured prominently in the later dispute over the Sanitary Fund. Clemens began his letter as a kind of burlesque of his own reporting on the legislature: "By authority of an invitation from Hon. Wm. M. Gillespie, member of the House Committee on Colleges and Common Schools, I accompanied that statesman on an unofficial visit to the excellent school of Miss Clapp and Mrs. Cutler, this afternoon. The air was soft and balmy—the sky was cloudless and serene—the odor of flowers floated upon the idle breeze—the glory of the sun descended like a benediction upon mountain and meadow and plain—the wind blew like the very devil, and the day was generally disagreeable." The passage was a forerunner of the beginning of chapter 4 of *The Adventures of Tom Sawyer* (1876) with its "benediction" shining down, and the function here was much the same as he described a school that is "not likely to be unfamiliar to the free American citizen who has a fair recollection of how he used to pass his Friday afternoons in the days of his youth." As he did in that later book, Clemens used the description of the schoolhouse to censure the oratorical style of the students, their compositions, and so on. Commencing with the typical editorial encomiums of a local institution, the sketch proceeded to burlesque of a general sort, but then went further. Clemens closed with a humorous critique of the school itself and its expenses. "Well, never mind—we must learn to take an absorbing delight in educational gossip; nine-tenths of the revenues of the Territory go into the bottomless gullet of that ravenous school fund, you must bear in mind." The procedure in this sketch was precisely what later landed Clemens into trouble with the "Ladies of Carson," and it was not really a misunderstanding. In other words, Clemens's criticism of the expenses behind Clapp's School, which he had joked was producing poor students, was not just part of the fun; rather, it was the point of the fun.[22]

In April, Sam's brother Orion, the secretary of the Nevada Territory, added to his list of titles president of the Sanitary Commission of Ormsby County, his wife Mollie serving as secretary. The ladies of Carson planned a Sanitary Fund Ball to raise money for the care of wounded Union soldiers, for such expenditures as bandages and chloroform, often in short supply or simply nonexistent in field hospitals. In his January 10, 1863 article "The Sanitary Ball," Clemens wrote with his usual verve and style, bordering always on chaotic comedy, about the dancing of the quadrille, during which "those long, trailing dresses . . . were under fire in the thickest of the fight for six hours." Given the circumstances, that the purpose of the ball was to raise money for the Union wounded, it is significant that Clemens described the dancing in military terms, as in this passage: "The dancers are formed in two long ranks, facing each other, and the battle opens with some light skirmishing between the pickets, which is gradually resolved into a general engagement along the whole line; after that, you have nothing to do but stand by and grab every lady that drifts within reach of you, and swing her." As a description of a ball during wartime, the sketch is priceless, the military argot fostering a sense of the ridiculous as the social interactions of male and female became the maneuverings of warring armies. Throughout the Civil War, Clemens employed military terms in humorous ways to portray relatively pacific pursuits such as dancing. In "Those Blasted Children" (1863), Clemens characterized the children as "cavalry" who were "mounted on broomsticks" and "attack my premises in a body." Similarly, the gusty chambermaid in "The Lick House Ball" (1863), became "a soldier in the army of the household" who reminded Clemens of a female Ulysses S. Grant, only if anything a bit more aggressive. General Grant had directed this terse response to Fort Donelson's defender, Confederate General Simon Bolivar Buckner: "No terms except an unconditional and immediate surrender can be accepted. I propose to move immediately upon your works." Clemens echoed the famous retort, writing that the chambermaid's visage "says in plain, crisp language, 'I don't want you here. If you are not gone in two minutes, I propose to move upon your works!'" In an environment of total war, misapplying military language became a comic outlet to dispel gloom. Thus the purpose of the fundraiser rendered Clemens's military imagery in "The Sanitary Ball" either altogether fitting or startlingly inappropriate. The potential inappropriateness of the military imagery made his writing all the funnier.[23]

The following year, in the "Letter from Mark Twain" of April 25, 1864, Clemens wrote about another ball, but his reporting in this instance sparked his flight from Nevada. "The ladies are making extraordinary preparations for a grand fancy-dress ball, to come off in the county buildings here on the 5th of May, for the benefit of the great St. Louis Sanitary Fair. The most pecuniary results are anticipated from it, and I imagine, from the interest that is being taken in the matter, the ladies of Gold Hill had better be looking to their laurels, lest the fame of their recent brilliant effort in the Sanitary line be dimmed somewhat by the financial achievements of this forthcoming ball."[24] Clemens's comments announcing the ball were innocuous enough, as he praised the ladies for their efforts and predicted their success. The comments were also somewhat noncommittal. Compare the comments above with this letter from the *Virginia City Union* for May 15, 1864. It announced an upcoming meeting with suitably patriotic language: "To-day, at 2 o'clock, the long deferred mammoth Sanitary meeting will be held at the Opera House. The announcement alone ought to fill the house, but when it is remembered that sweet singers, eloquent orators, pretty ladies, and a fine brass band will be in attendance, who can stay away? Turn out for the honor of Nevada! Turn out for the sake of loyalty and humanity.

Listen to the cry of suffering from our wounded thousands on the road to Richmond, and fill the building with an eager throng of humane, generous-hearted givers."[25] The *Union's* respect for the "sweet singers" and "pretty ladies" was as significant as the bathetic plea, "Listen to the cry of suffering from our wounded thousands." Clemens's letters were much better written, more entertaining, and superior in every conceivable way, yet they would not necessarily have been as appealing during wartime to some readers; in addition to occasionally questioning the motives of the fund's donors, he completely ignored the suffering cries of "our wounded thousands." Such an omission would certainly not have won friends among those already suspicious of his "secesh" leanings.

Clemens's disastrous interactions with the ladies of Carson were provoked by an article he wrote on the related issue of the Sanitary Flour Sack. In his letter of May 16, 1864 "History of the Gold and Silver Bars—How They Do Things in Washoe," Clemens described how "The Austin Flour Sack," a fifty-pound sack of flour donated to charity, was auctioned again and again to raise money for the Sanitary Fund. The auction of the flour was conducted by Reuel Colt Gridley, an old Hannibal acquaintance of Sam's who had gone to the Mexican War and then disappeared from view. Gridley surprised Sam one day while he was embroiled in his latest argument with a rival editor on the streets of Virginia City. Suddenly, Gridley growled from behind him, "Give him the best you've got, Sam. I'm at your back." Like Sam Clemens, Gridley was a Copperhead. In the better known version of the story of the Sanitary Flour Sack in chapter 45 of *Roughing It,* Clemens ignored Gridley's politics other than to misidentify him as "the Democratic candidate for mayor" instead of just an ardent supporter of the Democratic candidate. Be that as may be, even in 1872, "Democrat" was code for "disloyal." In the original "History of the Gold and Silver Bars—How They Do Things in Washoe," Clemens told the story more dramatically. The flour sack was inherently a matter of Civil War politics, for it began as a wager between Gridley, "a Copperhead, or as he calls himself, 'Union to the backbone, but a Copperhead in sympathies,'" and his rival, a supporter of the Republican candidate. Each backed his party's mayoral candidate in the Nevada town of Austin. They agreed that if Gridley's candidate lost, he would tote the sack through town "with a brass band at his heels playing 'John Brown.'" However, if the Democrat were elected, the band would have played "Dixie" while the Republican hefted the fifty-pound sack of flour.[26]

While Clemens wrote "History of the Gold and Silver Bars—How They Do Things in Washoe" with a patriotic and cheery tone, he hinted that behind the Sanitary Fund bubbled the ferment of political dispute amid the Civil War. If Clemens's discussion of Gridley's flour sack in chapter 45 of *Roughing It* was respectful, still more so was his 1870 *New York Tribune* obituary of Gridley, "The Famous Sanitary Flour Sack." Sam lauded his friend's "enviable reputation for integrity, benevolence, and enterprise" in service of the Sanitary Fund. The original sketch, however, differed from these later appreciations and contained his dig that the motivations for the wide popular support for the fund were rooted in something other than a sincere concern for the horrific conditions wounded Union soldiers experienced in field hospitals. As he wrote in his article, "you ought to see them roll out the twenty dollar pieces when their blood is up. It makes no difference what the object is, if you just get them stirred up once they are bound to respond." Donating to the Sanitary Fund was praiseworthy, but Clemens pointed out that donors were not thinking about the noble purposes of the charity; in fact, they were not thinking at all. They might have bid with equal enthusiasm for the "Genuine Mexican Plug," the cantankerous horse Clemens was suckered into purchasing at auction in *Roughing It*. Even those in charge of the Sanitary Commission recognized this. The Reverend Dr. Henry Bellows, who was the president of the commission and a Unitarian minister in San Francisco, characterized the Nevadans' support: "The feverish nature of mining life makes the population of every such country greedy of excitement in all their concerns. Sensation is the lifeblood of such a people." That craving for excitement certainly helped the Sanitary Commission do its good work. Reverend Bellows noted that the Gold Hill, Virginia City, and the other stars in that "constellation of gold and silver villages and towns . . . all shed benignant beams—and very substantial ones—upon the Central Treasury." Indeed, Nevada ranked third in donations in the entire United States, an astonishing fact given its remote location and sparse population. Only California and New York, in that order, gave more. Per capita, Nevada's contribution was the greatest, and it amounted to "over two dollars for every man, woman and child" in the Territory. The success of the flour sack auction, which Reverend Bellows referred to as "the wildest and most successful extravagance ever practiced in the interests of the Sanitary Fund," derived not from a desire to alleviate the tremendous suffering of the war wounded, but, as Clemens exclaimed, in the frenzy of mob psychology: "'Virginia's mad!' 'Virginia's got her back up!'"[27]

Clemens's approach in his Nevada journalism was a good example of what scholar Lawrence Berkove has termed the "Sagebrush style." Among the "Comstock Sagebrushers," he has suggested, arose an ethos that combined "strongly pro-Union" attitudes with the purposeful satire and impulse to burlesque seen in the classical cynics who "uncovered and examined the true agendas of individuals." During his reconstruction, Sam Clemens's impulse toward cynicism was, as a Rebel deserter with Copperhead leanings, pronounced. As he moved toward the Union, however, that impulse of the cynic to find those "true agendas" Berkove spoke of strengthened. Defeat of the "right, righteous, sacred" ideals of his boyhood generated this process, for any other such high-sounding words could have concealed lies in the guise of truth. Defeat of the Confederacy was making Sam skeptical of the "right, righteous, sacred" claims of the Union cause, too. Such minimal criticisms in "History of the Gold and Silver Bars—How They Do Things in Washoe" paled in comparison to what he wrote in the following days. In an article entitled "How Is It?—How It Is" (1864), of which only a tantalizing portion has survived, Clemens sought to explain why Carson had not outbid Dayton for the flour sack. To explain this embarrassing fact, he returned to the issue of the "grand fancy-dress ball" conducted by the ladies of Carson several weeks before. He explained "that the reason the Flour Sack was not taken from Dayton to Carson was because it was stated that the money raised at the Sanitary Fancy Dress Ball, recently held in Carson for the St. Louis Fair, had been diverted from its legitimate course, and was to be sent to aid a Miscegenation Society somewhere in the East; and it was feared the proceeds of the sack might be similarly disposed of." Of all the things Clemens might have said, there were few quite so inflammatory as alleging that the ladies of Carson had diverted the funds from their "grand fancy-dress ball" to a society promoting the amalgamation of the races. William Stewart, who along with territorial Governor Nye would be elected senator from Nevada and would share his Washington lodgings with Clemens during the Johnson impeachment crisis, complained that "Sam Clemens was a busy person. He went around putting things in the paper about people, and stirring up trouble. He did not care whether the things he wrote were true or not, just so he could write something, and naturally he was not popular. I did not associate with him." Many of Clemens's articles targeted Stewart, but roasting Judge "Petrified Man" Sewall, Thomas "the Silver-Tongued Orator" Fitch, or William "Bullyragging Bill" Stewart only raised some hackles and provoked occasional threats; seemingly allying himself with the "Peace Democrats" and the George B. McClellan ticket in 1864 while engaging in off-color humor at the expense of the ladies of Carson proved to be far more dangerous.[28]

Clemens's suggestion of financial impropriety would have been sufficient to elicit response. Emotions about the Sanitary Fund ran high, and charges had circulated in many parts of the country about possible misdirection of donations. Newspapers published notices, such as the one entitled "Rogues" that appeared in the *Sacramento Daily Union* for May 23, 1864, warning residents about "rascals" who have been "collecting contributions of money and goods for an imaginary Sanitary Fair." Reuel Gridley himself had been accused of defalcations from the Flour Sack funds, an apparently groundless accusation given the amount of money he raised and the fact that paying for his travel around the country left him destitute. In "The Gridley Sack of Flour and the Sacramento Star," an article that appeared in the May 31, 1864 issue of the *Reese River Reveille,* the paper defended their hometown hero (Gridley was from Austin, Nevada Territory, where the paper was published). The *Reveille* labeled accusations by the *Sacramento Star* "some of the most ungenerous and contemptible remarks that a respectable paper could be guilty of." Moreover, in defending the "bearer of the famous sack of flour," the *Reveille* expressed the opinion of many people: "The cause is one too sacred to be trifled with."[29]

Accusations of financial chicanery provoked indignant responses, but it was Clemens's innuendo involving the term "miscegenation" that ignited the blazes of controversy. In his *History of Nevada,* historian Hubert Howe Bancroft has pointed out that, despite the strong pro-Union sentiment in the territory, "Cohabitation with Indians, Chinese, or negroes was made punishable by fine of not less than $100 nor more than $500, or imprisonment in the county jail for not less than one month nor more than six." The hypocrisy inherent in this contradiction between Union politics and Nevada law provided the creative tension for Clemens's comments in a place where "we ain't for the nigger, but we are for the war." Clemens's use of the term "miscegenation" is interesting, too, for it had only been coined in December 1863 in a work entitled *Miscegenation: The Theory of the Blending of the Races, Applied to the American White Man and Negro.* This work, anonymously published by David Goodman Croly and George Wakeman, was misrepresented as the work of an ardent promoter of abolition. In reality, Croly and Workman were Copperheads, and the work was a hoax of the type Clemens himself often perpetrated. Croly and Wakeman hoped to do their little bit to sabotage Lincoln's reelection campaign. To do this, they drew on the Latin words *miscere* (to mix) and *genus* (race) to coin the neologism "miscegenation," defining the word as "the mixture of two or more races." The motive was the usual political dirty trick, but the word "miscegenation" was pure genius for Copperhead purposes (witness its extraordinarily rapid entrance into common usage). So rapid was its entrance into the language that the Goodrich and Porter 1864 revision of Noah Webster's *An American Dictionary of the English Language* included the word as well as this editorial comment: "A recent and ill-formed word. It should be *miscegeneration.*" By early 1864, the term was used in the press without bothering to define that it was neologism for amalgamation. Indeed, by April 1864, it was being used as a metaphor, as in the expression "political miscegenation," a phrase used to describe the idea that the Copperheads and radical abolitionists might "smoke the pipe of peace" to subvert Lincoln's reelection. Doubtless, part of the word's instant popularity owed something to the fact that the first three letters of *miscere*, to mix, naturally suggested the prefix *mis-*, used to indicate wrongness or impropriety. Croly and Wakeman certainly intended the word have such connotations.[30]

Indeed, the peculiar power asserted by the word "miscegenation" had as much to do with the concept of the purity of white ladies as it did with abolition politics. In the pamphlet *Miscegenation*, the author exhorted the Republican Party to proclaim "miscegenetic reform" as part of its platform in "the approaching presidential contest." Croly quoted—typically out of context—some of the leading figures among northern abolitionists: Wendell Phillips, Ralph Waldo Emerson, James Russell Lowell, Charles Sumner, Theodore Tilton, Harriet Beecher Stowe, and, repeatedly, Frederick Douglass. In *Miscegenation*, Croly adopted the abolitionist persona to praise the Republican Party as the "party of miscegenation," suggesting that life on the plantation was full of longing of master for maid and, more sensationally, of mistress for manservant. The pamphlet advocated the benefits of miscegenation, from New England to the South, and from the East to California, where Chinese men would be called upon to improve the human race by mating with white women. The pamphlet was condemned; endorsed; accepted as authentic by many, including Horace Greeley; and questioned by others. By the summer of 1864, the word had become the stuff of "off-color" jokes, so to speak, with newspapers throughout California and the Nevada Territory printing or reprinting witticisms involving southern miscegenation. In one of these, "Miscegenation Sent Home," a "Southern pro-slavery gentleman" sniped at an ex-slave, a free black man, saying, "I suppose you go in for amalgamation, miscegenation and what not?" The freed slave responded, "Oh yes, certainly . . . All Southern gentlemen do."[31]

While the pamphlet was not definitively revealed as a hoax in the United States until after Lincoln's reelection, many people, especially Republicans, were suspicious. One of them, the abolitionist Theodore Tilton, who was quoted in the pamphlet, "smelt a rat," as P. T. Barnum said in his discussion of the hoax in *The Humbugs of the World* (1865). Tilton wrote in the February 25, 1864 issue of *The Independent* that the work is "so absurd, that we are more than ever convinced such a statement was not written in earnest!" Others expressed similar skepticism of the document's authenticity. *The Methodist Review,* in its notice of the pamphlet's publication, labeled it "a piece of ingenious knavery quite worthy the followers of Fernando Wood and Sunset Cox. It produces physiological proofs of the ennobling results of commingling races; professes to advocate amalgamation." Fernando Wood and Samuel Sullivan "Sunset" Cox were infamous Copperheads, the former an important cog in New York's Tammany Hall Democratic machine and the latter a Democratic congressman from Ohio throughout the war and afterward a congressman from New York. By identifying the Copperhead congressmen as possible originators of the document, the Methodists had spotted the hoax. Others did, too. Western papers ran an article entitled "Miscegenation" at the same time Clemens was engulfed in trouble over his use of the word. "MISCEGENATION.—Mrs. Farnham, the authoress, now in the East superintending the publication of her 'Woman and her Era,' writes to a friend in Santa Cruz, as follows: 'The pamphlet Miscegenation proves to have been written by a pro-slavery Democrat for embarrassing the Republicans and giving such journals as the New York Herald fitting texts whereon to expend their virulence and vulgarity.'" Despite Republican doubts of its veracity, the pamphlet and its central term were used by the Copperhead press to further their case that Americans should cast their votes for McClellan and against President Lincoln. Croly, still in the guise of an enthusiastic supporter of President Lincoln and the Republicans, gushed that "[w]hen the President proclaimed Emancipation, he proclaimed also the mingling of the races." Another such publication sneered that amalgamation "used to be counted a crime; but now, in these ripe days of 'Republicanism' and miscegenation, this kind of intercourse between the whites and blacks has suddenly become a virtue which, if not *rare,* is the crowning and glorious triumph of the Republican party." Republicans responded in kind, by pointing out that the institution of slavery itself promoted the mixing of races; as in the joke cited earlier, Republicans "sent miscegenation home"—to the South. Congressman Mr. Kelly, a Pennsylvania Republican, cited government census statistics to prove this fact on the House floor when "Sunset" Cox gave a speech on February 17, 1864. Cox read directly from the pamphlet, charging the Republican Party with planning to adopt miscegenation as one of the planks in its platform for the upcoming presidential election. "The house simply laughed at him for his pains," as *The Independent* put it. Congressman Kelly responded with government statistics about "miscegens," the neologism for those of mixed race, arguing that "Sir, you are too late with your alarm! Your own friends have already done the work at the South; and, if they are permitted to go on with their iniquities without interference, as you contend they have the right to do, no black race will be left in the country. The slaveholders will bleach it white!"[32]

Suspicions and hints abounded, then, by May 1864, that the pamphlet was a Copperhead canard, and Clemens used the term knowing its connections to Copperheadism. Literary critic James Caron has naïvely concluded that had "Clemens confined his joking about the Sanitary Fund to the crack about miscegenation, his impending troubles would have been limited to mollifying the women from Carson City." It was, in fact, joking about miscegenation that created the furor, because it combined disloyal "secesh" talk with improper persiflage about white ladies during the tense months leading up to the November 1864 elections. This was a time in which, as Major G. W. Ingalls commented, "partisan politics became a full-fledged fixture in the valley." As Lincoln and McClellan supporters began declaring themselves, commented the major wryly, the "hair-pulling began." Middle ground disappeared into a line of demarcation, lamented the major, with "traitors, 'secesh,' and 'copperheads'" facing off against the "'black Republicans,' 'abolitionists,' and 'nigger worshippers'" on the other. Clemens's miscegenation article resembled Croly's and other related hoaxes, such as the slanderous articles claiming that "the ladies who left the North to teach the contrabands at Beaufort" had become pregnant by the ex-slaves they were teaching and had birthed sixty-four babies. Clemens blamed his publication of "How Is It?—How It Is" on being intoxicated, having written it after downing one too many whiskey cocktails at a social gathering. Doubtless, Mark Twain was a "water-less Twain" as they sometimes said. Nevertheless, his article is best understood in the context of election year Copperhead hoaxes and of his own early efforts such as "A Bloody Massacre Near Carson," "Petrified Man," and his reporting for the Third House. Clemens's Sanitary Fund hoax was on a much smaller scale than Croly's and did not seek to derail the reelection of President Lincoln, but his editorial "How Is It?—How It Is" was influenced by more than Virginia City whiskey.[33]

Clemens's calumny against the Sanitary Fund, a cause "too sacred to be trifled with," created the perfect storm of controversy, amalgamating, one might say, issues of money, patriotism, race, and sex during a time of war. His use of the term "miscegenation" demonstrated the remarkable celerity with which the word passed into the political lexicon, and his article provoked a western wildfire of controversy, with letters fired off to newspapers in the region, editorials written, and ultimately challenges exchanged. Four of the ladies in charge of the Sanitary Ball signed a letter to the editors of the *Enterprise*, calling the charges "a *tissue of falsehoods*, made for *malicious* purposes," and asserted that the proceeds would "go to the aid of the sick and wounded soldiers, who are fighting the battles of our country, *and for no other purpose*." The italicization of certain words and phrases expressed suspicion of Clemens's motives in making the allegations, for he employed a Copperhead term to undermine efforts for the sacred cause of the relief of Union soldiers in May 1864, during the heated presidential campaign. Copperhead publications routinely shot the term "miscegenation" across the bows to accuse Republicans of promoting the intermarriage of black and white. "Miscegenation is but another pet object of the Lincoln party," wrote the anonymous author of the pamphlet "Miscegenation Indorsed by the Republican Party." Clemens's hoax, however humorous, once again led to charges of disloyalty.[34]

Extricating himself from this entanglement was made more difficult for Sam because his brother, Orion Clemens, was in charge of the commission and his sister-in-law, Mollie, was one of the ladies in charge of the ball. In a private letter to Mollie Clemens, Sam claimed that the "item about the sack of flour slipped into the paper . . . when I was not sober," but that he could obviously not print such a retraction in the *Enterprise*. He apologized for making "the ladies angry" and requested that she privately ask them to either accept his unpublished explanation that he was drunk at the time "or else make them appoint a man to avenge the wrong done them, with weapons in fair & open field." The money had all been accounted for; on May 23, 1864, an accountant wrote in a ledger that the Sanitary Commission had received "Proceeds of Ball, by Ladies of Carson Valley, through Henry Epstein" a contribution of $425. That same day, Sam Clemens wrote a letter to Mrs. W. K. Cutler that suggests Mollie's peacemaking efforts had been successful. He opened by saying, "Madam—I address a lady in every sense of the term" and then apologized for "that unfortunate item of mine about the Sanitary Funds accruing from the ball." On the following day, he published a retraction of sorts, under the heading "Miscegenation." "We published a rumor, the other day, that the moneys collected at the Carson Fancy Dress Ball were to be diverted from the Sanitary Fund and sent forward to aid a 'miscegenation' or some other sort of Society in the East. We also stated that the rumor was a hoax. And it was—we were perfectly right. However, four ladies are offended." Even without the entire article, it is clear from the available fragment of "How Is It?—How It Is" that Clemens included the comment about the miscegenation society as a dig at the ladies. Whether or not any defalcations had occurred, the comment about a miscegenation society was calculated to draw fire but drew quite a bit more than Clemens had intended. A May 21, 1864 editorial in the *Virginia Daily Union* ("How It Is") labeled him "an unmitigated *liar, a poltroon and a puppy.*" Nor was this all. "Never before, in a long period of newspaper intercourse," asserted a second article ("The 'How Is It' Issue") "—never before in any contact with a cotemporary, however unprincipled he might have been, have we found an opponent in statement or in discussion, who has no gentlemanly sense of professional propriety, who conveyed in every word, and in every purpose of all his words, such a groveling disregard for truth, decency and courtesy, as to seem to court the distinction only of being understood as a vulgar liar."[35]

Clemens responded by repeated insults and challenges directed at James L. Laird, publisher of the *Union*. Laird, for his part, only made matters worse by pointing out that the actual author of the editorials critical of Mark

Twain, the disloyal Copperhead, was J. W. Wilmington, a veteran who had been "Captain of a Company in the Sixth Ohio Regiment, and fought at Shiloh." Over the course of several days, Clemens tried to extricate himself from the muddle by repeatedly challenging Laird, who consistently referred him back to Wilmington, the respected war hero, the venerated veteran, the Union soldier who had fought at Shiloh. Clemens faced several possible duels, not just from Laird and Captain Wilmington, but also from the husbands of the ladies he had maligned. Claiming in a letter to William K. Cutler, whose wife was president of the Sanitary Ball, that he was "ready to accept" a challenge from him but "Having made my arrangements—before I received your note—to leave for California," the affair of honor would have to be arranged immediately. As it transpired, Clemens fought no duel, but left the Nevada Territory in dishonor and disrepute, in a sense deserting for a second time a battle he had joined in Missouri. Sam expressed his frustration in a letter to Mollie in which he mourned, "the Sanitary expedition has been very disastrous to me."[36]

One can condemn Clemens's comments easily, of course. His appeal to racist discourse suggested he remained something of a "secesh" or at least a Copperhead in May 1864. James Caron has incorrectly averred that "the hoax by Mark Twain alleges malfeasance of funds and implies that the women of Carson City were disloyal 'Copperheads.'" Those who (conceivably) would be supporting miscegenation societies were Radical Republicans. Clemens's language was "copperish," "secesh," or, as scholar James Cox has phrased it, "somewhat 'Confederate.'" That was the point. Simply reacting to the details of the hoax, Nevadans (and many later readers) have missed the satire. The same thing had happened with "A Bloody Massacre Near Carson" and "Petrified Man," with readers accepting the hoaxes for true reportage and missing the satirical, polemical point. One can understand Clemens's motivation for the burlesque "How Is It?—How It Is" by asking this question: why was the miscegenation hoax so inflammatory? Scholars commenting on the contretemps seem anxious to suggest there was nothing at all funny about Clemens's miscegenation comments; they have disavowed them as speedily and as self-righteously as politicians distancing themselves from a formerly esteemed colleague in an election year. Scholar Fred Lorch has argued that Clemens's miscegenation claim "was, of course, intended to be humorous, but was in fact irresponsible and in bad taste." Fatout has chided Clemens as "wrong from the start." For Stephen

Fender, Clemens's motives during the whole debacle were "incomprehensible." Arthur Pettit has stated flatly that "Publicly, 'Mark Twain' used the Virginia City Territorial Enterprise as an organ for his prejudice." Christopher Wienandt, too, in considering Clemens as a journalist, has lamented that "serving the public" was not on his mind when he wrote that "money intended for the Sanitary Commission was to be diverted to a miscegenation society." Clemens, therefore, "can hardly be called a zealous reformer." Actually, Clemens's cynicism toward Union politics was increasing, as his own formative southern ideals collapsed on battlefields across the country. In fact, the process of reconstruction was well underway, perhaps ironically, as evidenced by the miscegenation hoax most particularly; Clemens's miscegenation hoax looked like the act of a Copperhead agitator, but it was in fact the act of a savage satirist. The reaction of the ladies of Carson City—and perhaps more particularly of their husbands—indicated that Clemens's judgment about the ardent supporters of the Union cause was correct. They endorsed Abraham Lincoln and the Republican Party. They organized fancy dress balls to demonstrate this support, rallied around and raised money for the relief of the wounded boys in blue, but were at bottom only very lukewarm supporters of abolition—even as a military necessity—and they most certainly did not believe blacks were the equals of whites. If they had, the miscegenation canard would have been just another of Sam's many hoaxes. Like the Republican congressmen listening to "Sunset" Cox read from Croly's pamphlet, Nevadans would have laughed him down. The bon ton of Carson City did not laugh, proving Sam Clemens's burlesque had struck home.[37]

"Hoity! Toity!!" exclaimed the editorialist in the Gold Hill *Daily News*, calling the dispute between Clemens, Laird, and Wilmington "emphatically a bad egg." The paper lamented dueling in the territory generally, but noted that the scrap with the *Union* was an especially poor example. "In the first place," the paper opined, "the cause of the quarrel was not one calculated to enlist public sympathy." An earlier editorialist during the "Bloody Massacre Near Carson" debacle had scolded Clemens on the pages of the Virginia City *Evening Bulletin*, arguing that "for the purpose of 'pointing a moral,' we would grant every license to the imagination of the scribe, but in matters that [a]ffect the character of a community or an individual, truth is an indispensable necessity." Later scholars have upbraided Clemens and so miss the genius of Mark Twain's reconstruction and the development of his persona.

Scholar Joseph Coulombe has claimed that as Clemens left Nevada, "[o]ne of the most noticeable changes was Twain's abandonment of the antisocial posturing of his earlier newspaper sketches." Clemens neither abandoned such posturing in his writing, nor can it be called antisocial. With society so frequently in the wrong, antisocial behavior was a potent corrective. Skepticism took the place of the "right, righteous, sacred" ideals of the southern system and became central to Clemens's artistic credo. With his miscegenation hoax, he had once again questioned the "character of the community." He had exposed its dirty little secret that their pro-Union stance was based not on principle but party politics. This time, Clemens lost his audience. In addition to being a deserter from a Confederate militia, Sam Clemens used the word "miscegenation"—"copperish" language, the neologism of disloyalty. He had proven himself no gentleman by accusing white ladies of supporting miscegenation. No, the cause of the quarrel would not enlist public sympathy, but that fact confirmed the hypocrisy Clemens attacked with "How Is It?—How It Is." Clemens truly saw "how it was," and the divergence between the high-sounding political rhetoric and the real attitude on the streets of Virginia City and in the convivial meetings of the Third House in Carson City was an important catalyst for his evolving public role. Such divergence gave rise to Mark Twain as a gadfly and agitator in the Nevada Territory and elsewhere, revealing always the "character of the community" by targeting hidden hypocrisies. The furor that followed his miscegenation hoax proved Clemens's instincts about the community's character were correct.[38]

It is interesting to note that a few months after Clemens's departure, Joseph Goodman, his editor at the *Enterprise*, was himself involved in a dispute with a rival paper. When the matter went to court, Goodman, according to Rollin Dagget, "almost precipitated a riot in the courtroom by objecting to Bennett's testimony on the ground that he had negro blood in his veins."[39] Those who know Goodman only as the genial, principled editor of the Virginia City *Territorial Enterprise* might be surprised to know that his pro-Union principles did not extend to full and equal civil rights for blacks. Indeed, his conversion to that cause came late—as it did with many Republicans, including the president. Clemens's article "How Is It?—How It Is" is best understood as a burlesque like Croly's pamphlet *Miscegenation*. One need not share Croly's or Clemens's politics as they were in 1864 to enjoy the spectacle of revealed hypocrisy. In later years, Clemens's politics changed, but his technique of allowing hypocrites to reveal themselves never altered. Clemens's southern leanings caused him to be angry at and skeptical of those who, ignorant of their own disloyal thoughts, mouthed the highest principles of Radical Republicanism and spied traitors behind every rock and sagebrush—or newspaper desk. Over time, his position as a skeptical outsider evolved into a permanent animosity toward power politics. Though in May 1864, Mark Twain's reconstruction was certainly incomplete, it was well underway, for "How Is It?—How It Is" foreshadowed, however astonishing the comparison may seem on the surface, his later anti-lynching editorials. Both exploited the disparity between the high-minded ideals society propounded and the reality tucked beneath the hypocrisy.

Sam Clemens left Nevada on May 29, 1864. Although he left pleading prior arrangements to travel to San Francisco, he certainly had motivation to light out *from* the territory. As he mordantly observed in his autobiography, "Well, it seemed to me that our society was no longer desirable in Nevada." Some papers expressed affection and understanding for the writer in his time of troubles. "Mark Twain has gone to San Francisco—doubtless to get time to review the 'situation' and mature his plans for the re-opening of the campaign," commented the *Humboldt Register*. "He got the 'women of America,' as they are in Carson, down on him—which is not pleasant; and he got mixed up in a chapter of follies with a cotemporary; and Mark, like a sensible fellow, has gone down to see how it all looks from a Bay view." The *Register* writer, while stepping around the miscegenation controversy, phrased the fracas in terms of a "campaign" and an issue of patriotism, as Clemens had infuriated the "women of America." Virginia City's *Daily Old Piute* was even more sympathetic but read like a mock obituary. "Left yesterday, for bluer skies and more verdant hills, S. L. Clemens, Esq., alias 'Mark Twain.' Yes, Mark has gone, and amid our fragrant sage brush, quartz-crowned hills and alkali hydrants we repose solitary and almost alone. The world is blank—the universe worth but 57½ and we are childless. We shall miss Mark; his bosom friend De Quille will miss him; Marshall will do ditto; every lunch house in the city, every brewery and every woman (who knew him)—and to know was to love him—will miss him. We can't dwell on this subject; we can only say—God bless you, Mark! Be virtuous and happy." It must have been wrenching, even for a competitor, to give up Mark Twain to California, and thence the world. The greatest tribute was that the *Old Piute* used the writer's facetious style: the burlesque of the sentimental style with the conventional suggestion that the "world is a blank" and that "we are childless"; the value of the universe given as a the report of a mining stock that has fallen to 57½; and the canny joke about his adventures in the less reputable parts of the city. It was as fond a farewell as Sam himself would have written of a beloved colleague.[40]

By contrast, the Gold Hill *Daily News* crowed that after having "played hell," Clemens "has vamoosed, cut stick, absquatulated," the last word being a hyper-Latinate western coinage for leaving the place one had been squatting on. The 1889 *Century* Dictionary deems it "[a] feigned word, of American origin, simulating a L. derivation" and defines it as meaning "To run away; abscond; make off." Ironically, given the reason for his departure, the paper also noted that "Mark Twain's beard is full of dirt, and his face is black before the people of Washoe." Puckishly, the editorialist included in the article a note of the meeting of the Ladies' Sanitary Society, in which the funds in question were specifically mentioned as having been "forwarded to Dr. Bellows, President of the National Sanitary Commission." The ladies were reported to have groaned three times for the "Enterprise as the vehicle of Mark Twain's abominations." On June 8, 1864, in an article entitled "What's The News?" the Gold Hill *Daily News* extracted further valuable lessons from the whole affair, gloating over the demise of the rival that had tricked them into reprinting "A Bloody Massacre Near Carson."

Such manufacturers, there be in the world, and such an one did upon a time abide in Washoe; but that man has disappeared from the land and has we fear disappeared from our gaze forever. Is it necessary to say that we allude to the lamented Twain? That loved and lost journalist, tortured by a demand for "news" when it was not, did manufacture some that he fondly believed would satisfy the public craving. He filled the pine forest at Dutch Nick's with the ghastly corpses of the Hopkins family, and sprinkled the road to Carson with gore from the vermillion scalp of the apocryphal mother of those mythical slain. That "news" satisfied the greedy mind of the public, and it stared itself out of countenance in frozen horror for a few brief hours, and was content. But mark the sequel: the indignation of the non-manufacturer and the diabolical damnation of the deceived. The fate of that unhappy man is ever before us, and warns us to avoid the rock upon which he split whenever we are asked "What's the news?"

Sam absquatulated from the territory and also from the Sanitary Fund. On May 25, 1864, he wrote to Orion: "Don't stump for the Sanitary Fund—Billy Clagett says he certainly will not. If I have been so unlucky as to rob you of some of your popularity by that unfortunate item, I claim at your hands that you neither increase nor diminish it by so fruitless a proceeding as making speeches for the Fund. I am mighty sick of that fund—it has caused all my d——d troubles—& I shall leave the Territory when your first speech is announced, & leave it for good." As president of the county Sanitary Commission, how could Orion avoid stumping for the fund? The querulous outburst unmasked Clemens's antagonism toward the fund, an antagonism that may help explain a number of burlesques he published a few months after his departure for San Francisco.[41]

A few years later, in "How I Escaped Being Killed in a Duel" (1872), Clemens recalled his "absquatulation" euphemistically as a "retirement" from the *Enterprise*. He transformed, mutated, or excised numerous details in his retelling of the events. James Laird became "Mr. Lord, editor of the rival paper." He related how his rival "flew up about some little trifle or other that I had said about him—I do not remember now what it was. I suppose I called him a thief, or a body-snatcher, or an idiot, or something like that." Clemens avoided the topic of miscegenation entirely, presenting himself as the trickster who challenged another to a duel, but then feared what he has brought on himself. To escape, he used chicanery, tricking Lord's second into believing he was a crack shot, when in reality "I practised and practised at the barn door, and could not hit it." In short, "How I Escaped Being Killed in a Duel" depicted Clemens as an older Tom Sawyer who reconstructed defeat into victory. In his autobiography, too, Clemens ignored the miscegenation scandal, commenting only that "I woke up Mr. Laird with some courtesies of the kind that were fashionable among newspaper editors in that region." In June 1864, Sam Clemens, Confederate deserter and "damned secessionist," could hardly have imagined that 1872, the year he would publish "How I Escaped Being Killed in a Duel," would find him married into a wealthy family that had supported the Underground Railroad; a respected author, the darling of the press; and the editor, and part owner of a Yankee newspaper, the Buffalo *Express*. Over the summer of 1864, President Lincoln's chances for reelection improved as Sherman commenced marching through Georgia, capturing Atlanta in September, and as Grant engaged Lee's Army of Northern Virginia in a series of devastating battles. Southern Rebels and northern Copperheads were in retreat. Samuel Clemens, too, found himself cobbling together writing assignments for a number of newspapers. His hasty retreat from the Nevada Territory had left him unemployed, at times depressed, but defiant. "Mark Twain has gone to San Francisco," observed the *Humboldt Register*, "doubtless to get time to review the 'situation' and mature his plans for the re-opening of the campaign." Mark Twain's *campaign* would continue on new ground. He would rise again.[42]

CHAPTER 3

"THE GENATIVE, DATIVE, AND ABLATIVE CASES OF TRAITORS"

Twain's San Francisco Satires, 1864–1866

> Dear Mother! burst the tyrant's chain,
>   Maryland!
> Virginia should not call in vain,
>   Maryland!
> She meets her sisters on the plain—
> "*Sic semper,*" 'tis the proud refrain,
> That battles minions back amain,
>   Maryland!
> Arise, in majesty again,
>   Maryland, My Maryland!
> —JAMES RYDER RANDALL, 1861

> But I have had a "call" to literature, of a low order—*i.e.* humorous.
> —MARK TWAIN, October 19–20, 1865

OLLOWING HIS "ABSQUATULATION" from the Nevada Territory, Sam Clemens's spirits were buoyant, his fortunes promising. All but ridden out of the territory on a rail, he might have exhibited a suitably chastened attitude. In fact, Clemens felt himself to be a success. While he suffered trying times of near-poverty, the two years leading up to his departure for Hawaii and later for a cruise to Europe and the Holy Land on the *Quaker City* were generally marked by increasing literary and financial good fortune. As he traversed the Sierra

Nevada Mountains, Sam found himself in Angel's Camp, where he heard a story about a frog named Dan'l Webster. That moment of great import for the future history of American literature was tagged only by a brief comment in his journal: "Met Ben Coon, Ill river pilot here." Ben Coon was probably the original of "Jim Smiley," and Clemens published the story "Jim Smiley and his Jumping Frog" on November 18, 1865, in New York's *Saturday Press*. Over the next few weeks, that story propelled Clemens toward the national and international success he craved.[1]

Following his ignominious departure from the Nevada Territory, Clemens wrote for a number of important publications, among them the San Francisco *Morning Call*, the *Californian*, the *Dramatic Chronicle* (later the San Francisco *Chronicle*), and the San Francisco *Golden Era*. He also served as the San Francisco correspondent for the paper that had given him his start in Nevada, the Virginia City *Territorial Enterprise*. Years later, Clemens used the term "lofty" to describe his character when he first arrived in California. It was due to that obstinate optimism that Clemens's many failures failed to make of him a failure. During that time he was fired from the *Call*, "the only time in my life that I have ever been discharged and it hurts yet." Instead of defeating him, the difficulties he endured made his career. Just as his earlier desertion from Missouri's Marion Rangers led to his becoming Mark Twain, Clemens's departure from the Nevada Territory and arrival in California turned that pseudonym into a household name. His confident letters, then, were prescient. In a letter dated September 25, 1864, to his mother, Sam hardly sounded defeated: "I quit the 'Era,' long ago. It wasn't high-toned enough. I thought that whether I was a literary 'jackleg' or not, I wouldn't class myself with that style of people, anyhow. The 'Californian' circulates among the highest class of the community, & is the best weekly literary paper in the United States—& I suppose I ought to know." Similarly, in October 1865, he boasted to Orion and Mollie Clemens: "And now let me preach *you* a sermon. I never had but two *powerful* ambitions in my life. One was to be a pilot, & the other a preacher of the gospel. I accomplished the one & failed in the other, *because* I could not supply myself with the necessary stock in trade—i.e. religion. I have given it up forever. I never had a 'call' in that direction, anyhow, & my aspirations were the very ecstasy of presumption. But I *have* had a 'call' to literature, of a low order—i.e. humorous." In January 1866, Sam exulted to his mother and sister of his ambitions: "I will only have to take the scissors & slash my old sketches out of the Enterprise & the Californian—I burned up a small cart-load of them lately—so *they* are forever ruled out of any book—but they were not worth republishing." In the same letter, Sam included a clipping about "The Jumping Frog" from the New York correspondent of the San Francisco *Alta California*: "Mark Twain's story in the *Saturday Press* of November 18, called 'Jim Smiley and his Jumping Frog,' has set all New York in a roar, and he may be said to have made his mark. I have been asked fifty times about it and its author, and the papers are copying it far and near. It is voted the best thing of the day." In San Francisco, Sam Clemens "made his mark" as Mark Twain. As he did so, significant changes in his public persona took place, changes traceable in the articles that providentially escaped his several attempts at burning. They showed that Sam's "call," which he contrasted with the call one would receive before becoming a minister, had something in common with that other, loftier profession after all. His "scribbling to excite the laughter of God's creatures" continued to develop his "prophetic function," as his friend William Dean Howells later termed his satirical attacks on society.[2]

While in San Francisco, Clemens again took on a sacred object of political life closely related to the Sanitary Fund. Some of these fugitive references involved his covering of the Ladies Fair of the Christian Commission, a specifically Christian version of the Sanitary Commission. Sam also befriended Reverend Henry Bellows, Unitarian minister and president of the U.S. Sanitary Commission. "Bellows is an able, upright & eloquent man," he wrote to his mother in December 1866, "a man of imperial intellect & matchless power—he is Christian in the truest sense of the term & is unquestionably a brick." Perhaps because Bellows was a "brick," Sam's comments on the commission's work tended to be ironical rather than satirical. When a massive "Sanitary Cheese" was displayed at the Mechanics' Fair to raise money for the fund, Clemens advised San Franciscans to attend and view it, for "it is worth twenty-five cents to look upon such a monument of kindly Christian charity." Describing a mountainous mass of cheese as "a monument of kindly Christian charity," Clemens smirked, however obliquely, at the type of gestures individuals and companies made to support the Union cause. Consider, too, his July 4, 1864 article in which he described a parade with a possibly fictitious glue factory wagon festooned with the motto, "We stick fast to the Union." Sometimes, his burlesque seemed to write itself. Clemens made no comment, nor did he need to.[3]

Clemens safely hid more pointed criticisms of Civil War-era politics in fiction. In December 1864, he published "Lucretia Smith's Soldier" in *The Californian*. In a "Note from the Author," he explicitly identified the article as a burlesque of "those nice, sickly war stories in *Harper's Weekly*." The work lampooned those sappy stories, true, but also aimed at the War Department, the reverence accorded wounded soldiers, and the cheap, jingoistic patriotism of the sort that served to enlarge the coffers of the Sanitary Fund. The burlesque jabbed at the Sanitary Fund's work as much as it did a particular subgenre of story, as the protagonist, Lucretia Borgia Smith, named for the notorious poisoner, became a nurse in a Union hospital. Moreover, Clemens's "Note from the Author" at the head of the story fairly announced that his targets were political and, with his thumb on his nose like that petrified man back in the Nevada Territory, he suggested the story's reliability was assured, "inasmuch as the facts it contains were compiled from the official records in the War Department at Washington." He then piled up the authorities and the acknowledgments, including "*Jomini's Art of War*, the *Message of the President and Accompanying Documents*, and sundry maps." As discussed in the first chapter, Clemens loved to joke about supposedly reliable sources, particularly maps. Comedic as such elements were, they necessarily elevated the text to the level of *national* satire. Of course, Clemens did not neglect to credit a local brewery "which enabled me in this production to soar so happily into the realms of sentiment and soft emotion." Invoking the flag and beer, Sam associated patriotism with drunkenness throughout the wear years.[4]

Details obscured the true target of burlesque, however. Clemens himself noted that hoaxes such as "A Bloody Massacre Near Carson" and "Petrified Man" were misread because, "the 'nub' or moral of the burlesque—if its object be to enforce a truth—escapes notice in the superior glare of something in the body of the burlesque itself." The public response to "Lucretia Smith's Soldier" was a prime example. Perhaps because readers so enjoyed laughing at the inflated sentimentality of the burlesque, they missed the covert target. During the Civil War, in the Union states, the jokes told by or about Union soldiers tended either to be sympathetic to the Union soldiers, directed against the military establishment, or aimed at the enemy. The *Alta California* for April 3, 1863, featured a literary burlesque of Job 14:1. Purportedly penned by a Union private, the joke was based on a similar Rebel version from *Southern Illustrated News* attributed to a soldier in

Stonewall Jackson's army named "Hard Cracker," which one suspects was a pseudonym. The *Alta California* version involved an Ohio infantry:

CHRONICLES OF THE ONE HUNDRED AND TWENTY-THIRD OHIO VOLUNTEER INFANTRY.
1. Man that is born of woman, and enlisteth as a soldier in the One Hundred and Twenty-third Ohio is of few days, and short of "rations."
2. He cometh forth at "reveille," is present also at "retreat," yea even at "tattoo," and retireth apparently at "taps."

The burlesque marched on for a number of verses, extracting humor from camp life and expressing great understanding and sympathy for the soldier whose "days are full of troubles." Several newspapers in the West also reprinted this somewhat humorous joke:

During the late battle of Shiloh an officer hurriedly rode up to an Aid and inquired for Grant. "That's him with the field-glass," said the Aid. Wheeling his horse about, the officer furiously rode up to the General, and touching his cap thus addressed him. "Sheneral, I vants to make von report: Schwartz' Battery is took." "Ha!" says the General, "how was that?" "Vell, you see, Sheneral, de t——d Shesheshnist come up in de front of us, and de t——d Shesheshnists come in de rear of us, and Schwartz' Battery vas took." "Well, sir," said the General, "you of course spiked the guns." "Vat!" exclaimed the Dutchman in astonishment, "schpike dem guns—schpike dem new guns? No, it vould schpoil dem!" "Well," said the General, sharply, "what did you do?" "Do?" "Vy, we tood dem back again, by—!"

This joke involved national character types, the stereotype of the Dutchman in America, but the humor targeted the Confederate enemy—"de t——d Shesheshnist." Clemens's jokes did not do this. Rather, they functioned as covert attacks on the government, society, or even the army itself, as in the 1864 story "Lucretia Smith's Soldier." There is truth to historian Daniel Aaron's assertion that Clemens "resisted the impious and impolitic urge to be *openly* irreverent about the War itself." Clemens's sallies were as covert as the actions of the militia he had once belonged to, and at times only slightly less ridiculous.[5]

Clemens set "Lucretia Smith's Soldier" in May 1861, in Bluemass, Massachusetts, a name obviously associated with the Union but also humorously with "Bluemass Pills," a common medication (a compound of mercury and rose petals) used to treat depression. President Lincoln had taken Bluemass Pills before moving into the White House. "Bluemass" was also a name for a type of soil commonly occurring with quartz, and Clemens may have been joking about that as well from his mining days in the Nevada Territory. From this storied city of Bluemass, Reginald de Whittaker dreamed of impressing the love of his life, Lucretia Borgia Smith, with his decision to enlist in the Union Army. Like a "Bluemass Pill," it seemed the right medicine to cure his depression.[6]

The confusion and separation typical of romance occurred when Reginald appeared before Lucretia to announce his enlistment, only to be criticized for his cowardice in not, as she believed, answering the country's "shout to you to fall in and shoulder arms." Accused of cowardice, Reginald pridefully withheld the fact that he had in fact already enlisted. This misunderstanding estranged the two, even as he has marched off to battle. The story's plot highlighted the old romantic standby of lovers separated by war and of a woman exhorting her young man to shoulder arms and defend his country. Moreover, the hackneyed plot complication hinged on the young man's decision that, having enlisted and been misunderstood, "he remembered that he was no longer an effeminate dry-goods student, and his warrior soul scorned to sue for quarter." Clemens's mocking treatment indicted the people who consumed the romances so avidly; they, too, elevated false sentiment in place of reality. Increasingly, Clemens saw the pious hypocrisy behind such sentiment, owing in part to the fact that what had been "right, righteous, sacred" in his own youth had been all but destroyed by late 1864, when he wrote the story. Sanctimonious, pro-Union sentiments became the stuff of burlesque, with Clemens frequently deriding popular expressions of patriotism. Clemens subjected both sides to satire during the months leading up to the November 1864 presidential election. Scholar Edgar Branch has noted that Clemens, in his reporting on the Democratic or "Copperhead" convention in San Francisco, was "wielding the hatchet" for the *Morning Call*, which supported the Republican ticket. Such articles were comparatively rare, however, for the skeptical Clemens directed his irony and satire most often toward authorities and, as the November elections neared, it was increasingly obvious that the Republican Party would continue to be in charge. In a series of articles written for the San Francisco

Morning Call, Clemens depicted drunken women (he insinuated they were prostitutes) as exceedingly patriotic and even as Union recruits. In "Calaboose Theatricals," written July 14, 1864, Clemens profiled "Anna Jakes, drunk and disorderly, but excessively cheerful" as she sang sentimental war songs "of the distorted, hifalutin kind" while another woman was "cursing like a trooper in a neighboring cell." Meanwhile, a male prisoner bellowed, "*Will* you dry up that infernal yowling, you heifer?" No one could enjoy the singing because, as Clemens noted, "the cruel war music was so fused and blended with blasphemy in a higher key." In "Enlisted for the War" (August 2, 1864), Clemens depicted a bevy of "old soldiers," women who have spent a great deal of time in prison, as combatants who have been "fighting the prisons." Using martial language throughout, he humorously crafted an alternate universe in which women mustered in as soldiers, gin was the chief weapon, and prison was the enemy. Cumulatively, such comic material undermined through pervasive irony the use of language glorifying war. That was one of the main effects of "Lucretia Smith's Soldier," too, and it foreshadowed Clemens's later burlesque of Emmeline Grangerford in *Adventures of Huckleberry Finn* (1885) as well as his friend William Dean Howells's brilliant story "Editha" (1905), in which the title character sent her beloved to battle—and death—with the words, "the man I marry must love his country first of all" ringing in his ears.[7]

In the world of "Lucretia Smith's Soldier," conformity created courage out of fear of censure. The "mass of blue" in the fictional town of Bluemass tacitly enforced conformity to the sacred cause of Union. Reginald quailed before "tempests of shot and shell" less than he feared appearing weak before Lucretia or indeed anyone else. Even a rudimentary sort of patriotism as noble or selfless was absent here, as social, rather than political concerns, motivated the soldiers. Hidden in the burlesque lurked Clemens's covert self-criticism of his actions in enlisting in the Marion Rangers three years before and some justification for his later desertion.[8]

Estranged as they must be in a romantic text, the lovers proceeded along separate narrative lines, Reginald fighting on in battle, "a morose, unsmiling, desperate man, always in the thickest of the fight," while Lucretia "nursed her grief in silence" and scanned the list of wounded for his name. Casualty lists appearing in newspapers or posted in public places were often the first means by which families learned that their husbands, fathers, sons, and brothers were wounded, killed, or missing in battle. They were an iconic part of Civil War culture, North and South. Lithographs were made of bereaved women receiving the news. Stereotypically, when reading "a long list of maimed and killed, poor Lucretia read these terrible words, and fell fainting to the floor: 'R. D. Whittaker, private soldier, desperately wounded!'"[9]

In its denouement, the sketch revealed itself, not as just a joke about the sick, but as *a sick joke*. Having located the wounded R. D. Whittaker in a Washington hospital, Lucretia, like a poisonous version of a Sanitary Fund nurse, tended his wounds for three weeks. The soldier had been horribly injured. "A ball had shattered his lower jaw," Clemens wrote, "and he could not utter a syllable." Moreover, "his head was so profusely bandaged that his features were not visible." These two details were central: he could not speak and his features were hidden. Finally, a doctor unwound the bandages, and the joke was sprung: the soldier Lucretia had been tending was *Richard Dilworthy* Whittaker, of Wisconsin, not her own *Reginald de* Whittaker of Bluemass, Massachusetts. Lucretia smashed her fist on the medicine table, bawling: "O confound my cats if I haven't gone and fooled away three mortal weeks here, snuffling and slobbering over the wrong soldier!"[10]

Clemens ended his story inconclusively, with Reginald still missing. The story's lack of conclusion contributed to the comic undercutting of the sentimental war story subgenre, but it also raised a number of ethical questions. Lucretia's comment that she had been "slobbering over the wrong soldier" may have been a covert way of contending that one ought to have lamented Confederate casualties in addition to the Union wounded. Both soldiers were Union soldiers, but the fact that the two soldiers were mistaken for each other suggested a war in which one could not discern one soldier from the next. The story germinated in a border state mentality of confusion and disorientation, and one witnesses here the mistaken identity, the doubling, twinning, and use of paired characters common to much of Clemens's subsequent work. What if the bandaged soldier had been a Confederate? Would Lucretia have been guilty of disloyalty to her country, not just her lover? More obviously, Clemens interrogated the motives of those who exhorted soldiers to enlist, of those who enlisted, and of those who cared for the wounded. Patriotism? Idealism? For Lucretia, caring for a wounded soldier was secondary to playing a romantic role. For Reginald, manly expectations deserved the credit. Nearly four decades later, in his 1901 speech on Lincoln's birthday, Clemens sounded the same note, but more positively: "We believed in those days we were fighting for the right—and it was a noble fight, for we were fighting for our sweethearts, our homes, and our lives."[11]

Clearly, "Lucretia Smith's Soldier" was certainly not solely a burlesque of "literary fashions and manners," as Edgar Branch has suggested. Beyond questioning the jingoistic patriotism of popular culture, Clemens undermined the motives and the sentiments behind them. Romanticizing war created a compound as deadly as the rose petals ground with mercury to make Bluemass Pills. Lucretia's love was as murderous as her name suggested, and her sentiment, connected to the high emotion evoked by the wounded Union soldiers, was self-indulgent. As historian Drew Gilpin Faust has suggested in *This Republic of Suffering* (2008), "the predominant response to the unexpected carnage was in fact a resolute sentimentality." Other responses appeared, too, due to the "reality of modern industrialized warfare" that seemed inherently at odds with the world of sentiment. The result, Faust has observed, was often burlesque or parody. Such was the case with Clemens's burlesque of "those nice, sickly war stories in *Harper's Weekly*." The fictional accounts of nurses caring for wounded soldiers staged a spectacle of the reader's empathic pain. As such, Clemens insinuated, they were pretty lies, like the frenzied bidding on Gridley's flour sack in Virginia City. When Lucretia's neighbor inquired, "Mercy! what in the nation's the matter with the girl?" the line advanced a double meaning. What ailed the girl ailed the nation—separation, disunion, the rejection of reality in favor of deceptive sentimentality. The story's cynicism is brutal. One wonders how Clemens could joke about wounded, maimed, missing Union soldiers during the Civil War, especially since "Lucretia Smith's Soldier" conveyed a message some must have regarded as anti-patriotic and possibly disloyal at a time when the nation was concerned with caring for the wounded. After all, when the burlesque appeared in December 1864, Walt Whitman was visiting Union hospitals and President Lincoln, recently reelected, was penning the immortal words of his Second Inaugural: "With malice toward none, with charity for all, with firmness in the right as God gives us to see the right, let us strive on to finish the work we are in, to bind up the nation's wounds, to care for him who shall have borne the battle and for his widow and his orphan, to do all which may achieve and cherish a just and lasting peace among ourselves and with all nations." The story was well received in a social context of widespread bereavement, a fact indicative of the irreverent spirit of western humor as well as a general trend of anti-Romantic writings, from burlesque to the rise of aesthetic realism. With the realities of the war ever-present, those "nice, sickly war stories" were being replaced by realistic presentations of sentiment as well as realistic battle scenes. "Lucretia Smith's Soldier" was one comic step on the march toward such realistic war novels as John W. De Forest's *Miss Ravenel's Conversion from Secession to Loyalty* (1867), Stephen Crane's *The Red Badge of Courage* (1895), and Ellen Glasgow's *Between North and South* (1902).[12]

The publication of "Lucretia Smith's Soldier" indicated the importance of Clemens's southern leanings to the development of his reconstructed persona as Mark Twain, for the story was a notable use of literature as a vehicle for political and social polemic. His Nevada writings certainly contained this element from the very beginning, but it is true, as scholar Ivan Benson has stated, that "[i]n San Francisco, Mark Twain's humor became more and more impregnated with social reproof." The surrender of Robert E. Lee to Ulysses S. Grant at Appomattox, the subsequent collapse of the Confederate government, and most particularly the assassination of President Abraham Lincoln accelerated the reconstruction of Mark Twain.[13]

On the night of April 14, 1865, John Wilkes Booth crept into the president's private box at Ford's Theater and shot him with a pistol. The assassin then leaped from the box to the stage shouting "Sic semper tyrannis," the state motto of Virginia, meaning "Thus always to tyrants." That June, Clemens began writing a series of columns under the heading "Answers to Correspondents" for the literary paper the *Californian*. As Clemens assumed his new position, the political environment in San Francisco following the president's assassination remained volatile. As in many large cities, mob violence had erupted, targeting Copperhead newspapers and sometimes their owners. In San Francisco, many newspapers were attacked, most particularly Beriah Brown's *Democratic Press*. The extent of the mob violence has led some to conclude that the fury was indiscriminate, and that, as historian Barbara Cloud has alleged, "innocent" newspapers were broken up "only because they happened to be in the way," identifying the paper *L'Union Franco Americaine* as one of them; in reality, Republican papers had frequently charged that paper with disloyalty. In an article the week prior to the president's assassination, the *Alta California* published an article denominating it a "French Secession Organ" that "has been in the habit of abusing the Administration and the nation, and justifying the rebels for a long time in articles such as would give the editor a good right to a lodging in Alcatraz." Even before the assassination of the president, popular sentiment in the North and the West was largely against such papers, and it was toward them and Copperheads generally that the famous lines from George F. Root's song "Just Before the Battle, Mother" (1864) were directed:

> Tell the traitors all around you,
> That their cruel words, we know,
> In ev'ry battle kill our soldiers
> By the help they give the foe.

The suppression of newspapers by military authorities was commonly discussed in San Francisco, with many Republican papers advertising the names of those that ought to be suppressed, as many in fact were. In short, the mobs, or at least their leaders, recognized their enemies and acted accordingly.[14]

Many loyal papers expressed satisfaction and qualified approval of the mob assaults. With its editorial title, "An Expression of Anger—A Word of Caution," the *Evening Bulletin*, for example, summed up the attitude. "Incited by an honest and natural animosity, several hundreds of the citizens of San Francisco joined in a sudden and destructive attack upon the publication offices and material of several newspapers in this city which had made themselves obnoxious to loyal sentiment long since by their opposition to the war for the Union, and their coarse strictures upon our murdered President." While approving of this "natural" feeling, the editorialist cautioned that such revenge was "not the best expression for heartfelt sorrow over the death of a good man." The *Alta California*, too, justified the violence against the "offices of certain obnoxious publications," calling the news of the president's assassination "more than men could bear." The *Dramatic Chronicle*, another paper Clemens wrote for occasionally, characterized the attacks as "'irregular justice,' which though not sanctioned by the courts will not be severely condemned by even the most moderate and law-abiding citizens." After nearly two weeks of reflection, another editorial in the same paper called the mob violence "not unnatural, nor is it to be harshly judged." The writer concluded by calling for the legal suppression of disloyal papers. During the war, many Copperhead newspapers were shut down throughout California.[15]

Years later, after his personal reconstruction was as complete as it could be and after southern Reconstruction was over, Clemens wrote that "Mr.

Lincoln's assassination gave the common globe a sense of personal injury." At the time, however, Clemens quickly revolted against what came to be called "waving the bloody shirt" of the Union dead, but particularly of the slain president. Many waved the bloody shirt of the slain president to advance the Union program, that is, using the fact that the president's murderer had been a Copperhead to suppress free speech, to enforce uniformity of outlook, and to garner votes for Republican candidates. Clemens's criticism of the "bloody shirt" erupted most forcibly in a series of articles he wrote for the *Californian*. He had written for the publication several times after his flight from the Nevada Territory. Bret Harte was a fellow contributor, and the editor was Charles Webb, the man who had christened Clemens the "Moralist of the Main." Clemens admired Webb, but to Radical Republicans the editor was "as bitter a Copperhead as ever went unhung." Webb was loyal, one critic admitted in a voice dripping with irony, "loyal to the Southern Conthieveracy, loyal to the Rebellion, and loyal to anything in opposition to our Government." Clemens, having been similarly traduced, had never shied away from accusations of disloyalty. Far from it. He had dealt with accusations directly when writing such articles as "Another Traitor—Hang Him!" Just as Clemens had been driven from the *Enterprise*, Webb was driven from his post as editor of the *Californian*. Not coincidentally, he resigned his position on April 15, 1865, the day the president died. Scholar Franklin Walker has suggested that Webb "came away with the feeling that it was not safe to walk down the street unless you clothed yourself with the star-spangled banner and slapped its folds in your neighbor's eyes." Shortly thereafter, the name Mark Twain began to appear on the "Answers to Correspondents" column for Webb's paper. Clemens used his column, for which he manufactured both the questions and the answers, to defend Webb, and by extension himself, by tackling all the sacred elements of Unionism: July 4th, war music, and the loyalty oath required of anyone (presumably even Clemens himself) who had borne arms against the Union or uttered disloyal statements. Moreover, in passages that still seem shocking, Clemens joked about John Wilkes Booth and the assassinated president. Given that Webb was labeled a Copperhead solely for his mildly derisive comments about Lincoln and the war effort *before* April 14, Clemens's comments *after* the 14th seem all the more shocking.[16]

In his columns, Clemens offered several statements concerning the post-assassination political climate, but the column on June 10 is the crucial one for understanding his response. He opened the column typically enough, with "Mark Twain" fielding questions from "AMATEUR SERENADER," "ARITHEMETICUS," and "AMBITIOUS LEARNER," among others. Ranging freely, he criticized serenading as "a wicked, unhappy and seditious practice" and joked about "a Georgia major's uniform, which is a shirt-collar and a pair of spurs." Clemens cut to the heart of his satire with a letter from "NOM DE PLUME," also called "the Frenchman." The use of the French phrase for a pen name functioned humorously as a surrogate for Clemens himself, for in the previous column, a question had been addressed to "MR. MARK TWAIN" and signed, with a misspelling of the French phrase, "Yours, without prejudice, NOMME DE PLUME." The "Frenchman" inquired why his parents named him Mark, for "had they known your *ardent* nature, they would doubtless have named you Water-less Twain." The joke referred to Clemens's reputation, created in great measure in his own columns, for heavy drinking. The name Mark Twain was also one that he had used in bars to put two drinks (or a double) on his tab. In the second column, Clemens resurrected this character to inquire about grammar.

> I read in the papers a few days since some remarks upon the grammatical construction of the sentences—"*Sic semper traditoris*" and "*Sic semper traditoribus*," and I procured a Latin grammar in order to satisfy myself as to the genative, dative and ablative cases of traitors—and while wending my weary way homewards at a late hour of the night, thinking over the matter, and not knowing what moment some cut-throat would knock me over, and, as he escaped, flourishing my watch and portmonaie, exclaim, "*Sic semper tyranis*," I stumbled over an individual lying on the sidewalk, with a postage stamp pasted on his hat in lieu of a car ticket, and evidently in the *objective case* to the phrase "how come you so?" As I felt in his pockets to see if his friends had taken care of his money, lest he might be robbed, he exclaimed, tragically, "*Si*(hic) *semper tarantula-juice!*" Not finding the phrase in my grammar, which I examined at once, I thought of your advice and *asked* him what he meant, said he "I mean jis what I say, and I intend to sti-hic to it." He was *quarter*-less, Twain; when I *sounded* him he hadn't a cent, although he *smelled* strong of a 5-scent shop.

Weaving back and forth like the drunken tragedian it described, this rollicking "Answers to Correspondents" made a number of critical points about the climate in San Francisco following Lincoln's assassination. Clemens targeted primarily four elements of the assassination. First, he needled the overly punctilious commentators with their picayune concerns. One thinks of the sententious way in which such recondite issues as the proper declension of a Latin noun or conjugation of a Latin verb are discussed. Such mundane concerns were ludicrous when put into the context of such a shattering event as the assassination of the president. This idea hinged on Booth's crying out "Sic semper tyrannis" after shooting the president. While there were many eyewitnesses to the assassination, those in the theater collectively reported hearing Booth's cry both before and after the shot, while some reported he cried "Sic semper tyrannis!" others "The South is avenged!" "The South shall be free!" and even "I have done it!" Still others reported that he said nothing or that he said something unintelligible. Others even claimed he said both "Sic semper tyrannis!" and "The South is avenged!" While grammar is always important, it is difficult to imagine an occasion when discussing the difference between "the genative, dative and ablative cases of traitors" would have been less appropriate. Clemens's creation of the character Nom de Plume, the Frenchman in the sketch, recalled Professor G. in the burlesque map of the "Grande Vide Poche," so taken with the minutiae that he missed the reality of the situation.[17]

At the same time, Clemens lampooned the figure of Booth himself, who appeared to some at Ford's Theater to have been drunk. In Clemens's version, Booth was so drunk that he slurred over the statement he yelled after firing the shot that killed the president: "Sic semper tyrannis." The Booth figure in Clemens's burlesque cried "*Si*(hic) *semper tarantula-juice!*" Tarantula juice was slang for whiskey. Clemens punned on his own nom de plume with jokes about the Booth figure being "*quarter*-less, Twain," that is, not having any money but also having presumably drunk from the whiskey bottle until it is "a quarter less Twain," the Mississippi riverboating term for one quarter fathom below level. In any event, the character had been drinking cheap whiskey, or "tarantula juice," and so "hadn't a cent" but did have a "scent" after drinking at a saloon known as a "5-cent shop." The popular press represented Booth as being depressed, drunken, even weaving about after the assassination. To many, Booth was "a crazy, drunken actor—the son, after all, of a famously crazy, drunken actor." The confusion of the Booth figure with the name Twain, however, suggested an identification of the two, as if Clemens again challenged those who had charged him with disloyalty.[18]

Clemens mocked as well Booth's exaggerated theatricality, highlighting the fact that Booth was an actor by having the drunken figure in the sketch say "tragically, '*Si*(hic) *semper tarantula-juice!*'" Saying the motto Booth had used during his attack on the president "tragically" emphasized the significance of the assassin's theatrical persona. Clemens drew this aspect of his sketch directly from news reports about the assassin. The *Territorial Enterprise* identified Booth as "the illegitimate son of the elder Booth, and half brother to J. B. Booth and Edwin Booth—both well known to play-goers of California and Nevada." The *Evening Bulletin* noted that Booth was "a son of the late Junius Brutus Booth, the tragedian, and a brother of Edwin and J. B. Booth, late of this city." Other papers made the connection as well. John Wilkes Booth was a well known and successful tragedian in his own right, particularly in the South, where playbills advertised him as "A STAR OF THE FIRST MAGNITUDE!—THE YOUNGEST TRAGEDIAN IN THE WORLD!" The attack itself was extraordinarily theatrical. All the papers recorded some version of Booth's cry at attacking the president, "Sic semper tyrannis." The news came by telegraph, and most western papers, including the *Alta* and the *Enterprise,* reprinted comments from the New York *World:* "The cry of the murderer, as he leaped from the President's box and ran across the stage, betrays no madness or frenzy. All circumstances show that the same political fury and hate which lit the flames of the great rebellion inspired these hellish deeds."[19]

Lincoln had his role, too, and was frequently compared to the slain Caesar. "Not all the blood of the Caesars combined," concluded the correspondent for the *Alta California,* "was honored, much less mourned, as have been the mortal remains of Abraham Lincoln." In the same vein, and more frequently asserted, was that Booth was the modern Brutus. The *Dramatic Chronicle* even connected the place and method of assassination, with Booth "likening himself to that of 'Brutus,' for whose representations, dramatically, his father was so famous. The manner in which he left the box in which the tragedy was committed, the brandishing of the dagger, and the exclamation, '*sic semper tyrannis*,' show that he had *studied for the part*." Indeed, he had. Booth's cry, "*sic simper tyrannis*," was the same used by Brutus when stabbing Caesar, according to traditional accounts. Booth even noted in his diary "Friday the Ides," connecting the timing of his Friday, April 14, 1865 attack on the president with Brutus's choice of the Ides of March for attacking Julius Caesar. During the twelve-day manhunt following the assassination, Booth complained that his action, which he deemed a blow against tyranny, had placed him beyond society. He defended the nobility of "doing what Brutus was honored for." Booth's April 14 letter to the editors of the Washington, D.C. newspaper the *National Intelligencer* detailed the reasons for his assassination of the president, concluding this way:

> If the South is to be aided it must be done quickly. It may already be too late. When Caesar had conquered the enemies of Rome and the power that was his menaced the liberties of the people, Brutus arose and slew him. The stroke of his dagger was guided by his love of Rome. It was the spirit and ambition of Caesar that Brutus struck at.
> "Oh that we could come by Caesar's spirit,
> And not dismember Caesar!
> But, alas!
> Caesar must bleed for it."
> I answer with Brutus:
> He who loves his country better than gold or life.
> John W. Booth

Ending his apologia with an imperfect rendering of lines from Shakespeare's *Julius Caesar*, Booth proceeded to Ford's Theater for his final role.[20]

Clemens took that figure of Booth, with all the exaggerated flourishes of the *tragédien*, and revealed him as a drunken, down-on-his-luck buffoon. It recorded Clemens's skepticism toward the elevated dramatism of Booth, just as the writer had lampooned similarly "right, righteous, sacred" notions of the Union in "Lucretia Smith's Soldier." Clemens's burlesque may also have had something to do with the many people arrested—often while intoxicated, not surprisingly—for expressing joy at the president's assassination. The figure of the drunken Copperhead with Booth's cry made unintelligible became in the sketch an object of humor rather than horror or outrage. While many were arrested for such disloyal statements, Clemens suggested these individuals were harmless, if ludicrous, drunks, more likely to be the objects of crime than perpetrators of one. Likewise, by associating his own name with the drunken state of the Booth figure, Clemens may not have associated himself with the act of assassination, but he certainly identified himself as a target of suspicion for some of his own earlier statements such as "Bigler vs. Tahoe" and "How Is It?—How It Is." Prior to the assassination, he had often been the target of such accusations, and it is likely he remained sensitive about the issue.

Just as Clemens had derided dishonest sentimentality in "Lucretia Smith's Soldier," he mocked Booth's excessive dramatism, but the apotheosis of Abraham Lincoln provided another target for Clemens, both in his "Answers to Correspondents" and in other works of the period. Clemens's burlesque of the president's assassination came less than two months after the event. Between the time of the assassination and the appearance of his article, Andrew Johnson had been sworn in as president, John Wilkes Booth had been tracked down and shot to death, and the trial of the co-conspirators approached its conclusion. Each day, the assassination made the news again. A series of announcements proclaimed an official period of mourning for six months. All soldiers and officials in all government installations in the Army, Navy, Revenue Marine, Department of State, the Treasury Department, the Post Office, and the Department of the Interior were instructed to wear "crape upon the left arm for the period of six months." Newspapers struck a fittingly funereal pose by using thick, black column lines. As President Johnson said, "our country has become one great house of mourning, where the head of the family has been taken away." President Johnson announced that June 1, 1865, would be appointed "for special humiliation and prayer in consequence of the assassination of Abraham Lincoln, late President of the United States." Clemens penned the burlesque "Answers to Correspondents" amid all the dark trappings of national mourning; indeed, with government officials wearing black armbands, he could not have purchased a postage stamp without being reminded of the tragedy at Ford's Theater.[21]

Booth seriously misread the American people, northerners most obviously, when he attempted to portray Lincoln as a Caesarean tyrant by attacking him on the classical "ides." Americans were much more cognizant of the fact that the "Savior of the Union" had been shot on Good Friday, the Christian commemoration of the Savior's crucifixion. Lincoln's death was an apotheosis. It was often explicitly stated, as when one editorialist proclaimed, "The stroke of the assassin was the apotheosis of the victim."

In the days following Lincoln's assassination, he was likened to Christ in papers throughout Nevada and California. "He lived to redeem his country," declared the *Territorial Enterprise*, "and then heaven made him a martyr that he might live forever in the hearts of his people." Paper after paper likened the president's assassination to the betrayal and crucifixion of Christ. The *Alta California*, its columns drawn in wide black margins to suggest mourning, soberly intoned that "the assassination of Abraham Lincoln was, save one, the blackest crime ever committed in the world— that one was the Crucifixion on Calvary." Ministers, too, compared Lincoln to Christ, and the papers published entire sermons, such as the Reverend Hamilton's sermon at Oakland's Presbyterian Church in which he identi- fied only "one greater crime . . .—that which crucified the Savior of the world." The *Daily Evening Bulletin* called the assassination "a wicked deed of treason, unparalleled since the hour when Judas betrayed the Savior of the World." Funereal poetry appeared, too, using similar language. Emilie Lawson's poem "Abraham Lincoln" appeared in the *Daily Evening Bulletin* on April 19, identifying the slain president as "the king whose name no shadow staineth! Who bore the people's cross." Most enduring were the words of Julia Ward Howe's "Battle Hymn of the Republic." The singing of this hymn during the funeral obsequies held in San Francisco immediately followed the sermon and concluded the service. Originally written in 1862, when the poem was reprinted in both the *Alta California* and the *Evening Bulletin*, the words attained a new meaning:

> In the beauty of the lilies Christ was born beyond the sea,
> With a glory in His bosom that transfigures you and me;
> As He died to make men holy, let us die to make men free,
>   While God is marching on.

Lincoln had become the American Christ.[22]

Such an outpouring of worshipful admiration contributed to what would be called the "bloody shirt" that dominated Reconstruction-era politics. For Judge Charles Mason, writing on April 23, 1865, even Lincoln's funeral evi- denced the "crafty skill of Mark Anthony in displaying to the Roman people the bloody mantle of Caesar." Whether Lincoln was Christ or Caesar, this martyrological drama created for Clemens the opposite effect of what one might have expected. Such events typically enforce conformity, but with

Clemens, ever the gadfly, the more reverence accorded a figure, the more inclined he was to doubt the sincerity of popular sentiment. This explained, in part, his burlesque of Lincoln's assassination in "Answers to Correspondents," but Clemens went on to burlesque other elements of patriotism during those months of mourning. With the June 24 column, his comments became more satirical, and he displaced the immediate context of the Civil War to a discussion of disloyalty in reference to the American Revolution. One letter writer queried, "Why is it that on this day, the greatest of all in the annals of the rights of man—viz: the Glorious Anniversary of the Battle of Bunker Hill—*our Great Ensign of Freedom does not appear on the Custom House?*" Another letter, written to the evocatively titled (fictitious) newspaper the *Flaming Loyalist,* raised further suspicions about government officials who failed to properly recognize "*the hallowed 17th of June.*" Scholar Edgar Branch has suggested that while the work directly addressed "a political wrangle" involving the appointment of Charles James to the Custom House, the writer made plain his ire at the politically charged atmosphere following the president's assassination when any deviation however slight might be condemned as disloyalty. Clemens had seen this before, when the *Enterprise* was accused of using "Copperish" language. More recently, he had seen it in San Francisco, when Charles Webb resigned his editorship the day after Booth shot the president.[23]

Little wonder, then, that when the writer to the *Flaming Loyalist* proclaimed "He don't keep up his lick!—he's DISLOYAL!" Clemens responded to his imagined interlocutor with this diatribe:

> Oh, stuff! a public officer has a hard enough time of it, at best, without being constantly hauled over the coals for inconsequential and insignificant trifles. If you *must* find fault, go and ferret out something worth while to find fault with—if John Doe or the Collector neglect the actual business they are required by the Government to transact, impeach them. But pray allow them a little poetical license in the choice of occasions for getting drunk and hoisting the National flag. If the oriental artisan and the sentinel agriculturalist held the offices of these men, would they ever *attend to anything else* but the flag-flying and gin-soaking outward forms of patriotism and official industry?

In this and other of his San Francisco writings, Clemens blunted accusations of disloyalty directed toward himself and others with stout irony; he did, however, something much more momentous. He took his stand precisely on the grounds where he was attacked. His comedy was not simply defensive, but offensive. Once again, Clemens associated patriotism with drunken emotionalism—"Getting drunk and hoisting the National flag."[24]

In his final "Answers to Correspondents" column, Clemens wrote about the July 4th celebration in San Francisco. This was the first Independence Day since the assassination of the president, yet he described the "INDEPENDENCE ARCH" in a hilarious burlesque centering on the figure of Abraham Lincoln himself. "I have seen arch-traitors and arch-deacons and architects," he began, but never an arch so ugly as this one. Clemens then derided the "cheap flags" and the "large medallion portraits of Lincoln and Washington—daubs—apparently executed in whitewash, mud and brickdust, with a mop." Throughout the description, he employed strikingly inappropriate diction, such as "execution," "sickly," "ghostly," and "monstrous." The arch itself reminded him of a "barber-pole," prompting his description of the "FOUNDERS AND SAVIORS OF THE REPUBLIC." "Washington is clean-shaved, but he is not done getting shampooed yet; his white hair is foamy with lather, and his countenance bears the expectant aspect of a man who knows that the cleansing shower-bath is about to fall. Good old Father Abe, whose pictured face, heretofore, was always serious, but never unhappy, looks positively worn and dejected and tired out, in the medallion—has exactly the expression of one who has been waiting a long time to get shaved and there are thirteen ahead of him yet." Clemens had reported the previous July 4th, 1864, in much the same way, describing houses that were "broken out all over with flags, like small-pox patients," but his depiction of Abraham Lincoln on the first July 4th since his assassination must have disturbed some readers. Clemens, as scholar Branch has phrased it, "cast a critical eye not only on the details of these festivities in San Francisco, but on the quality of the journalism that chronicled them." That is, Clemens began his July 8 "Answers to Correspondents" by providing his own depiction of the arch and surrounding events. He then quoted other publications, revealing how the truth had been filtered and distorted through the reporters' eyes. No one wanted to admit that the medallion of the slain president looked as bad as it did. Not three months after his martyrdom, Lincoln the icon had become "tired out." Through comedy, Clemens again pointed out to his readers that the reporter owed fealty only to truth. Here, he moved toward the persona of the reconstructed southerner who, like Colonel Sherburn in *Adventures of Huckleberry Finn* (1885), "was born and raised in the south, and I've lived in the north; so I know the average all around." Born in the South, Clemens had visited the North and had mingled with Yankee and Rebel alike in the West. By 1865, he was already attacking the "flag-flying and gin-soaking outward forms of patriotism" that would disallow honest commentary and criticism.[25]

Similarly, in an article "Mark Twain on the Colored Man," written for the *Territorial Enterprise* following that first July 4th after the president's death, Clemens described the participation of black citizens in the San Francisco parade. "I was rather irritated at the idea of letting these fellows march in the procession myself, at first," Clemens confessed before proceeding to attack those who persisted in that view, mimicking his own process of reconstruction. Ventriloquating the language of racism, Clemens referred to the black marchers by their "descriptive title" most frequently heard, "damned naygurs," which he explained satirically, was the "name they go by now." Intended to jeer at the racism seen in the Union camp, the article was designed to offend, for it launched another fusillade at those who elevated the martyred president without elevating the Lincolnian ideal of emancipation and racial justice. Clemens described the "strategy" of putting the lighter-colored blacks first in the march, "then glooming down by some unaggravating and nicely graduated shades of darkness to the fell and dismal blackness of undefiled and unalloyed niggerdom." One should not overlook the satirical value to this description, for Clemens expatiated on the miscegenation issue again. Implicitly, he contended that race was not binary, but a continuum, and even irrelevant. Clemens joked that "no man could tell where the white folks left off and the niggers began." Such pointed barbs targeted the insistence of those who contended that the "damned naygurs" had no place in the procession, for the continuum argued against white versus black. The presence of the black marchers at the parade was immensely symbolic and important at the first July 4th after President Lincoln's assassination and the end of the Civil War. Likewise, it was significant that Clemens, however comically, opposed racial separation and invoked integration. He was beginning to use his "scribbling to excite the laughter of God's creatures" even while developing "his prophetic function" in society beyond what he had attempted in the Nevada Territory.[26]

Clemens's reconstruction accelerated when he began attacking Albert Evans, a reporter for the San Francisco Morning *Call* and later the city editor for the *Alta California*. Evans was the writer who had poked fun at the writer, labeling him a "sage-brush Bohemian," and the *Call* was the paper that had fired Clemens. Vengeance doubtless contributed to Clemens's attacks, but the series of articles did much more than vent spleen. In them, Clemens clearly defined the function of the writer in society. In labeling the series directed at Evans "a personal tiff," scholar Franklin Walker has overemphasized the personal at the expense of the political. Clemens's anger at Evans, whom he referred to with the moniker "Fitz Smythe," stemmed from his belief that his rival had abdicated his responsibility as a reporter. Clemens concocted such hoaxes as "Petrified Man," "A Bloody Massacre Near Carson," and "How Is It?—How It Is" to trick the public into concern over political issues, but those were purposeful distortions to unveil hidden truths; Fitz Smythe lied to mislead, and did so from the perspective of a pro-Union, pro-police politics. The distinction appeared in the "Editorial Manifesto" printed in the *Enterprise* several years before: "Our duty is to keep the universe thoroughly posted concerning murders and street fights, and balls, and theaters, and pack-trains, and churches, and lectures, and school-houses, and city military affairs, and highway robberies, and Bible societies, and hay-wagons, and the thousand other things which it is in the province of local reporters to keep track of and magnify into undue importance for the instruction of the readers of a great daily newspaper." The manifesto, probably written by Clemens and Dan de Quille (William Wright), exhibited an ironically bemused tone toward the parochial nature of local news. It expressed a disrespectful attitude toward fact, but also suggested the legitimacy of magnifying, elaborating, and occasionally distorting for the purpose of "instruction." Humorous as the statement doubtless seemed to readers with its juxtaposition of murder and Bible study, it suggested the higher truth the reporter must serve. Sam Clemens understood that. Albert Evans did not.[27]

Clemens's initial criticism of Fitz Smythe came during the tempest surrounding Bret Harte's publication of *Outcroppings,* an anthology of California poetry. "Harte," as Patrick Morrow has mordantly observed, "had to sort through an avalanche of essentially two types of poetry: talentless imitations of late Augustan picturesque verse in a California setting, or high-sounding Victorian verse of general truths, general sentiments, and predictable rhymes." Western reviewers rightly called the book "hogwash," a "slop bucket," and "tailings . . . which would average about 33 1/3 cents per ton." Tagging the volume "tailings" was most unkind, for the term referred to the gravelly marl left after the silver or gold had been separated out. Seeking to mine western literary gold, Harte had struck a rich vein of slag.[28]

In an ironic turn of events, the poor quality of the poetry in *Outcroppings* led to widespread calls for more regional poetry inspired by the Golden State. All those who could lift a pen felt that their efforts, however juvenile, equaled the muck they had read in Harte's anthology; most were probably correct. Sam Clemens was still at this point a friend of Bret Harte's, still viewing the more established author as a mentor. Later, Clemens would find Harte "showy, meretricious, insincere," but when the *Outcroppings* reviews hit the paper, he went on the warpath. Albert Evans attacked the volume, and Clemens responded with his column "Caustic," written for the *Territorial Enterprise* of December 19, 1865. In this editorial, Clemens claimed that Fitz Smythe was critical of the anthology solely because his own poem "In Memoriam," published in the *Alta California* on April 17, 1865, had been excluded. Clemens proffered a burlesque of the poem that mourned the slain president, passing it off as the original.

> THE MARTYR
> Gone! gone! gone!
>   Forever and forever!
> Gone! gone! gone!
>   The tidings ne'er shall sever!
> Gone! gone! gone!
>   Wherever! Oh, wherever!
> Gone! gone! gone!
>   Gone to his endeavor!
> (RECAPITULATION.)
> Gone forever!
> To wherever!
> Ne'er shall sever!
> His endeavor!
> From our soul's high recompense!

Fitz Smythe's original poem was bad enough; Clemens's burlesque was worse. In the original, written a day after President Lincoln's death and published in the *Alta California* on April 17, Evans had written

> One mournful wail is heard from shore to shore;
> A Nation's heart is stricken to the core;
> And Freedom, kneeling, with uncovered head,
> Weeps by the altar of OUR COUNTRY'S DEAD.

If Clemens was truly burlesquing "In Memoriam," and not some other poem by Fitz Smythe or another eminent California poet, one can say that he adopted the bathos as he found it, while exaggerating the ridiculous formal elements. Like so many others who have discerned nothing behind Clemens's comic comments, biographer Albert Paine labeled Clemens's burlesque "a more or less pointless witticism." Purporting to quote a portion of the poem with its "Gone! gone! gone!" and "recapitulation" "Gone forever!" Clemens opined, "I consider that the chief fault in this poem is that it is ill-balanced—lop-sided, so to speak. There is too much 'gone' in it, and not enough 'forever.'" The poem is "bad," Clemens argued, so Fitz Smythe's judgments of *Outcroppings* were illegitimate. "[H]e never wrote but two poems in his life," Clemens complained. One of them was his lopsided elegy to Lincoln, "which he composed when the news came of the assassination of the President." The other was "The Dream of Norton I, Emperor." By linking the slain president with Emperor Norton, a fixture in San Francisco and a kind of half-mad drunk with delusions of imperial grandeur, Clemens began the process of debunking Fitz Smythe and, through him, continued to deride the rampant glorification of the president. The kind of genius that produced a poem like "The Martyr," Clemens contended, was "a dangerous kind of genius" and worthy of "capital punishment." Fitz Smythe, in other words, was guilty of a crime as bad as murder, as if his poor poem assassinated the president anew.[29]

Fitz Smythe's poem was just a single drop in a sea of such sentimental verse washing over the country, one of several unfortunate side effects of the president's death. Clemens referred to the controversy again nearly a month later in the *Territorial Enterprise* for January 18, 1866. His column, "The Righteous Shall Not Be Forgotten," probably referring to Psalm 112:6, announced that H. H. Bancroft planned "to tender justice unto all that legion of Californian poets who were defrauded of fame in being left out of 'Outcroppings.'" Clemens joked that the quantity will be greater than the quality of the poetry, noting also that "Fitz Smythe has contributed his stately anthem, 'Gone! Gone! Gone!' written in a lucid moment just subsequent to the assassination of the President." Clemens ended his ironic piece by speaking more directly so that the "one-eyed potatoes" would see the point of the burlesque, exhorting potential contributors: "Come on, you sniveling thieves! Fall into ranks and blast away with your rotten poetry at an unoffending people! Do your worst and vamoose-scatter-git!"[30]

In his various burlesques involving the slain president, Clemens assailed the tendency to deify Lincoln as the martyred Christ. Clemens's claim that "Gone! Gone! Gone!" was a "dangerous kind of genius" asserted that such vapid glorification of the president harmed the country partly because of its mindless jingoism and partly because of its jangling poetry that was just flat out, dreadfully, killingly "bad." One thinks of historian Edmund Wilson's description of Carl Sandburg's bathetic six-volume biography of Abraham Lincoln: "[T]he cruelest thing that has happened to Lincoln since he was shot by Booth has been to fall into the hands of Carl Sandburg." Clemens likewise responded with a biting humor unusual at a time when emotions about the slain president remained quite strong. Clemens's burlesque about the Lincoln elegy appeared in December 1865. President Johnson's sentiment in his First Annual Message of December 4, 1865, was more than mere rhetoric: "Our thoughts next revert to the death of the late President by an act of parricidal treason. The grief of the nation is still fresh."[31]

Union partisanship and pathetic poetry may have sparked Clemens's antagonism toward the man he called Fitz Smythe, but his attacks over the next half year centered on the duty of the reporter to the community. Fitz Smythe was a famous apologist for the San Francisco police. For Clemens, his opponent's staunch Unionism reflected his support for all the institutions of government without regard to their effect on the people. Fearing that "we are threatened with civil war in California," Evans had called for a "strong hand" to quell the first sign of unrest. One of the criticisms common among Confederates and Copperheads alike was that President Lincoln, by suspending the habeus corpus laws and restricting constitutional guarantees of free press and free speech, had become a tyrant and created a police state. Even when police abuses were apparent to all reporters, Fitz Smythe either kept quiet or defended the police. Clemens's denunciations of the police were, by contrast, quite explicit. In his January 23, 1866 article, he wrote, "I want to compliment Chief Burke—I do honestly. But I can't find anything to compliment him about. He is always rushing furiously around, like a dog after his own tail—and with the same general result, it seems to me; if he catches it, it don't amount to anything, after all the fuss; and if he don't catch it it don't make any difference, because he didn't want it anyhow; he only wanted the exercise, and the happiness of 'showing off' before his mistress and the other young ladies." Once again, such jokes landed him in trouble, for Chief Burke was irate both that the reporter would dare to compare his behavior to a frisky dog's and by insinuating his private life was that of a cur, too. Threats of legal action and even a retaliatory arrest for public intoxication failed to quell Clemens's ardor for attacking the police; on the contrary, they confirmed his belief that the police were corrupt and out of control. Admonishing Fitz Smythe for his failure to attack the police, and often including criticism of the reporter within articles denouncing police corruption, Clemens made the larger point that the press was a guarantor of political freedom only when it freed itself from allegiance to anything other than truth. His energetic sorties against Fitz Smythe were a means of attacking Union politics and governmental abuse of power. They stemmed ultimately from Clemens's Copperhead leanings, for he saw in the abuses perpetrated by the San Francisco police a type of the state itself, particularly the Union government's abrogation of habeus corpus and freedom of speech rights during and following the war.[32]

In a string of articles, Clemens let fly at Fitz Smythe's newspaper reports, deriding them as romances written "to glorify his god, the police." In "Gorgeous New Romance, By Fitz Smythe!" Clemens burlesqued an article about "koinickers"—counterfeiters—rounded up by the police. Fitz Smythe chose for his title "A Chapter in the History of the San Francisco Police," handing Clemens a convenient form for the burlesque, as the idea of a "chapter" in the "history" suggested less than objective reportage. The "Chapter in the History of the San Francisco Police" became, through Clemens's satirical sense of humor, the "Gorgeous New Romance." Clemens attacked both the form and content of his rival's writings, suggesting that his "terrible solid column romances about the hair-breadth escapes and prodigies of detective sagacity of the San Francisco police" were more fiction than fact. Clemens labeled his rival a "novelist" and begged "Fitz Smythe to re-publish another flaming 'chapter in the history of the San Francisco Police,'" but suggested adding a bit of realism, such as the facts about the police bungling. Clemens hilariously dissected Fitz Smythe's column as a romance novel, analyzing its ten sections as if they were chapters in a nail-biting, edge-of-your-seat potboiler. Clemens even used Fitz Smythe's chapter titles, but with his own twist. Where his rival indited "The New Decoy," Clemens exaggerated it as "'The New Decoy!'—the red hand of crime begins to show—somewhere."[33]

With his Fitz Smythe burlesques, Clemens perfected the system he used in many of his greatest works: apprehending a truth about a person, he exaggerated it into caricature or beyond, creating in the process a character for his own work. Worse than the sensationalist pap Fitz Smythe wrote was the fact that the writer overlooked mistakes by the police that had allowed the criminals to slip through their fingers in the first place. Indeed, Clemens made that complaint so clear in his burlesque that even a "one-eyed potato" had to see the nub. At one point, he blandly stated his criticism:

> The romance is gotten up with several objects in view. One is to show how mean a thing it is to call for investigations of police affairs as Dr. Rowell is doing; another is to try and bolster up the Grand Jury's recent "vindication" of the Police Department—the other day—a "vindication" which the public did not accept with as much confidence as they would if it had come from Heaven; another is to show that the stool-pigeon Ned Wellington—"Indian Ned"—who was appointed a special officer by Burke, is no more of a thief or a rascal than many another man on the force, and I think that is unjust to Wellington; and another object, an eternal one with Fitz Smythe—is to glorify his god, the police. This latter is a disease with him; it breaks out all over the *Alta* every day; and it phazes Smythe worse than the small-pox.

During his fight with Evans/Fitz Smythe, Clemens contracted to write travel letters for the *Alta California* during the *Quaker City* excursion to Europe and the Holy Land, letters that eventually became his first book *The Innocents Abroad* (1869). At this point, however, the *Alta* was the "Daily Morning Blanket," as he called it, and Fitz Smythe, who had become its city editor, was its chief producer of bombast. Clemens's criticism was both stylistic and political. He had learned during the Nevada years how demagogues used inflated romantic language to hide disturbing policies.

The more elaborate and inflated the language, whether in defense of the sacred cause of slavery in his youth, the sacred cause of Unionism in the Nevada Territory and San Francisco, the sacred cause of the police, or the sacred cause of anything, the warier Clemens became that the speaker was trying very hard to conceal something. "The unfilagreed facts in Smythe's column romance," Clemens contended, could have been recited in a brief paragraph, which he then did. Moreover, he appended a section titled "Another Romance" in which he drew attention to numerous police scandals involving larceny, prostitution, and theft. Clemens credited those who captured the counterfeiters, but argued that focusing only on the "glory" of the police officers while ignoring "the scallawags" (also spelled scalawags) was abdicating a city reporter's responsibilities. He questioned the motives that led Fitz Smythe to write this romance that has "ten distinct chapters, and occupies more room and flames out with a grander sublimity in the *Alta* than did the capture of Richmond and the Southern armies, as published in the same paper. How marvelous are thy ways, O Lord!"[34]

Clemens connected the police "romance" with the inflated descriptions of the "capture of Richmond and the Southern armies" to ally the war effort with a corrupt civil authority, linking the *Alta*'s effusive patriotism with its advocacy of a strong civic power, the police force. Moreover, Clemens's use of the term "scallawags" was noteworthy. As historian James McPherson has pointed out, "scalawag" and "carpetbagger" were "among the most pejorative words in the American political lexicon." "Scalawags" was used "to describe Southern whites who joined the Republicans" and were considered to be traitors to the Confederacy, the South, and their race. Albion Tourgée, a Union officer and a later "carpetbagger" himself, defined "scalawags" in *A Fool's Errand* (1879) as "the native whites who were willing to accept the reconstruction measures." Allied with corrupt police "scallawags," Fitz Smythe was a scalawag, too, because he turned his back on the people in favor of law enforcement; in this equation, Clemens characterized the abusive, corrupt San Francisco police as more of an occupying force than collaborators—like the Union Army in the South. Clemens insistently connected Fitz Smythe's pro-police stance with his pro-Union politics, registering his concern at the potential for a police state in which loyalty oaths were required and outward expressions of disloyalty were aggressively suppressed. In "Take the Stand, Fitz Smythe," Clemens again attacked this "Excuser and Explainer-in-Chief to the Police" for excessive praise and for neglecting his duty as a reporter. Clemens reprinted an article from the San Francisco *Morning Call* with the heading "WHERE ARE THE POLICE?" Clemens chose this article probably because it described "a terrible onslaught" by a "band of soldiers" attempting to break into the home of "a peaceable citizen." Accompanied by his neighbors, the man had to search high and low before finding any police officers to help them. Clemens clearly linked the police and the military as rogue forces ignoring or trampling on the rights of private and "peaceable" citizens. Clemens was in fact responding to numerous outrages by Union soldiers in San Francisco, outrages that were excused by many because, as Clemens inquired with heavy irony, "Didn't they fight for their country, and haven't they *saved the country?* Well then. Very well then. After having saved the country, ain't they entitled to help themselves to just as much of it as they want?"[35]

Clemens continued to roast his rival, the police, and the military in a paired article, "Fitz Smythe's Horse" and "What Have the Police Been Doing?" Clemens humorously described how Fitz Smythe fancied himself a cavalry officer, "with his soldier coat on, and his mustashers sticking out strong like a cat-fish's horns," yet gave his horse "nothing to eat but them old newspapers." The newspapers provided insufficient "food" for the horse—Clemens's dig at the poor quality of the reporting. Another target was the editor's preening. Fitz Smythe obviously "thinks he looks like old General Macdowl," the officer in charge of suppressing newspapers and treasonous statements in California and Nevada. In his rhetoric, Evans did seem to think he himself wielded such power. Clemens followed his comments in "Fitz Smythe's Horse" with "What Have the Police Been Doing?" a masterful burlesque in which he imitated Fitz Smythe by seemingly praising the police who "infallibly snaffle every Chinese chicken-thief" even as far more serious crimes remained unsolved. Indeed, during his time in the Nevada Territory and San Francisco, Clemens grew increasingly aware of racism directed toward Chinese as well as African Americans. This is not to say that he forswore stereotypes in producing his humor; far from it. Likewise, he continued to react negatively to miscegenation, writing in the *Call* of a "most infernal description of miscegenation" in which a Chinese man married a white woman. However, he also endorsed the responsibility of the police to protect everyone, and he recognized his own responsibility as a reporter to draw attention to their failure to do so. Clemens nursed an irritation at the *Call* partly for firing him but also for editing his articles on the Chinese. Even in 1870, Clemens would write "Disgraceful Persecution of a Boy," in which he criticized anti-Chinese sentiment in California, where "a Chinaman had no rights that any man was bound to respect." With this line, a close paraphrase of Chief Justice Roger Taney's argument in the *Dred Scott* decision that blacks had "no rights which the white man was bound to respect," Clemens rejected the decision about the slave from Missouri, a decision he had once applauded. Imbued with a sense of outrage at injustice, Clemens's San Francisco satires were crucial to his developing narrative voice. Scholar Edgar Branch has traced the colloquial style of the later masterpieces *The Adventures of Tom Sawyer* (1876) and *Adventures of Huckleberry Finn* (1885) to these early sketches. Indeed, in writing his articles on Fitz Smythe, Clemens joined the colloquial style with a sledgehammer irony. In "What Have the Police Been Doing?" Clemens's ventriloquation of Evans's style (as Fitz Smythe) culminated with this ironic plea: "Can't you find somebody to pick on besides the police? It takes all my time to defend them from people's attacks."[36]

When Clemens penned "Remarkable Dream" in early February 1866, he made a major leap toward his reconstruction. In this sketch, he adopted the comedic prophetic persona, imagining a dream in which Ananias, the "Prince of Liars," appeared to him to commend Fitz Smythe's reportage. A figure in early Christianity, Ananias sold land and then donated a portion of the proceeds to the church while claiming he had donated it all. Peter rebuked him, saying, "thou hast not lied unto men, but unto God" (Acts 5:4). Like Ananias, Fitz Smythe lied and betrayed those he was supposed to serve. Implicitly, he lied to God, too, in his "war against truth." Clemens, who had identified his calling as being of "a low order—i.e. humorous," here insisted that being a reporter really was a higher calling. So, too, with the work of a satirist who reminded journalists of this. The prophetic form was central to the reconstructed persona Clemens created. The reconstruction of Mark Twain visible in these years was not self-serving, though it served him well. As he attacked Fitz Smythe, the police, and violence against the Chinese, he agitated for justice. As the Fitz Smythe series of articles appeared, readers could see the transformation accelerating as Clemens took the charge of disloyalty and redefined it. The writer cannot be a toady, the stooge of the powerful, but must be a dissenter, a heretic, an apostate. Disloyalty to the government was loyalty to the people when the government forsook the principles it proclaimed.[37]

Politically, reconstruction of states involved ceasing hostilities, recognizing the Union, and passing state constitutions that guaranteed the rights of black American males to vote, the "free nigger Constitution" that had been so controversial when defeated in the Nevada Territory in 1863. These elements were required for a return to "normal relations to the Union." Twain's reconstruction would never return him to such a state of normalcy; rather, at its most basic level, Sam Clemens's experiences in the Nevada Territory and California made of him a responsible gadfly, constantly stinging the state. As he left San Francisco, not harried out of town this time, but to embrace a national audience, his attitudes toward race remained conflicted. Still, his awareness of the hypocrisy of many Union officials and voters in the West initiated a larger criticism of culture. Sam Clemens's social criticism proved to be self-criticism as well. Some have suggested that Clemens's move toward the Republican Party, completed when Grant defeated Johnson in the 1868 vote, was craven political calculation. In fact, his movement toward the dominant political party of his era was provoked precisely by his antipathy toward the Union and its political champions. Calling the reunited country to account for its hypocrisy in not living up to its loudly and oft-proclaimed ideals, Clemens crafted the role for himself of something more than a mere humorist and became a skeptical satirist viewing society with a jaundiced eye. Through his reconstruction, Sam Clemens, first forced to be an outsider as a border-stater, became a writer on all sides and against all sides, entrusted with a special commission to criticize all facets of the reunified nation. In a notebook entry written sometime during July 1866, Clemens recalled President Abraham Lincoln's Second Inaugural Address: "Eloquence Simplicity—Lincoln's 'with malice toward none, with charity for all, & doing the right as God gives us to see the right, all may yet be well.'—very simple & beautiful." Clemens's close paraphrase of Lincoln's words proved they lived in his heart. The striking contrast between Lincoln's "Simplicity" and the inflated hyperbole directed toward him as the martyr of the Union cause struck Sam Clemens, just as the disparity between pro-Union principles and the lack of racial justice had struck him as far back as Virginia City, Nevada. After the Union victory, the southern cause became for Clemens not the "Lost Cause" that demanded an aggressively unreconstructed adherence to prewar southern ideology; the cause itself underwent reconstruction and became a mission to reconstruct the politics of the nation. His personal reconstruction well underway, it remained for Mark Twain to report on the country's Reconstruction. Many writers went South for such a project, but for Sam Clemens, there could have been no better base of operation than the nation's capital, Washington, D.C.[38]

SEEKING A REPUTATION "THAT SHALL STAND FIRE"

Twain, Reconstruction, and the Impeachment
Crisis in Washington, 1866–1869

As we have observed before, events are fast taking this question of reconstruction out of the hands of politicians and deciding it practically in the best manner. It will have little difficulty for the next Congress.
—*Daily Evening Bulletin,* April 20, 1865

I believe the Prince of Darkness could start a branch hell in the District of Columbia (if he has not already done it), and carry it on unimpeached by the Congress of the United States.
—MARK TWAIN, April 7, 1868

ARK TWAIN'S RECONSTRUCTION took place alongside the national Reconstruction that began before the Union's military triumph and before the tragedy and turmoil of President Abraham Lincoln's assassination. Even as the Civil War and Reconstruction remade the nation, they remade Mark Twain. Politicians discussed what Reconstruction would mean for the Confederacy long before the final surrender of its armies in April and May 1865, but Reconstruction was not just for the Confederate states. Before the war's end, several border states underwent various forms of Reconstruction. One of them was Clemens's home state of Missouri, which President Lincoln singled out in his Fourth Annual Message given in 1864. "Important movements have also occurred during the year to the effect of molding society for durability in the Union. Although short of complete success, it is much in the right direction that 12,000 citizens in each of the States of Arkansas and Louisiana have organized loyal State governments with free constitutions, and are earnestly struggling to maintain and administer them. The movements in the same direction, more extensive though less definite, in Missouri, Kentucky, and Tennessee should not be overlooked." The president had good reason for expressing doubts about Missouri. This "molding society for durability in the Union" involved structural changes in what were formerly Confederate states as well as in border states, like Missouri, of uncertain allegiance. Missouri had contributed 109,000 men to the Union Army and an estimated 30,000 to the Confederacy, in the form of enlisted soldiers or irregulars, and the state was constantly subjected to the depredations of bushwhackers and militias like Quantrill's Raiders. "The political fight for control of Kansas, characterized by violence and bitterness," as historian Edwin McReynolds has observed, "had made Missourians excessively partisan." When the Confederate General Sterling Price invaded the state in 1864, he found some enthusiastic recruits, forced others, and was met by a Union force likewise comprised of soldiers whose loyalties were not unmixed. Missouri did undergo an "internal reconstruction" during the war, but as historian Eric Foner has pointed out, it was the "last border state" in which the process was complete.[1]

Throughout the border states and the South, "Reconstruction" was on everyone's lips even before the final defeat of the Confederacy, but what it meant varied from one person to the next. For many southerners Reconstruction consisted largely of external forms, changes such as rewriting the state constitution to recognize the emancipation of the slaves. The state of Missouri passed its laws officially emancipating the slaves on January 11, 1865, an action that led Frederick Douglass to exult, "Missouri, the state of Claiborne Jackson and Sterling Price . . . Missouri, the home of guerillas, is a free State to-day." Reconstruction also included taking the loyalty oath. Sometimes, such changes were outward signs of an inner reconstruction. George Washington Cable was an exceptional case. Having first taken up arms to defend the South, he later took up his pen to attack its legacy of racism—for which he became persona non grata in southern society. For others, however, taking the oath was a pragmatic decision to preserve their property from confiscation. Many took the oath "as a matter of precaution," as one Confederate lieutenant colonel explained when advising his mother to do so. She did so reluctantly, her attitudes remaining as staunchly Confederate as they had been when she had christened the assassination of President Lincoln "righteous retribution" and the "[o]ne sweet drop among so much that is painful." Outwardly, many southerners were reconstructed "for durability in the Union," but that only meant assenting to policies that had become unavoidable.[2]

Like southern society in general, Sam Clemens was reconstructed, molded for "durability in the Union." As with southern society generally, however, even as he craved and sought, as he wrote a friend, a "reputation that shall stand fire," Reconstruction was to some degree imposed from without. It was also highly complex, highly personal. Even the idea of a reputation that could "stand fire" recalled Sam's earlier desertions, instances in Missouri and Nevada where he failed to "stand fire," but fled. Some of Clemens's descriptions of the country in the immediate postwar era seemed to embrace the "politics of forgetting," as historian David Blight has called the country's hasty reunion between the North and the South. In his 1867 letters to the *Alta California* prior to his departure on the *Quaker City* voyage to Europe and the Holy Land, Clemens invoked images of a quick reconstruction of the country. He did comment on the situation in St. Louis where "the political bitternesses engendered during the war are still about as strong as they ever were," joking that even "Church congregations are organized, not on religious but on political bases; and the Creed begins, 'I believe in Abraham Lincoln, the Martyr-President of the United States,' or 'I believe in Jefferson Davis, the founder of the Confederate States of America.'" In the main, however, Clemens expressed surprise at the quick accommodation to the new political reality. He marveled at the way the country, North and South, simply got back to work. He related what a fellow correspondent had told him about Richmond, Virginia, where "he saw rebel Colonels, Majors and Captains, connected with the new express enterprise, helping the porters handle heavy boxes and barrels, and with their coats off and sleeves rolled up, too!" "Our Alexanders," Clemens opined, "do not sit down and cry because there are no more worlds to conquer, but snatch off their coats and fall to shinning around and raising corn and cotton, and improving sewing machines." Visiting New York's "Blind Asylum" on Ninth Avenue, Clemens watched as a blind girl assembled a wooden map of the United States by touch. She "pulled this map to pieces and jumbled the States up like a pile of bricks, and then the young disunionist repented of her work, and quickly reconstructed her country again."[3]

As Clemens prepared to embark on the *Quaker City* with a high-toned passenger list that boasted General William Tecumseh Sherman, who later withdrew from the cruise, and former Confederate Colonel William Denny, he often sketched such hopeful images of a quick and easy reconstruction. He was not alone. The *Daily Evening Bulletin,* less than a week after the president's assassination, claimed that "events are fast taking this question of reconstruction out of the hands of politicians and deciding it practically in the best manner. It will have little difficulty for the next Congress." The prediction would prove overly sanguine, but Clemens, too, saw cause for hope. "By some wonderful process or other," he wrote in his April 30, 1867 letter to the *Alta California,* "the soldiers of both armies have been quietly and mysteriously absorbed into civil life." Army statistics tell some of the story. On May 1, 1865, the Union Army *alone* totaled 1,000,516 troops. By 1871, the U.S. Army of the reunited country had shrunk to a postwar head count of 28,953 men; the population of that standing army in 1871 was but a few thousand more than the combined casualties on the *first day* of the Battle of Antietam. The demobilization of the Union and Confederate armies was indeed a marvelous transformation, even more unreal in its way than the rapid mobilization of the country for war. Even when Jefferson Davis, once president of the Confederacy, was released from Fort Monroe, Clemens was surprised and gratified as he watched the "fallen Chief" and the "extinguished sun" enter the New York Hotel with "no crowd around, no torchlight processions, no music, no welcoming cannon—and better than all, no infuriated mob, thirsting for blood and vengeance." All of these evidences were cause for hope.[4.]

Clemens's Reconstruction letters charted the course of a reconstructed American identity, both for the country and for the writer himself. When Clemens commented on "WHAT SIX YEARS HAVE WROUGHT" in the February 23, 1867, letter to the *Alta California,* he expressed wonder and admiration at how the war had changed American life. In New York City alone, the six years had dramatically increased the population, witnessed the construction of "acres upon acres of costly buildings," and "made five thousand men wealthy." His comments were a rehearsal for the memorable passage in *The Gilded Age,* the novel he wrote in 1873 with his neighbor Charles Dudley Warner: "The eight years in America from 1860 to 1868 uprooted institutions that were centuries old, changed the politics of a people, transformed the social life of half the country, and wrought so profoundly upon the entire national character that the influence cannot be measured short of two or three generations." Clemens continued to marvel at the changes taking place in the country because of the Civil War. In 1883, when he took a trip down the Mississippi to refresh his impressions of the river while writing *Life on the Mississippi,* he commented continually on the changes he witnessed, frequently struggling to recognize what had been old, familiar landmarks. The Civil War introduced the subject of historical change in Clemens's writing. The concept of historical change influenced *Adventures of Huckleberry Finn* (1885), in which the protagonist struggled with old definitions of race loyalty versus a higher loyalty to justice, and *A Connecticut Yankee in King Arthur's Court* (1889), where a mechanic named Hank Morgan, a self-styled "Yankee of the Yankees," traveled back in time to Arthurian England to completely industrialize and democratize the country in three years. Hank lamented that the land "reminded me of a time thirteen centuries away, when the 'poor whites' of our South who were always despised, and frequently insulted, by the slave lords around them, and who owed their base condition simply to the presence of slavery in their midst, were yet pusillanimously ready to side with the slave lords in all political moves for the upholding and perpetuating of slavery, and did also finally shoulder their muskets and pour out their lives in an effort to prevent the destruction of that very institution which degraded them."[5]

The abolition of slavery aside, not all of the changes "wrought so profoundly upon the entire national character" were positive, and in Clemens roiled the warring currents of American nationalism and American idealism. At the heart of this conflict was a new definition of loyalty that had commenced during his years as a western reporter. Just as he denounced the hypocritical racism of Republicans who were rabidly anti-southern (not just anti-Confederate), Clemens identified many elements unleashed during Reconstruction that led to the excesses of the era he and Warner named with the title of their book, *The Gilded Age.* In his *Alta California* letters, he also commented on other changes, such as the "upstart princes of Shoddy" whom the war had propelled to commercial success and the "good round million of her citizens" for whom the war had necessitated "the closest kind of scratching to get along." Clearly, there were many changes in the country, but Sam Clemens, too, had changed a great deal since his visit to

New York in 1853 when he had expressed only revulsion for the "human vermin" infesting its streets. No longer did he identify with the southern "slave lords," but neither did he identify with northern "upstart princes."[6]

Throughout the 1860s and 1870s, politics and social justice issues increasingly preoccupied Clemens. In his writings about Hawaii, which he visited in 1866, he commented on the condition of the "abused and insulted natives." When he went on the lecture tour in 1869–1870, his topic was "Our fellow Savages of the Sandwich Islands." That lecture sparked a minor uproar among clergymen, who were offended by Clemens's satirical suggestion that, as the native Hawaiian population had dropped from 400,000 to 55,000, America ought "to send a few more missionaries and finish them." After the Civil War, Clemens commented on all the major social and political issues from capital punishment to women's suffrage. In later years, he formed the habit of clipping newspaper articles and using them to write his running commentary on world events as diverse as American adventurism in the Philippines, massacres of missionaries in China, King Leopold's atrocities in Africa, and Russian pogroms against the Jews. With the end of the Civil War, Clemens's attempts to defend himself against charges of disloyalty became instead a campaign to charge the nation with disloyalty to its own ideals, a motive for which the persona of the reconstructed southerner was peculiarly appropriate. Clemens exploited his identity as a reconstructed southerner to criticize American culture, often specifically a northern culture. "Barnum's First Speech in Congress (By Spiritual Telegraph)," published in the New York *Saturday Evening Express* on March 5, 1867, was a prime example.[7]

In "Barnum's First Speech in Congress," Clemens transmuted his position as a reconstructing southerner to effective literary and social use. In 1865, P. T. Barnum, the "Great Showman" and "Prince of Humbugs," served as a Connecticut state legislator. Best known today for creating the American Museum and the "Greatest Show on Earth," Barnum achieved fame during the war for defecting from the Democratic Party to become a Radical Republican. On May 26, 1865, Barnum delivered a speech to the state legislature demanding that the word "white" be stricken from the state constitution, for it restricted enfranchisement to white males. Barnum's speech, while high-minded and, frankly, on the right side of history, failed to convince his fellow legislators. As historian A. H. Saxon has sardonically observed, the change was made only when "the 15th Amendment was about to become the law of the land anyway." Such hesitancy gave credence to charges of hypocrisy because southern states had to adopt "free constitutions" to reenter the Union. In October 1865, North Carolinian Thomas Settle, running for Congress, energized voters by declaring, "This is a white man's government, and intended for white men only, as even Connecticut, in New England itself, has just decided." During Barnum's unsuccessful 1867 campaign for the U.S. Congress, his candidacy was greeted with howls of derision from people unwilling to accept the "Prince of Humbugs" as a legitimate politician. Appropriately, the elections that year happened to fall on April Fool's Day. A writer in *The Nation* hailed Barnum as "THE TWO HUNDRED THOUSAND AND FIRST CURIOSITY IN CONGRESS." The *New York Herald* scoffed that he would be "a fitting representative for the wooden nutmeg State, which would lose nothing of the character it already enjoys by sending him to Congress." Indeed, the paper suggested that Barnum would be suited for Washington, because he "has been used to menageries all his lifetime." More seriously, the paper complained that "Under the leadership of Barnum the radical party will be thoroughly reconstructed on the grand historical principle of philosophical humbug." Even those who shared his principles found something laughable in his candidacy.[8]

By 1867, Clemens *may* have accepted Barnum's argument in favor of voting rights for African Americans, but he found his political rhetoric reminiscent of his professional patter as a carnival barker luring customers to view the "Fiji Mermaid," "the tattooed man," General Tom Thumb, and the "Ethnological Congress of Savage and Barbarous Tribes." It was this carnival language that Clemens lampooned in "Barnum's First Speech to Congress," published during Barnum's unsuccessful 1867 congressional bid. Clemens apprehended this "speech" from the future, reporting that Barnum will cry, "NO! Even as one sent to warn ye of fearful peril, I cry Help! help! for the stricken land!" Like the news reports of Barnum's candidacy, Clemens focused on the hilarity of having a bona fide huckster in Washington, patterning the work rather obviously after both prophetic political rhetoric and a showman's patter. References may have been to bearded women, dwarves, and giants, but Clemens presented them in biblical patterns, with the expression "the pride of his strength," invocations such as "O, spirit of Washington!," repeated use of the word "ye," laments such as "The country is fallen!" and the concluding exhortation, "Rouse ye, my people, rouse ye! rouse ye! rouse ye!" Clemens lifted the phrase "the pride of his strength" straight from Ezekiel 30:6: "Thus saith the Lord; They also that uphold Egypt shall fall; and the pride of her power shall come down." In the context of Barnum's support for Radical Reconstruction, those Egyptian slaveholders of the allusion were really unreconstructed Rebels and Copperheads attempting to win the peace after having lost the war.[9]

Clemens's Barnum was a caricature of the real man, but the famous May 26, 1865 speech P. T. Barnum delivered before the Connecticut legislature had contained many elements that cried out for such exaggeration.

> Suppose an inhabitant of another planet should drop down upon this portion of our globe at mid-winter. He would find the earth covered with snow and ice and congealed almost to the consistency of granite. The trees are leafless, everything is cold and barren; no green thing is to be seen; the inhabitants are chilled, and stalk about shivering from place to place;—he would exclaim, "Surely this is not life; this means annihilation. No flesh and blood can long endure this; this frozen earth is bound in the everlasting embraces of adamantine frost, and can never develop vegetation for the sustenance of any living thing." He little dreams of the priceless myriads of germs which bountiful Nature has safely garnered in the warm bosom of our mother earth; he sees no evidence of that vitality which the beneficent sun will develop to grace and beautify the world.

Barnum persisted in grandiloquent style for some time, describing how spring eventually arrived, causing the extraterrestrial visitor much wonderment. "So it is with the poor African," Barnum concluded. "You may take a dozen specimens of both sexes from the lowest type of man found in Africa; their race has been buried for ages in ignorance and barbarism, and you can scarcely perceive that they have any more of manhood or womanhood than so many orang-outangs or gorillas."[10]

Clemens seized on the oddities of Barnum's speech, exaggerating them for his own imagined congressional address. Commenting on the political turmoil during Reconstruction, Clemens's Barnum viewed congressional and presidential quarreling over radical reconstruction as a return of "grim Treason." Barnum lamented that "once more helpless loyalty scatters into corners as do the dwarfs when the Norwegian giant strides among them!" The imagery is some of the most comic Clemens ever created, but had a sharp point, however grotesque. "Where is the poor Negro?" queried Barnum, answering his own question: "he is free, but he cannot vote; ye have only made him white in spots, like my wonderful Leopard Boy from the wilds of Africa! Ye promised him universal suffrage, but ye have given him universal suffering instead!" Clemens parodied the inflated political language and its hyperbole that Barnum had used in his speech when asking, "Will they let a mulatto vote half the time, a quadroon three-fourths, and an octoroon seven-eighths of the time? If not, why not? Will they enslave seven-eighths of a white man because one-eighth is not Caucasian? Is this democratic?" Clemens referred to "my wonderful Leopard Boy from the wilds of Africa," a burlesque image that captured Barnum's political argument as well as his identity as a showman of freaks and oddities.[11]

The tone of Clemens's take on Barnum's speech was so comic that it threatened to overwhelm serious satire in a wash of humor. It came dangerously close to causing people to miss the satirical jab just as they had with "Petrified Man," "A Bloody Massacre Near Carson," and "How Is It?—How It Is." "By the close of the speech," scholar David Sloane has noted, "Twain has completely submerged Barnum's radical Republicanism in the museum curiosities dominating the burlesque rhetoric." While Clemens did broach the important issue of enfranchisement for former slaves, his use of the "Leopard Boy" analogy made Barnum's rhetoric even more ridiculous than it might have seemed on its own. Likewise, his Barnum hysterically cried, "the Happy Family of the Union is broken up!" The "Happy Family" referred to Barnum's vision of a peaceable kingdom where all animals lived together amicably. Clemens had lampooned this idea in a letter for the *Alta California* of March 2, 1867, three days before "Barnum's First Speech in Congress," saying that the "Happy Family remains, but robbed of its ancient glory." In the speech, he had jeered at the very idea of different animals living happily together as hopelessly idealistic, having Barnum invoke the "celebrated Happy Family, consisting of animals of the most diverse principles and dispositions, dwelling together in peace and unity." This burlesque expressed Clemens's cynicism, for his Barnum ended by crying, "O, snake the seditious miscreant out of the national feed-tub and reconstruct the Happy Family!" The "miscreant" was President Johnson, whose removal Barnum demanded: "Impeach! impeach! impeach!"[12]

Clemens's references to Johnson, which were not in Barnum's 1865 speech, derived generally from the president's hostility to the Reconstruction Acts and the first call by Congress to impeach him in January and February 1867. More specifically, Clemens responded to the president's veto of a bill "to provide for the more efficient government of the rebel States" on March 2, 1867, three days before "Barnum's First Speech in Congress" appeared on March 5. In his veto message, President Johnson's explanation involved his opposition to the enfranchisement of the liberated slaves:

> If in the exercise of the constitutional guaranty that Congress shall secure to every State a republican form of government universal suffrage for blacks as well as whites is a *sine qua non,* the work of reconstruction may as well begin in Ohio as in Virginia, in Pennsylvania as in North Carolina.
>
> When I contemplate the millions of our fellow-citizens of the South with no alternative left but to impose upon themselves this fearful and untried experiment of complete negro enfranchisement— and white disenfranchisement, it may be, almost as complete—or submit indefinitely to the rigor of martial law, without a single attribute of freemen, deprived of all the sacred guaranties of our Federal Constitution, and threatened with even worse wrongs, if any worse are possible, it seems to me their condition is the most deplorable to which any people can be reduced.

Thus, Clemens really responded to two disreputable figures, one the Republican huckster Barnum and the other the Democratic President Johnson, a "usurping tyrant," "seditious miscreant," and "dread boss monkey." Clemens's addition of Johnson to Barnum's speech was topical and had to do with the president's swipes at northern states, like Barnum's Connecticut, that would impose on the defeated South what they were unwilling to accept for themselves. Clemens showed no mercy to either side, viewing both national parties as unprincipled and hypocritical. Clemens had sparked the miscegenation controversy in Nevada for much the same reason; his attacks on Johnson paralleled his earlier attacks on Unionists who had failed to embrace equal rights for black citizens. Sam Clemens may have marveled at the rapidity of Reconstruction he witnessed in some parts of the country, but in "Barnum's First Speech in Congress" he expressed skepticism at the idea that the Republican Congress and the Democratic President Johnson could work together to "reconstruct the Happy Family."[13]

From June to November 1867, Clemens was out of the country, having shipped with the *Quaker City* on its trip to Europe and the Holy Land. Along the way, he wrote the letters for the *Alta California* that became the basis for his first full-length book, *The Innocents Abroad* (1869). Interestingly, the book contained little commentary on the recent war, and even less on politics. Clemens seemed to have endorsed the traditional American dictum, "Politics stops at the shore." Other than a few passing comments, mainly for a humorous rather than a satirical point, he eschewed critical comments about the government or the recent war. In fact, the overall point of Civil War material in *The Innocents Abroad* seemed to be how little the war mattered when one was abroad. Clemens became more emphatically American as he saluted the stars and stripes at sea or celebrated July 4th with the other passengers. Regional differences disappeared in the context of national ones. In *Mark Twain and the American West*, scholar Joseph Coulombe has stated that *The Innocents Abroad* "set him at odds with Europeans rather than defined him against other Americans (even while it accented his western origins)." This was certainly accurate, and Clemens patriotically saluted the American flag flying on the *Quaker City* as "my true passport."[14]

Equally as important, the war simply did not register as much with the people Clemens met in foreign lands, for whom the outcome was less momentous. "A Portuguese of average intelligence," Clemens noted, "inquired if our civil war was over." The writer's incredulity erupted in the passage, but against the panorama of ancient ruins and the vast sweep of history, the American Civil War faded, along with other historical events, into merely "the history of something or somebody." Clemens even poked fun at a painting of Jefferson Davis because the German artist transformed the Confederate leader's rather distinctive visage to make him appear German. Along the same lines, Clemens cast his mind forward four thousand years and imagined an encyclopedia entry in the year 5868: "URIAH S. (or Z.) GRAUNT—popular poet of ancient times in the Aztec provinces of the United States of British America. Some authors say flourished about A. D. 742; but the learned Ah-ah Foo-foo states that he was a cotemporary of Scharkspyre, the English poet, and flourished about A. D. 1328, some three centuries *after* the Trojan war instead of before it. He wrote 'Rock me to Sleep, Mother.'" Even the American Revolution and the great General Ulysses S. Grant disappeared into irrelevancy in this historical hodgepodge. Clemens's joke that "Graunt" had written "Rock Me to Sleep" (its actual title) was topical and significant. Elizabeth Akers Allen had written the poem in 1860, and it became immediately popular when set to music. The song swept the country, with its maudlin lyrics capturing the public imagination. It was precisely that rank sentimentality that captivated Clemens, too. In fact, he referred to the "operatic affectation" of amateur performances of the song in the very first work he had signed with the pen name "Mark Twain." In his burlesque encyclopedia of "Graunt," Clemens attributed the poem to the general because of the controversy surrounding the its authorship. The song was written by Elizabeth Akers Allen, but it was claimed by a Mr. Ball, among many others. The dispute over the authorship of the poem seems today insignificant, as Clemens recorded in "Is Shakespeare Dead?" (1909), but the "authorship was claimed by most of the grown-up people who were alive at the time." Clemens wrote of the controversy many times throughout his life, and even satirically claimed authorship for himself in "An Important Question Settled" (1868).[15]

If the reference to "Rock Me to Sleep" served to underscore great contests that, over time, evaporate into triviality, the poem also seems to have been powerfully evocative for Clemens.

> Backward, turn backward, O Time, in your flight,
> Make me a child again just for to-night!
> Mother, come back from the echoless shore,
> Take me again to your heart as of yore;
> Kiss from my forehead the furrows of care,
> Smooth the few silver threads out of my hair;
> Over my slumbers your loving watch keep;—
> Rock me to sleep, mother,—rock me to sleep!

Written on the threshold of the Civil War, "Rock Me to Sleep" evoked the pathos of a culture wishing to turn back the hands of time. For Clemens, as for many of those living through the Civil War, the idea of turning back the hands of time seemed a magical, wondrous balm that would have healed the physical and psychological wounds of war. While he often lampooned the poem as overly sentimental, Clemens was clearly taken with it and used it frequently as a symbol of the desire to escape history. In "No. 44, the Mysterious Stranger" (1905–1908), Clemens had the character No. 44 (a figure of Satan, Christ, or a prophet) quote the poem as a magical incantation to turn back the hands of time. No. 44 and the character August began speaking backward, and then history proceeded to reverse itself: "[W]here there was war, yesterday's battles were being refought, wrong-end first." However poor a literary production the work was, "Rock Me to Sleep" provided Clemens with a poignant metaphor of the pain of historical change. In his literature, at least, Clemens could imagine a time when the political divisions that had so vexed him would no longer matter.[16]

Upon his return to the United States, Clemens entered the Washington phase of his writing career, and it was a remarkable time for a writer to report from the nation's capital. "How the cauldron *does* boil," he exclaimed from his vantage point in Washington, D.C. After President Lincoln's assassination, Andrew Johnson, a Democrat from the border state of Tennessee, took the oath of office and became the country's seventeenth president. Johnson had opposed slavery and, though a Democrat, seemed of the president's party when it came to government policy toward the South. As President Grant wrote in his *Memoirs*, however, Johnson defected soon after Reconstruction commenced.

> I do not believe that the majority of the Northern people at that time were in favor of negro suffrage. They supposed that it would naturally follow the freedom of the negro, but that there would be a time of probation, in which the ex-slaves could prepare themselves for the privileges of citizenship before the full right would be conferred; but Mr. Johnson, after a compete revolution of sentiment, seemed to regard the South not only as an oppressed people, but as the people best entitled to consideration of any of our citizens. This was more than the people who had secured to us the perpetuation of the Union were prepared for, and they became more radical in their views.

With a "complete revolution of sentiment," Johnson vetoed one Reconstruction bill after another. In 1866, when Johnson vetoed the Freedman's Bureau Bill, a bill to fund the bureau that served as a buffer between the emancipated southern slaves and the frequently hostile southern officials, Republicans were stunned. To many, the action smacked of betrayal, and they compared Johnson to that arch-traitor Benedict Arnold. Johnson vetoed the bill because he feared the rise of federal power, but it was precisely federal power that the Radical Republicans required to codify in law and secure in actual practice the gains won by the Union war effort. Blacks were free, true, but guaranteeing those freedoms was proving to be more difficult than declaring them. The Civil Rights Bill sought to both define and protect those freedoms, but it, too, was vetoed by Johnson. The veto of the Civil Rights Bill marked the final break with the president. No further accommodation would be attempted, and Congress overrode the president's veto, "the first time in American history," as historian Eric Foner has asserted, that "Congress enacted a major piece of legislation over a President's veto." Similarly, Johnson irked former Republican allies by granting many pardons to former Confederates. Historian David Blight has noted Johnson's role in the hasty reunion of North and South after the war: "More than fifteen thousand Southerners submitted applications for individual pardons, with many applicants visiting the White House in person. By September 1865, pardons were being issued wholesale, occasionally hundreds in a single day. By 1866, seven thousand ex-Confederates excluded under the $20,000 provision had received pardons." Johnson's erratic and unstatesmanlike behavior provoked discord, too. During the "swing around the circle," a historic whistlestop tour through the country in which he tried to garner support for his own views of Reconstruction, he hectored, harangued, and incited. Historian W. E. B. Du Bois has recorded that in Cleveland, "his audience became a mob while the President himself increased the hubbub . . . Someone cried, 'Why not hang Thad Stevens and Wendell Phillips?' 'Yes,' yelled Johnson, 'why not hang them?'" The brawl between the increasingly radicalized Republican Congress and the increasingly reactionary executive branch of the government began tumbling toward the impeachment crisis.[17]

Clemens was in Washington for much of this time, working briefly in the office of Nevada Senator William Stewart, whom he had known from the days of the constitutional conventions in Carson City and while serving as "his Excellency Gov. Mark Twain, of the Third House." Clemens adored spoofing Stewart's florid political rhetoric, having depicted him as "Bullyragging Bill Stewart" in "The Great Prize Fight" (1863). Stewart, according to Albert Bigelow Paine, Clemens's biographer and literary executor, "thought it would be considerably to his advantage to have the brilliant writer and lecturer attached to his political establishment." Senator Stewart described their reunion in Washington this way:

I was seated at my window one morning when a very disreputable-looking person slouched into the room. He was arrayed in a seedy suit, which hung upon his lean frame in bunches with no style worth mentioning. A sheaf of scraggy black hair leaked out of a battered old slouch hat, like stuffing from an ancient Colonial sofa, and an evil-smelling cigar butt, very much frazzled, protruded from the corner of his mouth. He had a very sinister appearance. He was a man I had known around the Nevada mining camps several years before, and his name was Samuel L. Clemens . . . After that he drifted away, and I thought he had been hanged, or elected to Congress, or something like that, and I had forgotten him, until he slouched into my room, and then of course I remembered him.

The description was jeering enough to have come from Clemens's pen, and Stewart's record of their time together captured the humorous rivalry the two shared. By this point in his career, Senator Stewart was an important figure in the Senate and in the Republican Party. He was one of three people present at Andrew Johnson's emergency swearing-in after President Lincoln's assassination, and he was later one of the Radical Republicans who pushed for Johnson's impeachment. Senator Stewart sponsored the Fifteenth Amendment to the Constitution, which proclaimed universal male suffrage. As one contemporary described his position, Stewart "was one of the bulwarks of his party in the senate on all the questions that were sprung in reconstruction days. He was a stalwart of stalwarts. Grant leaned on him, so did Conkling, Chandler, Carpenter—all of them."[18]

Clemens showed little respect for Stewart's elevated position and turned the senator's rooms into a circus, driving his landlady to distraction by "lurch[ing] around the halls, pretending to be intoxicated." Stewart threatened physical violence, Clemens was affronted, and the two quarreled. Clemens's friend, William Gillis, reported that Stewart fired the writer, who retorted that while Stewart had been "a howling success as a lawyer" in Nevada, "you wasn't worth a damn as a United States Senator." Clemens later lampooned Stewart in Roughing It (1872) as bribing him with mining stock back in the Nevada Territory, only to renege when the value increased. Stewart "placed the guilty proceeds in his own pocket," complained the outraged Clemens, illustrating the story with a sketch of the senator sporting an eye patch to lend him the air of a gentleman desperado.

It is unclear whether Clemens's depiction of Stewart in *Roughing It* was a result of a quarrel or even how serious the rift was. Stewart, in his memoirs, seemed to find it all very amusing. As Vincent L. Eaton, chief editor of the Library of Congress, has suggested, the description "appears merely to be a bit of buffoonery done with Mark Twain's own way of telling a story." Clemens joked about his departure from Stewart's employ in "The Facts Concerning the Recent Resignation" (1867), where he claimed to have been appointed as "The HON. MARK TWAIN, Clerk of the Senate Committee on Conchology." Clemens also wrote a comedic treatment of his experiences in "My Late Senatorial Secretaryship" (1868), where he substituted his old nemesis James W. Nye, the former governor of the Nevada Territory who had called him "a damned Secessionist." Along with Stewart, Nye was a senator from the new state, in which capacity, he once chided a heckler who remonstrated, "senator, the war is over." The diehard Nye justified the Reconstruction Acts this way: "Yes, but for an original unrepentant rebel there is no cure save through death; no justification save through ages of hellfire." In Nye's employ, according to the sketch, Clemens completely muddled correspondence with constituents, insulting those who requested a post office at Baldwin's Ranch by telling them that it would be an "ornamental folly" because none of them could read. He suggested something more practical. "What you want is a nice jail, you know—a nice, substantial jail." After his fictional firing, Clemens vowed, "I never will be a private secretary to a senator again. You can't please that kind of people. They don't know anything."[19]

Clemens delighted in the satirical possibilities of Washington even while personally he found living there barely tolerable. In a letter to his family, November 25, 1867, he groused, "—I room with Bill Stewart & board at Willard's Hotel," but also, "Tired & Sleepy—been in Congress all day & making newspaper acquaintances . . . Am hob-nobbing with these old Generals & Senators & other humbugs for no good purpose." Humbugs they may have been, but that was all the more reason to have a Mark Twain, a Will Rogers, or an Art Buchwald on hand. From late 1867 through early 1868, Clemens served as the Washington correspondent for such newspapers as the Virginia City *Territorial Enterprise* and the New York *Herald* and as a special correspondent who often reported from Washington for the Chicago *Republican* and the *Alta California*. In his Washington correspondence, Clemens commented on the political situation in the capital, the progress of Reconstruction, and the impeachment crisis. The political environment suited him, for, as he wrote on January 24, 1868, "There are lots of folks in Washington who need vilifying."[20]

Even as Clemens reported on the fluid political situation in Washington, his public persona of a reconstructed Mark Twain took shape. In his letter to the *Enterprise* of December 4, 1867, he connected the weather in Washington with its politics. "As politics go, so goes the weather," he wrote. "It trims to suit every phase of sentiment, and is always ready. To-day it is a Democrat, to-morrow a Radical, the nest day neither one thing nor the other. If a Johnson man goes over to the other side, it rains; if a Radical deserts to the Administration, it snows." Clemens himself experienced some such political weather during his months in Washington, and he, too, walked a fine line between the two political parties, often reserving judgment, but just as frequently criticizing both as he had done in his burlesque of P. T. Barnum. Likewise, Clemens included in the letter the same kind of burlesque he had practiced in Nevada during his reporting on the Constitutional Convention. In fact, he cracked some of the same jokes, as when claiming that the House of Representatives was comprised of men who "pay only questionable attention while the Chaplain is on duty, but they never catch flies while he is praying." Clemens's humor was especially biting when he brought up one of President Johnson's most controversial speeches, his Third Annual Message to Congress, delivered on December 3, 1867. Clemens reported to the people back in Nevada that the message "is making a howl among the Republicans" and that while "[i]mpeachment was dead, day before yesterday," the speech may have awakened the corpse. Attacking the Reconstruction laws, Johnson appealed to the Constitution, as when he opposed continued military rule in parts of the South. In one of his more impassioned moments, Johnson fulminated that such occupation "binds them hand and foot in absolute slavery, and subjects them to a strange and hostile power, more unlimited and more likely to be abused than any other now known among civilized men." Calling the Federal Army "a strange and hostile power" was bad enough, but using the figural image of "absolute slavery" to characterize the plight of white southerners ignored the actual fact of slavery as it had existed in the South. Nor was this all. Johnson decried the enfranchisement of African Americans, saying that "Negro suffrage was established by act of Congress, and the military officers were commanded to superintend the process of clothing the negro race with the political privileges torn from white men." This line led to one of Clemens's choice bits of political humor, when he reported to the *Enterprise* readers that he had crossed paths with Harry Worthington, a former Nevada congressman, who "dresses mighty well for a white man in these universal suffrage times." That is, even though white men have had their privileges "torn" from them for the purpose of "clothing the negro race," Worthington seemed properly attired. The joke was likely funnier for contemporary readers who were attuned to the fact that President Johnson had been a tailor before entering politics. Clemens just shook his head, wondering what the weather would be like the next day, vowing to "stand by with parasols, umbrellas and overcoats until the weather is reconstructed."[21]

Against the backdrop of the first impeachment crisis, a historical moment when many were calling for the president to be tried for "high crimes and misdemeanors," Clemens wrote yet another "resignation burlesque." Published in the New York *Citizen* on December 15, 1867, "The Facts in the Case of the Senate Doorkeeper" was a clear dig at the Senate's sniping at the president. After much thought, Clemens "rejoined Mr. Johnson's Administration as Doorkeeper of the Senate." Clemens adopted the persona of a slightly dimwitted figure who mistakenly viewed the role of the doorkeeper as a "ticket taker," charging senators fifty cents admission apiece. The only one who gained entrance without charge was "the ringmaster of the circus," Senator Benjamin Wade, a Radical Republican from Ohio. During the Reconstruction era, as historian Eric Foner has noted, Democrats commonly "described constitutional conventions and legislatures with black members as 'menageries' and 'monkey houses.'" Clemens used related terms, but not to serve such racist ends. He employed words like "menagerie" and "circus" frequently when discussing Congress to suggest a conglomeration of wild legislators, uncontrolled and uncontrollable. One has to laugh at the figure of the Radical Republican Benjamin Wade, the man next in line for the presidency if Johnson were impeached, as a ringmaster of the circus. Clemens's burlesque rollicked wildly, with the doorkeeper constantly interrupting the proceedings with all manner of insignificance. This laid the groundwork for his impeachment, and the Senate prepared a document fraught with the ponderous title, "Articles of Impeachment against the Doorkeeper of the United States Senate." Among other crimes, Clemens is tried for continually reciting lines from canto 6 of Sir Walter Scott's *Marmion:*

Oh, woman! In our hours
Of ease, uncertain, coy,
And hard to please—

The charges read that "In that, after disrupting and disorganizing the Senate time and again by repetitions of the aforementioned speech, commencing 'Woman! Oh, woman!' I incited the said Senate to rebellion and insurrection by still another attempt to inflict that speech upon them, and thus materially retarded the reconstruction of the aforesaid Senate at the period of its most promising progress." Clemens found the spectacle tremendously amusing, but implicit here were the minute details of the complaint, the jockeying for power, and the use of seemingly minor figures (elsewhere the secretary, here the doorkeeper) to target the chief executive. This impertinent sketch appeared as the Republicans in Washington deliberated, considering whether the president ought to be impeached. The debates, while occasionally high-minded, involved a good deal of pious posturing of the sort Clemens had come to distrust. For good reason had Clemens named Senator Benjamin Wade the "ringmaster of the circus."[22]

Through late 1867 and early 1868, Clemens tended to render judgment in a largely even-handed way. "This is the place to get a poor opinion of everybody in," Sam wrote his brother, Orion, in February 1868. Clemens referred to the legislators collectively and ironically as "the national wisdom" and "these Solons," after the wise Athenian lawgiver. In contrast, the lawmakers in Washington simply ignored most of the difficult issues. As the presidential race heated up and the impeachment proceedings stalled, he joked that at least Congress managed to pass legislation about the use of stationery. Clemens had great fun punning on the meaning of "stationary" versus "stationery" legislation before concluding that with their economies on government letterhead, "they have saved the country. God will bless them." Clemens's attitude toward Washington politics became increasingly cynical as Congress struck him, as later Congresses have struck many, as a "do-nothing Congress." In December 1867, he wrote, "Congress adjourned yesterday. I don't know whether they have done anything or not. I don't think they have." In another article, he avoided actual political matter to illustrate just how niggling many political debates in the capital were. In "Congressional Poetry," he analyzed a portion of a sentimental poem, before offering his judgment of the work in the form of a congressional resolution beginning, "*Be it resolved*, That all after the third stanza," the poem be revised to include this material:

> This is the house that Jack built,
> Congress adjourns the fourth of March;
> Then never more shall we parties part,
> Pop goes the weasel.

As Clemens admitted, this "is not poetical, but it has at least the merit of being instructive," and with his doggerel, he captured the absurdity of politics where the "house divided" still tottered and Congress, "the House," wasted time.[23]

Frustration at congressional inaction has spanned the history of that institution, but Clemens's vexation did not arise from the typical inactivity of legislators. Even in "Barnum's First Speech in Congress," his burlesque was pointed, over the top, and overwhelmingly comic; in his Washington letters, the tone grew outraged and hectoring as the Reconstruction crisis worsened with riots, lynchings, and Ku Klux Klan activity in many southern states. Against this backdrop, Clemens employed the comic-prophetic persona he had used in "Barnum's First Speech in Congress" with ever greater urgency. In April 1867, he published "Female Suffrage," which discussed the attempt by women in Missouri to gain the vote. The sketch featured a legislator who berated suffragettes as "a pack of padded, scraggy, dried-up, snuff-dipping, toothless, old maids" and was attacked and left with "hardly hair enough left on his head to make a toothbrush." This, Clemens suggested, caused him to "shudder," for it may be "that this revelation of the spirits is a prophecy." Attempts by women to gain the vote "along with us and the nigs, you know" contributed to the feeling of living in revolutionary times. He constructed many of his newspaper sketches with such elements, as burlesque of bombastic political rhetoric but also because the turmoil of secession, the Civil War, the assassination of the president, disputes over Reconstruction, and initiatives for black and female suffrage during the Johnson administration all contributed to a rush of change and a cumulative sense of crisis. In the *Chicago Republican*, Clemens described meeting a congressman who sounded like a cheap imitation of Elijah or Jeremiah: "Treason! Ha-ha! Treason is feeding at the very vitals of the land! . . . Sir, prophetic voices sound in my ears, and lo, they chant the requiem of the great Republic!"[24]

For much of 1867 into early 1868, Clemens reserved his greatest ire for "the government—which is another word for Congress in these days." Congress, dominated by Republicans, had overridden presidential vetoes, quelled President Johnson by the first threat of impeachment in 1867, and passed laws limiting presidential power. One of these, the Tenure of Office Act, was intended to limit the president's power to remove officials from their government positions. Johnson had been subverting the Reconstruction Acts by replacing officials he deemed too harsh with the South, officials such as Secretary of State Edwin Stanton and General Philip Sheridan, the military commander in charge of Reconstruction in Louisiana and Texas. Both the attempted removal of Stanton and the removal of Sheridan provoked disputes with Ulysses S. Grant, whom Clemens first met during this time. It is important to point out that, in his criticisms of Congress, Clemens was not endorsing Johnson. One might suspect that, as a fellow border-stater with similarly divided loyalties, he might have sympathized with Johnson. Only at one point did Clemens betray any sympathy for the president, when meeting him at a White House reception after the articles of impeachment had passed. On that occasion, the president "looked so like a plain, simple, goodnatured old farmer, that it was hard to conceive that this was the imperious 'tyrant.'" Clemens responded to the president in this instance on a human level, not on a political one. "I never saw a man who seemed as friendless and forsaken," he wrote, "and I never felt for any man so much." More striking was Clemens's sympathy with Johnson's skepticism about the constitutionality of the Reconstruction Acts. Clemens often expressed disquiet that "government" had simply become "another word for Congress in these days," a worry he shared with the president. Due to Johnson's hostility to the Reconstruction Acts, the Republican Congress labored to limit presidential, and even judicial, power. Clemens criticized the Republicans more than he did President Johnson in many of his sketches during this time precisely because they wielded power.[25]

"The truth is, that the more Congress reconstructs, the more the South goes to pieces," Clemens wrote in his aptly titled byline, "The Political Stink-Pots Opened." In many respects, the South was going to pieces, certainly for the emancipated slaves who found themselves targeted by a resurgent rebel nationalism. In his article, written on January 11, 1868, Clemens referenced the Sermon on the Mount and the parable of the foolish man who built his house on the sand: "And every one that heareth these sayings of mine, and doeth them not, shall be likened unto a foolish man, which built his house upon the sand: And the rain descended, and the floods came, and the winds blew, and beat upon that house; and it fell: and great was the fall of it" (Matthew 7:26–27). In Clemens's retelling of the story, he adopted a folksy tone, blending political argot with the biblical language and cadences of the backwoods preacher.

> You see, they started in to build a good, substantial reconstruction house, but there were some sandy places under it which did not look well. They thought maybe they might not be as risky as they looked, however, and concluded to chance them. But it was not a good idea. The house was hardly built, before one corner began to sink a little, and they had to jackscrew it up and put in an amendment prop. Then another corner began to sink, and they had to put in a similar prop there. Next the chimney began to lean, and they had to prop that mighty quick with a powerful brace; right away the kitchen began to cave in and the gable end to bulge out, and immediately some more jackscrews and braces had to be called into use . . . Such is the new house, and such the efforts made to save it. And of course it never rains but it pours—in the midst of all this vexation, along comes the Grand Jury, otherwise the Supreme Court, to examine it, and the owners and builders in fancy already hear the disastrous fiat: "Gentlemen, she won't do; she will have to come down; there is too much sand and not enough Constitution under her!"

With great trepidation, Republican papers waited in fear of the Supreme Court rulings on Reconstruction cases, dreading that the entire "reconstruction house" might prove to have been built on sand after all. If the very principle of reconstructing the South was rejected by the Supreme Court as unconstitutional, efforts by Republicans to fix the problems that had dogged American politics for so long were doomed to failure. Surely, it could not have been possible that the Civil War had been fought and hundreds of thousands killed, only to restore to the South its former prerogatives? Democrats dreamed of such an outcome. Republicans feared that if the Supreme Court ruled against the Reconstruction Acts and "obstructs the regeneration of rebeldom," as Clemens phrased it, southerners would hang "Union men upon any and every pretext, or upon none at all."

Moreover, "to admit them to power, unreconstructed and unrestrained, would be to acknowledge that the war for the Union was an iniquity, a crime." Consequently, both sides counted votes, trying to anticipate which justices would vote in favor of the Reconstruction Acts. Clemens, after detailing the differing opinions, cited the Radical Republican congressman from Pennsylvania, Thaddeus Stevens who had always maintained that "the Reconstruction Acts were 'outside the Constitution.'"[26]

Clemens, border-stater that he was, saw both sides to the issue and wrote his article explicitly to offer "a fair and honest exhibit of the Democratic side," even while increasingly aligning himself with the Republicans. Clemens, like the Democrats, sensed danger in the Reconstruction Acts, citing the case of William McCardle, whom he described as "a ferocious Vicksburg editor." Having disparaged the Reconstruction Acts in print, McCardle was arrested, jailed, and held under the very acts he had opposed, in particular the right of the army to rule in the South. While McCardle's case was on its way to the Supreme Court, Congress repealed the act in March 1868, out of fear that the case would provoke the entire collapse of the "reconstruction house." Before they repealed the portion of the law under which McCardle was imprisoned, however, the Supreme Court was very much a wild card. Had they ruled that the military had no jurisdiction in the southern states, the Reconstruction Acts would have tumbled, one after the other. Clemens probably identified with McCardle to some degree; after all, Sam himself had suffered a few scrapes as a journalist, some of them for espousing seemingly disloyal sentiments. In a practical sense, at least, he appreciated McCardle, for the case was "a splendid sensation, and is most palatable food for newspaper correspondents." After joking about the case as a good way to fill out newspaper columns, Clemens discussed the Supreme Court in a more serious vein. "If the Reconstruction Acts are Constitutional, we ought to believe they will sustain them; if they are not, we ought to hope they will annul them." This was sound reasoning. Throughout Reconstruction, Clemens stood for the separation of powers, a recognition of the integrity of each branch of government under the Constitution. From the perspective of decades, Clemens's views are sound, but at the time his view was unpopular. It was the argument of the Democratic minority and of that bugaboo of the Republicans, Andrew Johnson himself. It was Johnson who continually insisted on the application of the constitutional test to the Reconstruction Acts. "To me the process of restoration seems perfectly plain and simple," Johnson declared in his Third Annual Message to Congress. "It consists merely in a faithful application of the Constitution and laws." Sam Clemens was in rather dubious company.[27]

All of this is to say that Clemens held "nuanced views" on the subject of the Reconstruction Acts and on the related subject of impeachment. His skepticism of both parties had deep roots in the soul of the border state of Missouri. His attitudes during the impeachment crisis foreshadowed his later emergence as a Mugwump, an Independent Republican. He was clearly uncomfortable with the imbalance of power in Washington, where the legislative branch dominated the executive branch, and he just as clearly supported the authority of the judicial branch to set things right. At the same time, Clemens was no fan of Johnson's, disparaging him as "the obnoxious President." Clemens chided Congress for not using its power to remove the president and enact sound legislation. Instead, as he noted, "Whisky [is] taken into Committee rooms in demijohns & carried out in demagogues." In his private notes, he depicted the leading politicians of the day satirically and showed no favorites. Senator Eldridge of Wisconsin was the "leading & malignant copperhead," while Mr. Bingham of Ohio was a "nervous, severe & ready debater" who had a "sharp beak of a nose" and combed his hair, "apparently with a harrow." Clemens found General John A. Logan of Illinois especially disturbing. Logan responded to President Johnson's threat that the country was approaching a constitutional conflict between the legislative and executive branches of government by suggesting that the Senate should dismantle the "corps of pages that now constitute the 'military force' of this house." "Better suited to war than making jokes," Logan was "undignified," Clemens asserted. Clemens discerned, too, that even Logan's japes had "tiger's play" in them. Clemens tweaked Logan mercilessly in "The Facts Concerning the Recent Important Resignation," which appeared in the February 13, 1868 issue of the New York *Tribune.* Clemens wrote a burlesque that drew on his experiences at the Nevada Territorial constitutional conventions and the meetings of the Third House, depicting sessions of the House of Representatives as if he belonged to the "Pacific Delegation" from California. Immediately, he vowed to "settle this Reconstruction business." With his maiden speech, however, trouble erupted when Senator Logan farted in the House Chambers. Clemens failed to get past "Mr. Speaker—When the proud bird of freedom spreads his broad pinions—" before the untoward interruption. The character Mark

Twain went on the offensive, directly addressing Senator Logan: "I scorn also the feeble wit of savages from the wilds of Illinois." Ultimately, the character Twain was forced to resign from Congress by the Newspaper Correspondents Club, which was concerned that hobnobbing with gassy senators who have "feeble wit" demeaned the more august profession of the reporter.[28]

Clemens forever altered the popular image of Senator Logan, but his depiction of General Benjamin F. Butler seemed to fit with the existing impression. General Benjamin "The Beast" Butler was infamous for hanging a Confederate who insulted the American flag and for his "General Order No. 28" while military governor of New Orleans. He was also bald, and Clemens likened his head to "a water blister." Butler, Clemens continued, was "dismally & drearily homely, & when he smiles it is like the breaking up of a hard winter." Of them all, Clemens found the leader of the Radical Republicans, Congressman Thad Stevens of Pennsylvania, the "ablest man." The reporter had a cynic's disrespect for the leaders on all sides, and he may have felt the imbalance of power was unconstitutional. Given such an imbalance in favor of the legislative branch, its vacillation struck Clemens as cowardly: "Andrew can scare it with a growl."[29]

That Clemens favored impeachment by mid-February was made plain by his letter to the Chicago *Republican* of February 19, 1868. Clemens wrote a mock obituary for "our beloved brother, IMPEACHMENT" who passed away from "general debility." He blamed the nurses who "fell asleep and neglected him." He gave the nurses' names as "Mrs. Farnsworth, and also Mrs. Boutwell, and also Mrs. Stevens, the same that is called Thad." Throughout the piece, Clemens adopted the biblical cadences he affected in much of his writing during Reconstruction, but more significantly, he cast the central figures in the impeachment effort as women. He expected a manlier effort, it seemed, from Thaddeus Stevens, the Republican congressman from Gettysburg, Pennsylvania, who was chairman of the House Reconstruction Committee and spearheaded the impeachment effort. Later in the same article, he again attacked Stevens, who "could not impeach the President—because, as Mr. Stevens says—they were afraid." In an article for the *Territorial Enterprise*, Clemens expressed greater admiration for Stevens, calling him "the bravest old ironclad in the Capitol" who, against a wavering Congress, "fought hard for impeachment, even when he saw that it could not succeed." When Stevens called congressional Republicans

"Damned Cowards," Clemens identified it as "the finest word painting any Congressional topic has produced this season." With impeachment dead, Congress voted to remove the president's secretarial staff, an action Clemens derided as "simply boys' play." Instead of impeachment, they have embraced "retrenchment," he wrote. "Everybody is willing to see a fair fight between the President and his Congressional master," he editorialized, "but nobody is willing to see either of them descend to scratching and hair-pulling." More clearly than before, Clemens mocked Congress not just for doing nothing, and not just for botching Reconstruction, but for failing to impeach the president. "So endeth the second farce," wrote Clemens, disgusted at the failure of the second impeachment effort.[30]

As it turned out, the "beloved brother, IMPEACHMENT" was not quite dead. Clemens's February 21, 1868 "Letter from Washington" for the *Chicago Republican* fairly crowed: "LAZARUS IMPEACHMENT, COME FORTH!" Drawing on Christ's command to his dead friend in the tomb, "Lazarus, come forth" (John 11:43), and employing biblical cadences, Clemens's prose crackled: "The wild excitement that pervaded the capital that night, has not had its parallel here since the murder of Mr. Lincoln . . . And out of the midst of the political gloom, IMPEACHMENT, that dead corpse, rose up and walked forth again!" The immediate cause of this renewed impeachment attempt was Johnson's violation of the Tenure of Office Act, which had been passed, according to historian Samuel Eliot Morison, in order to severely restrict presidential power "by denying the President the right to remove civil officials, including members of his cabinet, without the consent of the Senate." In defiance of the act, Johnson tried to remove the lone staunch Republican left in his cabinet, Edwin M. Stanton. A holdover from the Lincoln administration, Stanton was crucial for the successful implementation of the Reconstruction Acts because, as secretary of war, he oversaw the Union generals who wielded military rule in the South. Continuing the farce, Stanton barricaded himself in his office and was "lauded by Republicans for sleeping in the War Office and holding the political fortress," as Clemens wrote in his article "The Grand Coup d'Etat" for the *Enterprise.* Calling Johnson's act "an open defiance of Congress—a kingly contempt for long settled forms and customs—a reckless disregard of law itself!" Clemens characterized the atmosphere in the capital as "intense," the thoroughfares thronged with people. "Old citizens remembered no night like this in Washington since Lincoln was assassinated," he wrote.[31]

Clemens captured the drama of the scene by writing a parody of Othello's speech from Act V, Scene ii. "When it was moved to-day, to read Washington's Farewell Address," he reported, "Mr. Ingersoll inquired of a neighbor if it would not be more appropriate to read Andrew Johnson's Farewell Address!" The next day was George Washington's birthday, providing the context for reading the "Farewell Address." Clemens claimed to have found the parody "in one of the lobbies." Here is the original with Clemens's burlesque below it.

Shakespeare's version of Othello's speech:

> Soft you; a word or two before you go.
> I have done the state some service, and they know't.
> No more of that. I pray you, in your letters,
> When you shall these unlucky deeds relate,
> Speak of me as I am; nothing extenuate,
> Nor set down aught in malice: then must you speak
> Of one that loved not wisely but too well:
> Of one not easily jealous, but being wrought
> Perplex'd in the extreme; of one whose hand,
> Like the base Indian, threw a pearl away
> Richer than all his tribe.

Clemens's burlesque of Othello's speech:

ANDREW JOHNSON'S FAREWELL ADDRESS.

> Soft you; a word or two before you go.
> I have done the State some damage, and they know it;
> No more of that:—I pray you, in your letters,
> When you shall these unlucky deeds relate,
> Speak of me as I am; some things extenuate,
> But set down naught in malice; then must you speak
> Of one that ruled not wisely nor too well;
> Of one, easily jealous, and, being wrought,
> Perplexed in the extreme, did,
> Like the base Judean, throw a pearl away,
> Richer than all his tribe!

In Clemens's version, Othello's "I have done the state some service" became "I have done the State some damage." Rather than being one who "loved not wisely but too well" like Othello, Johnson "ruled not wisely nor too well." Clemens's use of *Othello* was particularly interesting given the play's racial situation, for the title character was the "Moor of Venice." This foregrounded many of the issues at work in the impeachment crisis: miscegenation, racial equality, and political equality. Moreover, at this point in the play, Othello has just killed Desdemona and is preparing to kill himself. To put Othello's words in Johnson's mouth was a bit of a joke at the expense of the politician who had vetoed Republican legislation that would have recognized the political equality of blacks. In so doing, Clemens intimated, Johnson had committed political suicide. The conflict between Stanton and the president reanimated the Radical Republicans, and the next day, February 22, 1868, Congress heard a resolution from Representative Thaddeus Stevens calling for the impeachment of the president of the United States.[32]

Throughout his time in Washington, Clemens understood that in 1867–1868 the great political confrontation between the executive and legislative branches of government was an extension of the Civil War. He used military metaphors to describe the conflict between the branches of government, often invoking specific battles. Still, as the impeachment debacle approached crisis level on February 22, Clemens deemed the day one of tremendous import for the country. It was Washington's birthday, a day when legislative work usually involved the reading of Washington's "Farewell Address" and other suitably patriotic activities. "This birthday of Washington was historical before," he declared, "it is doubly so now." Clemens vividly described how during the morning, hours before Congress was scheduled to meet, "long processions of men and women were wending their way toward the Capitol in the nipping winter air." When Clemens arrived at the "reporters' gallery," there was hardly room for him to squeeze through the packed Capitol building. After several failed attempts by Democrats to adjourn due to the holiday, Thaddeus Stevens entered the room, and the "buzzing and whispering died out, and an impressive silence reigned in its stead." Clemens demonstrated both his understanding of the drama inherent to the scene and his ability to effectively convey it.

> Then the one man upon whom all interest centered, read the resolutions the multitude so longed to hear: and when he came to

where it was resolved that "THE PRESIDENT OF THE UNITED STATES BE IMPEACHED FOR HIGH CRIMES AND MISDEMEANORS," the prodigious words had something so solemn and so awe-inspiring about them that the people seemed inclined to think that the expected thunder-clap *was* about to crash above the pictured ceiling! The strong lights and shadows, augmenting distances and creating deceitful prospectives, the ghostly figure of the reader, the eager interest that marked the sea of faces, the impressive silence that pervaded the place, and the historic grandeur of the occasion, conspired to render the scene one of the most striking and dramatic that has ever been witnessed in the Capitol.

Over the days to come, Clemens reported on the speeches delivered by Democrats opposing impeachment and speeches by Republicans favoring it. As he reported on the closing debate before the vote on Tuesday, February 25, 1868, he noted that even Democrats dismissed Johnson as "a lost cause." The expression linked the president with the Lost Cause of the Confederacy, implying that his political defeat was an extension of the North's conquest of the South. The resolution to impeach the president, that is, to conduct an impeachment trial before the Senate for "high crimes and misdemeanors," passed. Even then, however, with President Johnson now facing trial and possible removal, largely for opposing the Reconstruction Acts, Clemens recalled Saturday, February 22, Washington's birthday, as more evocative, if not more significant, for that was the day Stevens read the Articles of Impeachment. "The resolution passed," Clemens mused, "and that was a momentous event; but Saturday was still the great day, after all. It was the day most to be remembered; its pictures were the most striking to the eye, and its events the most sensational, because of their novelty."[33]

Throughout the impeachment crisis of 1867–1868, Clemens increasingly sided with the Republicans against Johnson and the Democrats. Even in his moments of more straight reportage, he rather enjoyed the "striking" spectacle of the president's impeachment. In the *Chicago Republican*, Clemens expressed his opinion freely, joking about the type of support the president was receiving during his trial. In a section of a Washington letter titled "TELEGRAPHIC THUNDER AND LIGHTNING," the reporter claimed that "[t]elegrams offering support and encouragement to the President are still arriving constantly." He claimed to know this because he served as "Private Secretary *ad interim* to the Chief Magistrate." Congress, it will be remembered, had stripped Johnson of his private secretaries, so Clemens would necessarily be *ad interim*. This was yet another instance where Clemens identified with Johnson for satirical purposes. That identification made sense because of their shared backgrounds as border-staters, but it was also part of Mark Twain's reconstruction. In identifying with Johnson for the purpose of jest, Clemens differentiated himself from him as a "reconstructed southerner." The telegrams supporting Johnson were all humorous, some poking fun at Johnson's administration generally, such as the telegram from Alaska, the purchase of which had been arranged by William H. Seward, Lincoln's secretary of state who remained on under Johnson. He was considered a traitor by Radical Republicans. "Thermometer at 78 deg. below zero, but Democratic patriotism at a hundred and sixty above." The telegram was signed by one "C. Green Iceberg." Most of the telegrams were more pointed, for they came from parts of the country that had been either part of the Confederacy or that were notorious pockets of Copperheadism in the North. The Irish and New York City sent their support, and even General P. G. T. Beauregard wrote Johnson from Richmond, "We are with you, heart and soul!"[34]

Sam Clemens left Washington in March 1868, returning to San Francisco to untangle copyright issues with the *Alta California*, the original publisher of the letters that he hoped to revise for his first full-length book, *The Innocents Abroad*. He eventually extracted from them a promise not to republish them in book form and received permission from them to use the letters in his own book. That departure meant that he missed the heart of the second impeachment attempt, the one that actually summoned the president before the Senate, charged with "high crimes and misdemeanors." Votes held on May 16 and 26, 1868, fell one vote short of removing President Johnson from office. The acquittal resulted from the defection of seven Republican senators, one of whom died the next year, while the remaining six suffered political deaths and were not returned to the Senate by their constituents. Interestingly, the decisive vote against impeachment was cast by a fellow Missourian, General John Henderson, a Republican.[35]

Clemens welcomed his premature departure from Washington, for after his eviction from Senator Stewart's lodgings, he had changed lodgings at least five more times. Sam found the company of his old friend from San

Francisco, John Henry Riley, more to his liking. "We lodged together in many places in Washington during the winter of '67–'8, moving comfortably from place to place, and attracting attention by paying our board—a course which cannot fail to make a person conspicuous in Washington." None of his lodgings could compare with either a convivial miner's cabin at Angel's Camp or with San Francisco's Occidental Hotel, which he had once described not as just "Heaven on the half shell" but "Heaven on the entire shell." In a February 21, 1868 letter to his mother, Sam summed up the Capitol tersely: "Shabby furniture & shabby food—*that* is Washington—I mean to keep moving." Move he did, but his sudden departure did not prevent him from taking occasional political potshots. Some were the merest drive-by comments, such as the newspaperman's objection in "The Story of Mamie Grant, the Child-Missionary" (July 1868), when the title character suggested that the *Morning Gazette,* "a Democrat" paper, ought to "drop the follies of this world and make the Gazette a messenger of light and hope, a Baptist benediction at every fireside." The newspaperman remonstrated, "Saving your presence, Miss, Democrats don't care a damn about light and hope." In November 1868, Clemens published "Cannibalism in the Cars," a darkly humorous yarn featuring passengers on a snowbound train who resort to cannibalism. Clemens saved the joke from irrelevancy by infusing it with topical political content. Twain, as a character, traveled on the train, chatting with several passengers, who were intrigued when they discovered he hailed from Washington, D.C. One of them proceeded to tell the story of how he had once been snowbound on a train with congressmen. Ever adhering to House rules, they debated in a most civilized way the question of whom they should eat. This joke over whom to cannibalize owed much to the almost constant impeachment debates and the vigorous presidential campaign of 1868 that landed Ulysses S. Grant in the White House. "On the first ballot there was a tie," the narrator reported, and "there was some talk of demanding a new ballot." As the congressmen debated which of their number to eat, commenting on the size or stringiness of each individual, they adhered to congressional protocol: "Mr. A. L. Bascom, of Ohio: 'I move that the nominations now close, and that the House proceed to an election by ballot.'" Clemens discovered that the passenger who related the story had been "a member of Congress once, and a good one. But he got caught in a snowdrift in the cars" and was forever marred by the experience. "I had only been listening to the harmless vagaries of a madman," sighed the relieved narrator, "instead of the genuine experiences of a bloodthirsty cannibal." Clemens crafted his humor here with a surprisingly light touch, given the cannibal content, ending with the unspoken irony that the entire story was cast as a House debate but that the narrator was *only* an insane congressman and not an authentic cannibal. Clemens published the piece in the November 1868 edition of *The Broadway* in what one might call "The Election Issue." He sharpened his knives to comment on the cannibalistic nature of the American political process.[36]

After a bitter election that justified Clemens's cannibalistic satire, Ulysses S. Grant defeated his Democratic opponent, Horatio Seymour, a man accused of being a Copperhead during the war. Although Grant won by an impressive electoral margin, a slim three hundred thousand vote margin separated him from defeat. This was no mandate. Indeed, Grant's campaign slogan had been "Let us have peace," but there was little peace in either the election or in what followed. Clemens turned the collective discomfort of the country into humor in his New York *Tribune* sketch, "Concerning Gen. Grant's Intentions," which was published in December 1868 during the interregnum between Grant's election and inauguration. In an imagined interview, he adopted the pose of a journalist peppering the president-elect with one loaded question after another. Part of the humor arose from the burlesque of the interview form itself, with Clemens reporting that General Grant was "speechless" because he insistently answered each question with either silence or with some variant of his campaign slogan, "Let us have peace." Clemens captured something of Grant's personality. He first met Grant at a Washington reception in 1866, but "had no conversation," as he wrote later. During Grant's first term in office, Senator Stewart introduced the two, a meeting during which the president was again "speechless." "I shook hands and then there was a pause and silence. I couldn't think of anything to say. So I merely looked into the General's grim, immovable countenance a moment or two in silence and then I said: 'Mr. President, I am embarrassed. Are you?' He smiled a smile which would have done no discredit to a cast-iron image and I got away under the smoke of my volley." In all fairness, Clemens was only slightly less "speechless" than the president, but he was again struck by the man's implacable quiescence. In "Concerning General Grant's Intentions," he depicted the soldier-turned-politician as resembling a "cast-iron image" and as perhaps less embarrassed than angered by the string of questions that disrupted his quest for peace.

Peace, of course, was the last thing the president-elect had when beset by reporters. "Go to the—mischief! I have a thousand of your kind around me every day. Questions, questions, questions!" Clemens poked some good-natured fun at the exasperated general, contending that "If a man isn't about speechless who never says anything but Let us have peace, pray what is he."[37]

Clemens created far more than a simple burlesque, and his humor was the same type of "tiger's play" he had imputed to General John A. Logan. Clemens seemed out of patience with the president-elect for not sharing more of his plans for governance, other than to bring a nebulous peace to the country in general and Washington, D.C., in particular. It is well to remember that throughout the 1870s, Clemens leaned toward the reformist wing of the Republican Party, the "liberal Republicans." By the 1880s, this tendency developed into Clemens embracing the title "Mugwump," becoming a Republican who supported the Democratic ticket at the presidential level. The criticism of Grant revealed Sam's border state mentality. Historian Walter A. McDougall has noted that the party division that would cost the Republican Party the 1884 presidential election "began, significantly, in Missouri, Tennessee, and West Virginia."[38]

Clemens's primary targets in "Concerning General Grant's Intentions," however, were Democrats, northern and southern, who failed to support the Republican Party's plans for Reconstruction. Even if a bit suspicious of Grant, Clemens clearly took sides in this piece. He adopted the persona of a Copperhead reporter asking questions that left no doubt where that fictional reporter's sympathies resided. He directed a barrage of questions, such as "Sir, what do you propose to do about returning to a specie basis?" and "Sir, do you mean to stop the whisky frauds, or do you mean to connive at them?" He followed these with even more pointedly partisan questions.

> Do you intend to do straightforwardly and unostentatiously what every true, high-minded Democrat has a right to expect you to do, or will you, with accustomed obstinacy, do otherwise, and thus, by your own act, compel them to resort to assassination? . . . Sir, shall you insist upon stopping bloodshed at the South, in plain opposition to the Southern will, or shall you generously permit a brave but unfortunate people to worship God according to the dictates of their own consciences? . . . Sir, do you comprehend that you are not the President of a party?—that you were not elected by your own

strength, but by the weakness of the opposition? That, consequently, the Democrats claim you, and justly and righteously expect you to administer the Government from a Democratic point of view?

These were not Clemens's ideas, but ideas that he adopted for the purpose of a satiric persona. Why would Grant, a Republican, act in ways to please "every true, high-minded Democrat"? When Clemens suggested that if Grant neglected to kowtow to the Democrats and the southerners more generally, he would "compel them to resort to assassination," he did something Grant's campaign had done in winning the election: wave the slain president's bloody shirt. Clemens's reference to assassination was a comedic version of "waving the bloody shirt," a tactic that blamed southerners and Democrats for President Lincoln's assassination in particular and the Union dead more generally in order to increase support for the Republican Party. In Clemens's presentation, the Reconstruction Acts were contrary to "the Southern will" as, at least when enforced, they stopped the killing of Republicans and blacks in the South. Clearly, Clemens did not believe that letting former Rebels act "according to the dictates of their own consciences" would create a just society in the South.[39]

During the impeachment crisis of 1868, Clemens's political allegiances remained those of a critic of power even as he shifted increasingly to the Republican Party. His allegiances always remained in this twilight borderland. "Joining the Republican party constituted the most obvious form of capitulation, particularly after the passage of the Reconstruction Acts in March 1867," historian Gaines M. Foster has suggested. Yet for Clemens, the identification was never complete and never preeminent. His roles as cynic, satirist, and reconstructed southerner were paramount. In later years, Clemens remained cynical of politics and often disagreed with his own party. Important milestones along the way included his 1869 satires about the lame duck President Johnson. Neither of these, however, was truly partisan. In the context of Reconstruction, they were anti-Johnson as well as anti-moderate Republican. These pieces revealed a Clemens who identified, not with the politics of the laconic Grant, but with the politics of the firebrand Thad Stevens and his Radical Republicans. The first of the Johnson satires was "L'Homme Qui Rit," or "The Man who Laughs." This work was both a jab at Johnson and a burlesque of Victor Hugo's novel of the same title. Clemens's protagonist, "a poor tailor boy," was a very thinly veiled version of Johnson. On a dark midnight, he discovered a "putrid carcass" with the words "AFRICAN SLAVE TRADE" written on it. After other adventures, the tailor boy met the "Stranger Confederacy," who led him to forsake the love of his life, "Democracy." Clemens made passing references in the allegory to Johnson's drinking, speeches, and impeachment. Scholar Franklin Rogers has rightly argued that "L'Homme Qui Rit" proved that Clemens "had become a Radical Republican." At the same time, Rogers noted the presence of "other clues pointing toward a continuation of his loyalty to the South during Johnson's administration." That conflict of seemingly contradictory positions sprouted in the border state soil of Missouri and flourished in the Nevada Territory and California. Clemens always saw both sides, just as the historian Thucydides did, and gained wisdom from the perspective of defeat. The vantage point from which he viewed politics was in reality neither that of a Radical Republican, a Copperhead, or a Rebel, but had become the perspective of a reconstructed southerner. Loyalty to the Union did not mean disloyalty to the South. Nor did it imply toeing the Republican Party line.[40]

Even more biting was Clemens's late 1869 dramatic monologue, "The White House Funeral," a posthumously published satire of President Johnson's final cabinet meeting. Just as he had done with "Barnum's First Speech in Congress," Clemens wrote the burlesque in the first person, from the point of view of the public figure. With "The White House Funeral," however, he lampooned not a Radical Republican, but a succession of turncoats: William Seward, Gideon Welles, and, finally, "Andrew Johnson, that grand old second Washington, that resurrected Moses" himself. (Johnson had promised freed slaves he would be their "Moses.") Twain's Johnson began his speech with his infamous drunken performance at the inauguration, a moment when "I was too full for utterance." Clemens ventriloquated Johnson's voice, creating a type of philippic in which the leader himself catalogued every misdeed he had been guilty of over the course of his four-year term, concluding with acts taken just in the previous weeks, such as his pardoning of Dr. Samuel Mudd in February and of Edward Spangler and Samuel Arnold on March 2, 1869, following their convictions for aiding and abetting John Wilkes Booth in his attempted escape from Federal authorities. "The White House Funeral" was relentlessly severe; Clemens matched the tone nearly three decades later in his anti-lynching and anti-imperialist diatribes. Clemens had Johnson admit to "violating my oath," "obstructing the laws," and "nursing anarchy & rebellion." The irony reached its apex, however, when Johnson listed his "great deeds," and they read much like the Articles of Impeachment the Republicans in Congress had leveled against him in 1868.

> My great deeds speak for themselves. I vetoed the Reconstruction acts; I vetoed the Freedmen's Bureau; I vetoed civil liberty; I vetoed Stanton; I vetoed everything & everybody that the malignant Northern hordes approved; I hugged traitors to my bosom; I pardoned them by regiments & brigades; I was the friend & protector of assassins & perjurers; I smiled upon the Ku-Klux; I delivered the Union men of the South & their belongings over to murder, robbery, & arson . . . I rescued the bones of the patriot martyr, Booth, from the mystery & oblivion to which malignity had consigned them, & gave them sepulcher where I & many a generation of sorrowing worshippers may go & do honor to the brave heart that did not fear to strike a tyrant, even when his back was turned; I have swept the floors clean; my work is done; I die content.

However justified some of the complaints were, "The Funeral in Washington" was a savage attack. Scholar Louis J. Budd has suggested that "during the months when there was no obvious successor to the dying Johnson regime," Clemens engaged in a delicate "balancing act" that ended only with "The White House Funeral." Calling this article "searing," Budd has concluded that it showed that its author "had finally hoisted a party banner." Curiously, however, Clemens attacked, not the Democratic Party per se, but those politicians who had been turncoats, disloyal to the Republican cause. William H. Seward, who served as secretary of state under both the Lincoln and Johnson administrations, defended his actions in the piece during this final cabinet meeting. "I have always been consistent. I have always stood by the party in power. I was always the first to desert it when it lost its prestige." The same was said of Johnson, a Democrat who seemed to be Republican in sympathy until his inauguration. For the previous ten years, Clemens himself had grappled with issues of loyalty and disloyalty, but in "The White House Funeral," Clemens specifically attacked Johnson and the members of his cabinet who failed to live up to Republican ideals. In many ways, this foreshadowed Clemens's role within the Republican

Party for the next forty years. Much of his ire would be directed at those within the Republican Party who failed to live up to the idealism of Radical Republicanism.[41]

"The White House Funeral" was not published during Clemens's lifetime. He submitted it to the New York *Tribune*, where it was set in galley proofs and slated for publication, but cancelled at the last minute. "The White House Funeral" was probably shelved, as scholars Fischer and Frank have surmised, because reports had appeared in the press stating that President Johnson was actually near death. Under such circumstances, an article entitled "The White House Funeral" would have been too grotesquely insensitive even when directed at the much-derided Johnson. In "Concerning Gen. Grant's Intentions" and "The White House Funeral," Clemens emerged as a voice for the radical wing of the Republican Party, but he did so from the perspective of a reconstructed southerner. Significantly, in both pieces, he created a burlesque persona for himself as a disloyal southerner. The nature of the satire thus served to differentiate him from Copperhead journalists and from Johnson. Yet, Clemens still claimed an aversion to politics. In a letter to Mary Mason and Abel W. Fairbanks, whom he had met on the *Quaker City* cruise, Sam again expostulated, "I always did hate politics." Consistently, however, during our country's greatest trials, Samuel Clemens addressed the great political issues of the day, often obliquely, occasionally directly, and always with humor. Through the Reconstruction years, Clemens used his persona as a reconstructed southerner for satirical purposes, to criticize individuals, society, and politicians in particular for failing to live up to their most cherished beliefs.[42]

CHAPTER 5

THE "LINCOLN OF OUR LITERATURE"

The Reconstructed Mark Twain, 1870–1910

A Patriot is merely a rebel at the start.
—MARK TWAIN, 1908

ORCED TO CHOOSE SIDES in Missouri in the early months of the Civil War, Sam Clemens enlisted in the Marion Rangers and swore to defend the "right, righteous, sacred" principles of the South, including slavery. His desertion condemned him to choose sides again and initiated an ongoing, evolutionary process that moved him to identify with Radical Republicanism during and following President Andrew Johnson's impeachment trial.

Clemens's writing of "The White House Funeral" signaled a true shift in his political allegiances, but it by no means denoted a conclusion. Sam remained a border-stater at heart and always retained the blessing and the curse of seeing the world from all sides. In the later years of Reconstruction, viewing events from all sides was not always considered praiseworthy, but Clemens increasingly criticized the American government, and in the 1870s, that meant the Republican Party. In such works as "Disgraceful Persecution of a Boy" (1870), "John Chinaman in New York" (1870), and "Goldsmith's Friend Abroad Again" (1870–1871), Clemens satirized the treatment of Chinese immigrants in New York City, San Francisco, and America generally. Echoing Chief Justice Roger B. Taney's decision in *Dred Scott v. Sanders,* Clemens ironically proclaimed that "a Chinaman had no rights that any man was bound to respect." While each of the satires targeted the Irish, who were mainly Democrats, as part of the problem, Clemens could not, after his time in Washington, neglect Congress. In "Goldsmith's Friend Abroad Again," Clemens's Chinese protagonist Ah Song Hi related how money was extorted from him illegally by the American consul. Because "the Government at Washington know of this fraud, and are so bitterly opposed to the existence of such a wrong," they planned to legalize the extortion, rather than ending the practice. "It is a great and good and noble country," Ah Song Hi opined, "and hates all forms of vice and chicanery." Even more pointed than this irony was Clemens's "Fourth of July Speech in London" (1873), a good-natured diatribe in which he ironically lauded America for the heroes it has produced, luminaries such as George Washington and Benjamin Franklin as well as his contemporaries William M. "Boss" Tweed and the noted robber baron, Jay Gould. He chided the U.S. Army, "which conquered sixty Indians in eight months by tiring them out," and concluded by praising America's politicians: "I think I can say, and say with pride, that we have some legislatures that bring higher prices than any in the world."[1]

If such performances reproved American culture and government generally, in other venues, Clemens expressed a more partisan outlook that served the Republican agenda. In "The Revised Catechism" (1871), Clemens parodied the *Shorter Catechism* used in his own Presbyterian Church as well as in many other churches of the Reformed tradition. In the original, the first question directed to the young person was "What is the chief end of man?" The proper response was, "To glorify God and enjoy him forever." Not so, in Clemens's revision.

What is the chief end of man?
A: To get rich.
In what way?
A: Dishonestly if we can; honestly if we must.
Who is God, the one only and true?
A: Money is God. Gold and greenbacks and stock—father, son, and the ghost of the same—three persons in one: these are the true and only God, mighty and supreme; and William Tweed is his prophet.

Clemens aimed the parody very precisely at the Democratic Party in New

York City, commenting on specific instances of graft, corruption, and over-charging the city for "imaginary carpets," "apocryphal chairs," and "invisible printing." He scolded Democrats again in "The Secret of Dr. Livingstone's Continued Voluntary Exile" (1872). The noted physician and missionary Dr. David Livingstone had disappeared in Africa for a period of five years. After Stanley first uttered his famous salutation, "Dr. Livingstone, I presume," he had to "give him five years' news." Clemens had a great deal of fun with the kind of news Stanley had to provide the doctor, including such startling events as the election of General Grant, the Great Chicago Fire, the Tammany Hall scandal, and so on. Only when Stanley mentioned the Democratic Party's pick to run against Grant in his 1872 reelection campaign did Dr. Livingstone protest.

> "Horace Greeley is the democratic candidate for President of the United States, and all rebeldom hurrahs for him. He—"
>
> "Hold on! You have told me stupendous things, and with a confiding simplicity born of contact with these untutored children of Africa, I was swallowing them peacefully down; but there is a limit to all things. I am a simple, guileless, christian man, and unacquainted with intemperate language; but when you tell me that Horace Greeley is become a democrat and the ku-klux swing their hats and whoop for him, I cast the traditions of my education to the winds and say, I'll be d——d to all eternity if I believe it. (After a pause.)—My trunk is packed to go home, but I shall remain in Africa—for these things *may* be true, after all; if they are, I desire to stay here and unlearn my civilization."

If Mark Twain's reconstruction was more evolutionary than revolutionary, Horace Greeley's *volte face* after the war was as shocking a reversal as one can find in that era of public and personal cataclysm. Beginning as a revolt within the Republican Party, Greeley's candidacy for president against the incumbent Grant nearly split the Grand Old Party. Greeley, as historian Eric Foner has observed, "had spent much of his political career denouncing the Democratic Party," but found himself first as the Liberal Republican candidate nominated in a rogue convention and then elevated as the Democratic candidate. During his campaign, Greeley freely "flip-flopped" from positions he had held earlier on many substantive issues: "I was, in the days of slavery, an enemy of slavery, because I thought slavery inconsistent with the rights, the dignity, the highest well-being of free labor. That might have been a mistake." Such statements suggested Greeley might reverse Emancipation, and Clemens attempted to highlight the jarring surrealism of the man's comments by showing how they would strike someone who had been in Africa for the past five years. Having to "unlearn my civilization" also suggested that, if the electorate embraced Greeley's views on slavery and race, then African civilization was truer than American civilization.[2]

Perhaps because of these more partisan articles attacking Democrats and the Democratic Party, some contemporaries considered Clemens something of a political operative. This was especially true in the election of 1876. Having campaigned strongly for the Republican Rutherford B. Hayes in the highly contested election with Samuel J. Tilden, Clemens seemed the "Radical Republican" some had called him. But the Republican Party had changed. One interviewer for the Democratic New York *World* subjected Clemens to some of his own style of political burlesque, in a probably spurious exchange bearing the suggestive title, "A Connecticut Carpet-bag." The interviewer prefaced his discussion by reminding readers of the "active part" Clemens had taken in the election of President Hayes.

At the moment of his discovery Mr. Twain may not have been reading a special dispatch from Zach Chandler, but he was certainly not reading the Bible. It may not have been a note from Kellogg instructing him to indite a hymn for the downtrodden Republican negroes of Louisiana that he crumpled into a wad behind his back on seeing the reporter, and subsequently devoured in mouthfuls, his eyes meanwhile fixed religiously on the gas fixtures overhead, but this by no means proves that it wasn't; indeed, there was an air of guilt about Mr. Twain that no extraneous observations about the state of the Sabbath school in New Zealand availed in the least to dispel.

"Mr. Twain," said the reporter, "what have you to say on the political situation?"

"Sir," replied Mr. Twain, bundling a long white garment into his valise, "it is mixed."

"And?" said the reporter.

"I didn't mix it, and I don't know who did and I can't straighten it, and I don't know who can, and—what do you think, sir, of having Broadway with—"

"Excuse me, Mr. Twain, now there are the Southern outrages—"

"Never heard of them; never, never, never."

"Never heard of them, Mr. Twain?"

"No, sir, I never did (by this time Mr. Twain had one side of his bag packed, and was sitting on it); ain't in my line; let's talk about something else."

"Mr. Twain, I understand you voted the Republican ticket?'

"Yes, sir; where's the whiskbroom? Ah, here it is, in you go. Sir, would you journey through life swiftly and in peace?"

"Yes," replied the reporter; "but Mr. Twain—"

"Never mind the buts. You must make a rule of packing the whiskbroom first. Now for the pipe and the Bible, and there I'm all packed; must go; got to catch a train in three minutes; good bye"; and in a twinkling Mr. Twain was on his way to Hartford.

The "interviewer" depicted Clemens as the representative carpetbagger, as a *northerner* who went South to solve the problems of Reconstruction. Clemens, of course, was never in reality a carpetbagger, but his allegiance to the Republican Party, particularly in the recent campaign where Hayes was elected to clean up, or "sweep," Washington, made the depiction at least symbolically plausible. The charges in the "interview" were that Clemens, like the Radical Republican Senator Zach Chandler mentioned in the interview, were actually "sweeping away all the problems" (note the symbolic "whiskbroom") in order to claim that people should vote for Hayes. Finally, Clemens's close friend William Dean Howells was the campaign biographer for Hayes. He exhorted his friend to "come out with a letter, or speech, or something, for Hayes." For a time, Clemens demurred, even falling back on his perennial claim of disinterest in politics. "It seems odd," he wrote Howells, "to find myself interested in an election. I never was before." On September 30, 1876, Clemens addressed a Republican rally, replete with Civil War veterans, a brass band, and a torchlight procession. Ignoring the need to protect the rights of America's newest voters, the freed slaves of the South, Clemens advocated civil service reform. "That is exactly what we hope to do with our civil service under Mr. Hayes. We hope and expect to sever that service as utterly from politics as is the naval and military service, and we hope to make it as respectable, too." The only criticism Clemens made of the Democratic Party was that it created the "grotesque" system of civil service. He said nothing about the desperation felt by former slaves in the South. The situation in Louisiana referenced by the interviewer was just one of many, but was perhaps an order of magnitude greater than in other states of the former Confederacy. Historian Eric Foner has called the Colfax, Louisiana massacre in 1873, an event in which blacks were killed after surrendering to a group of whites, the "bloodiest single act of carnage in Reconstruction." William Pitt Kellogg was the Radical Republican governor at the time, and his election was only made possible by the votes of the newly enfranchised black citizens. An 1874 gubernatorial coup deposed Kellogg. Riots in New Orleans left fifty-six people dead, and Grant sent in the troops. The president, in a message to the Senate delivered July 31, 1876, referred to the situation: "In regard to Louisiana affairs, murders and massacres of innocent men for opinion's sake or on account of color have been of too recent date and of too frequent occurrence to require recapitulation or testimony here. All are familiar with their horrible details, the only wonder being that so many justify them or apologize for them." Some of those justifying the crimes were Republicans. Others simply ignored them, sweeping them under the carpet in order to ensure the election of Hayes. When questioned about "southern outrages," and there were many outrages such as voter intimidation, lynchings, and the rise of the Ku Klux Klan, the fictional Clemens in the "interview" responded by saying, "Never heard of them; never, never, never."[3]

Clemens was no political hack, however. He actually considered the 1876 election to have been a great blot on the Republican Party. He recalled November 1876 as a "vast political conflagration [that] was blazing at white heat which was presently to end in one of the Republican party's most cold-blooded swindles of the American people, the stealing of the presidential chair from Mr. Tilden, who had been elected, and the conferring of it upon Mr. Hayes, who had been defeated." Tilden had won the popular vote, but a special commission awarded Hayes the electoral votes from disputed state elections, giving Hayes the election by a single electoral vote. Scholar Shelley Fisher Fishkin has noted that this "Compromise of 1877" was arrived at only because Hayes made "certain concessions to the Southern Democrats—which included his word that the federal troops would be out of the South." The action, Fishkin concluded, "was a potent symbol—one which signaled, to the white South's delight, that Reconstruction was over." Clemens concluded that the Republicans stole the election despite the fact that, as he himself proclaimed, "I was an ardent Hayes man."[4]

Clemens's judgment of the Republican Party became radicalized even as the party of Lincoln moved away from Radical Reconstruction. His disillusionment with Hayes had much to do with the president's failure to secure the freedoms of the former slaves in the South, the "downtrodden Republican negroes" referred to in the *World* interview. Historian Edward J. Blum has identified a shift in the Republican's "southern policy from appealing to black voters and seeking to uphold their voting privileges" to one of conciliating whites. Hayes ended the military occupation of the South and, in his Second Annual Message, delivered on December 2, 1878, proclaimed that the "recent Congressional elections have furnished a direct and trustworthy test of the advance thus far made in the practical establishment of the right of suffrage secured by the Constitution to the liberated race in the Southern States. All disturbing influences, real or imaginary, had been removed from all of these States." The Republicans had, with their great whiskbroom, brushed away the very serious problems facing the emancipated slaves. All was well. Reconstruction was over.[5]

The removal of federal troops may have ended Reconstruction, but it did not end Mark Twain's reconstruction. The battles had just begun, as this "desouthernized southerner" became more radical than the Republican Party, castigating it for not living up to its ideals. In so doing, he again left himself open to charges of disloyalty—charges he had dealt with ever since he had joined and then deserted the Marion Rangers and gone West. In the campaign of 1880, Clemens again took an active part in the canvass, speaking up for Garfield. "I am going to vote the Republican ticket, myself, from old habit," he told an audience in Hartford. Clemens treated taxes and tariffs primarily, but asserted that these were crucial issues that relate to "our actual *bread and meat.*" In a fable, Clemens compared the tariff to "a family of eagles living near the sparrows" that would eat both birds and eggs. The fable made for an unusual campaign speech, but Clemens conveyed the fear of government power that emerged from the Civil War experiences of what, at times, seemed a police state. The fable's eagle, after all, devoured everything. Following Garfield's victory, Clemens spoke on November 2, 1880, at the "Republican Jollification." Clemens's speech on this occasion was also highly unusual and recalled his spoof of Johnson in "The White House Funeral." Speaking in somber tones as if at a funeral, Clemens delivered the "Funeral Oration Over the Grave of the Democratic Party." "The aged and stricken Democratic party is dying," he intoned soberly. He referred to the party in stock Republican terms, but also as a dying actor. "In the South he played 'The Assassin of Freedom,' and mouthed the sacred shibboleths of liberty with cruel and bloody lips." Clemens made oblique references to President Lincoln's assassination, comparing the Democrats to the actor-assassin Booth.[6]

In 1884, Clemens refused to support the Republican nominee for president of the United States, James G. Blaine. Clemens did not like Blaine's running mate, General John A. Logan of Illinois, recalling his "tiger's play" in the Senate during the impeachment proceedings. The passing years had not changed his opinion of Logan. In a letter to William Dean Howells, he recalled the general's emotive and very long 1879 speech that was "unimaginable torture" for the audience. The head of the ticket, however, was far worse. Clemens wanted a return to honest government and believed, along with the other Mugwumps, Republicans that refused to support their party's national candidate, that Blaine was corrupt. In her study of liberal reform in the nineteenth century, historian Leslie Butler has noted that "Liberal reformers had distrusted Blaine for years and had repeatedly threatened to leave the party of Lincoln if it made this enemy of reform its standard-bearer. The Democratic nominee, Grover Cleveland, did not merely represent the lesser of two evils: he had already proven himself a key ally, leading efforts for civil service reform while serving as governor of New York." When evidence appeared proving that Blaine had abused his position as House Speaker to engage in land, stock, and loan swindles, liberal Republicans defected. Staunch Republicans derided them as Mugwumps, "an Algonquin word for 'great chief,'" as Butler has observed, "that their detractors used to ridicule the bolters' pretensions (and that the reformers themselves quickly embraced)." While Blaine won the Republican nomination, he lost the election. When asked to stump for Blaine, Republican Senator Roscoe Conkling responded acerbically: "I am not practicing criminal law." Clemens referred to the Republican nominee as "the paltry scoundrel Blaine" and as "Blaine the Nickel-plated statesman." In "Turncoats," a speech given in Hartford in October 1884, Clemens defended his position. "I easily perceive that the Republican party has deserted us, and deserted itself; but I am not able to see that *we* have deserted anything or anybody. As for me, I have not deserted the Republican code of principles, for I propose to vote its ticket, with the presidential exception; and I have not deserted Mr. Blaine, for as regards him I got my free papers before he bought the property." Drawing on his southern background to justify his identity as a Mugwump, Clemens figuratively waved his "free papers" and refused to be a slave to party loyalty. The Mugwump defection landed Grover Cleveland in the White House in 1884, an outcome that, as historian Gaines M. Foster has recorded, was greeted as a liberation in the South: "For southerners only the election of Democrat Grover Cleveland in 1884 established reunion, or, as one of them phrased it, allowed the South's 'escape from captivity and humiliation.' Towns throughout the region held parades, fired cannons, lit bonfires, and generally rejoiced." Clemens felt liberated, too, for he had rejected the need to be a Republican, to identify himself with a particular candidate, even while staunchly adhering to "the Republican code of principles." And he made his declaration precisely on the grounds that he was a reconstructed southerner, that he had his free papers. By invoking slavery, Clemens subtly suggested that the Republican Party had lost the election because it had lost its dedication to ensuring the benefits of Reconstruction—civil rights for the freed slaves.[7]

Similarly, in his essay "The Character of Man" (1885), Clemens inveighed against Blaine and suggested that "what is called party allegiance, party loyalty . . . turns voters into chattels, slaves." Here, Clemens expressed an anger similar to what had motivated his attacks on Unionists in the Nevada Territory: hypocrisy. The tirade became strident, as he attacked the hypocrisy of people who are "shouting rubbish about liberty, independence, freedom of opinion" while demanding conformity and party loyalty. Clemens reminded readers that their "fathers and the churches shouted the same blasphemies a generation earlier when they were closing their doors against the hunted slave, beating his handful of humane defenders with Bible-texts and billies, and pocketing the insults and licking the shoes of his Southern master." Acquiescence to southern demands, as the Republican Party was increasingly doing, struck Sam as the same sort of northern hypocrisy the world had witnessed when Daniel Webster colluded with southern politicians to pass the Fugitive Slave Act. Sam had cheered those laws in the 1850s and demanded their strict enforcement; by the 1880s, he used it as another means of whipping northerners for their hypocrisy. During the 1880s, Twain's reconstruction became more obviously that of the patriotic cynic, the gadfly intent on questioning everything. The reconstruction Mark Twain experienced did not parallel the national experience in this regard. Historian Foster has contended that

The rapid healing of national divisions and damaged southern self-image, however, came at the cost of deriving little insight or wisdom from the past. Rather than looking at the war as a tragic failure and trying to understand it, or even condemn it, Americans, North and South, chose to view it as a glorious time to be celebrated. Most ignored the fact that the nation had failed to resolve a debate over the nature of the Union and to eliminate the contradictions between its equalitarian ideals and the institution of slavery without resort to a bloody civil war. Instead, they celebrated the war's triumphant nationalism and martial glory. Southerners participated in the celebration, even though they had lost the war. Surprisingly, they never questioned whether defeat implied something was wrong with the cause or their society. Their cause had been just and the failure the result only of overwhelming numbers, they concluded. Conceivably, defeat might have impelled them to question the morality of slavery and, in the process, of southern race relations. It might have led southerners to be more skeptical of their nation's sense of innocence and omnipotence. But it did not. Late nineteenth-century southerners gained little wisdom and developed no special perspective from contemplating defeat.

Clemens's experience deviated from Foster's analysis significantly. There were many other exceptions, such as the author's southern, Confederate friend George Washington Cable. His novels and essays made him a pariah in southern society, and he retired in the North. Clemens became skeptical and gained that privileged vision, that "special perspective from contemplating defeat" that Foster has outlined. Words like "patriotism" and "loyalty" had to be redefined; Sam could not define them in the same way as those who had labeled him "disloyal." Patriotism did not involve waving the flag, and it did not involve "slavery" to party. In "Mock Oration on the Dead Partisan" (1884), Clemens called a partisan of a political party a "slave . . . meek and docile, cringing and fawning, dirt-eating and dirt-preferring slave." Once more, Clemens delivered a mock-eulogy on a political rival, but he directed this philippic against the Republican, James G. Blaine. "People seem to think," Clemens wrote in his notebook in 1888, "they are citizens of the Republican party & that that is patriotism & sufficiently good patriotism. I prefer to be a citizen of the United States." Clemens's emergence as a Mugwump was as momentous as his identification with the Republican Party in 1869. That identification was never truly complete, for Clemens always saw both sides, a vantage point forced upon him by history as a border-stater during the Civil War. "I was born a Mugwump, and I shall probably die a Mugwump," Clemens asserted in 1893. Identifying himself as a Mugwump returned Clemens to the border, back to the region he was born in, and into the political territory history had forced him into, however much he had tried to escape it.[8]

Redefining himself, Sam Clemens redefined patriotism, for the antebellum definition offered by preacher, pedagogue, and parent in that little village on the Mississippi River no longer worked. "It was a little democracy," Clemens wrote, "which was full of Liberty, Equality, and Fourth of July; and sincerely so, too, yet you perceive that the aristocratic taint was there." So, too, were the sermons preaching the justice of slavery. Reconstruction forced a reexamination of all political allegiances. In "Man's Place in the Animal World" (1896), Clemens rejected that nexus of church and state in defining patriotism: "For many centuries 'the common brotherhood of man' has been urged—on Sundays—and 'patriotism' on Sundays and week-days both. Yet patriotism *contemplates the opposite of a common brotherhood*." Clemens, as he did so frequently in the postwar years, connected this patriotism to slavery. "Man is the only Slave. And he is the only animal who enslaves . . . Man is the only Patriot. He sets himself apart in his own country, under his own flag, and sneers at the other nations, and keeps multitudinous uniformed assassins on hand at heavy expense to grab slices of other people's countries, and keep *them* from grabbing slices of *his*. And in the intervals between campaigns he washes the blood off his hands and works for 'the universal brotherhood of man'—with his mouth." For Clemens, slavery was a universal problem. Misplaced patriotism had prolonged slavery in his own childhood; and in the postwar era, misplaced patriotism expanded slavery through the world in the form of imperialism. The lesson in "Man's Place in the Animal World" was general, universal. The "uniformed assassins" were soldiers, fighting under any national flag. Just as the pious hypocrisies of southern nationalism went unquestioned in Hannibal in the 1830s–1850s, the pious hypocrisies of American nationalism were accepted as truth in the 1890s.[9]

In "As Regards Patriotism" (1901), Clemens again extended his criticism of his society to argue that "Patriotism is merely a religion," but its authority makes one turn "Traitor to keep from being called Traitor." "Traitor" was a word he had been hearing for a long time. "Training does wonderful things . . . Before the Civil War it made the North indifferent to slavery and friendly to the slave interest; in that interest it made Massachusetts hostile to the American flag, and she would not allow it to be hoisted on her State House—in her eyes it was the flag of a faction. Then by and by, training swung Massachusetts the other way, and she went raging South to fight under that very flag and against that foretime protected-interest of hers." Here, in such texts as these, Twain's reconstruction, though it was always ongoing, may be said to have approached its final stage, for he used his own pre-reconstruction experiences and his identity as a reconstructed southerner as the basis for calling all society to account. He repeatedly drew upon his own background as a Confederate as a prerequisite for true loyalty, however strange that may seem; unlike those Unionists who had never questioned their loyalties, Clemens had undergone a heartfelt reconstruction. "A patriot is merely a rebel at the start," he wrote in 1908. "In the North before the war, the man who opposed slavery was despised and ostracized, and insulted." Clemens's theory that a patriot started as a rebel had roots in his own experiences, for he had to rebel against the false ideals of society in order to be a patriot. A true patriot in Missouri in the 1850s would have opposed slavery. A true patriot in the Nevada Territory a decade later would have pointed out the hypocrisy of Unionists who refused to embrace emancipation and enfranchisement of slaves. A true patriot in Washington would criticize both parties for their failures. "In any civic crisis of a great and dangerous sort," Clemens charged, "the common herd is not privately anxious about the rights and wrongs of the matter, it is only anxious to be on the winning side." Clemens understood that winners never have to come to terms with the meaning of triumph. Victory leaves no legacy; defeat grants wisdom and insight. This is so because the fact of defeat foists introspection upon the defeated. For Clemens, loss remained ever-present, an open wound, and healing was impossible when surrounded by all the evidence of defeat, that the "right, righteous, sacred" ideals had been destroyed. Only a rebel could oppose society and escape what Clemens insistently referred to as "training." Clemens used the examples drawn from slavery for he himself had experience with it, having witnessed its desperate consequences. Abraham Lincoln reached the same conclusion when seeing the slave markets of New Orleans. Sam's journey took longer, but the changes were just as profound.[10]

Clemens's post-Reconstruction writings used his southern background, even his brief stint as a Confederate bushwhacker, to create a prophetic persona judging all society. In "The Private History of a Campaign That Failed," he debunked the ethos of heroism and patriotism central to other contributions to the *Century* series. In its place, Clemens concluded that war was just "the killing of strangers against whom you feel no personal animosity." As a border-stater and as a reconstructed southerner who championed the platform of Radical Republicanism at its best, he could support such a judgment. His rhetorical positioning in this and other works required that he emphasize his southern roots, a strategy Clemens used time and again. One very fine example came in 1874, when Clemens published "A True Story, Repeated Word for Word as I Heard It" in the *Atlantic Monthly*. In this story, Clemens based the character "Aunt Rachel" on "Auntie Cord," who worked as a cook for his sister-in-law, Susan Langdon Crane at Quarry Farm. Clemens spent at least twenty-four summers at Quarry Farm, his summer writing retreat in Elmira, New York. Sam wrote William Dean Howells, his close personal friend and editor of the *Atlantic Monthly*, that the story "has no humor in it," making it "rather out of my line." Clemens started the story with his own teasing laughter directed at Aunt Rachel. The joking abruptly ceased, however, when "Misto C—," as he was called in the story, inquired, "Aunt Rachel, how is it that you've lived sixty years and never had any trouble?" "Has I had any trouble? Misto C—, I's gwyne to tell you, den I leave it to you. I was bawn down 'mongst de slaves; I knows all 'bout slavery, 'case I ben one of 'em my own se'f. Well, sah, my ole man—dat's my husban'—he was lovin' an' kind to me, jist as kind as you is to yo' own wife. An' we had chil'en—seven chil'en—an' we loved dem chil'en jist de same as you loves yo' chil'en." Reprimanding Clemens, Aunt Rachel told the story of seeing all of those children sold at auction. Clemens had been "bawn down 'mongst de slaves," too, but his experience of slavery had been very different from Aunt Rachel's. Clemens obviously crafted this story carefully, and it was not "Repeated Word for Word as I Heard It," as the title claimed; "I have not altered the old colored woman's story," Clemens commented to William Dean Howells, "except to begin it at the beginning, instead of the middle, as she did—& traveled both ways." It was, however, a "true story." Clemens included something in this story that had been lost from the public discourse during Reconstruction: the slaves' perspectives on slavery, the Civil War, and its aftermath. Aunt Rachel told about losing her family at a slave auction, but then becoming a cook for a Union general. One evening, "a *nigger* ridgment" showed up "a waltzin' an a-dancin'" and she scolded them for disrupting her kitchen. "'Look-a-heah!' I says, 'I want you niggers to understan' dat I wa'n't bawn in de mash to be fool' by trash! I's one o' de ole Blue Hen's Chickens, *I* is!'" The reprimand struck a chord of memory with one young black man. He was her youngest child. William Dean Howells rightly said that "A True Story" was "a study of character as true as life itself, strong, tender, and most movingly pathetic in its perfect fidelity to the tragic fact." As Aunt Rachel told the story from the perspective of a now former slave, she unfolded the history of an era, with all the sorrows caused by slavery and with all the joys of emancipation. The story's conclusion, with its painful separation salved by euphoric reunion, was one of the finest Clemens ever wrote: "Oh, no, Misto C—, *I* hain't had no trouble. An' no *joy!*"[11]

Clemens adopted a similar tactic in his masterpiece, *Adventures of Huckleberry Finn* (1885), with the character of Colonel Sherburn staring down a southern lynch mob: "Do I know you? I know you clear through. I was born and raised in the south, and I've lived in the north; so I know the average all around. The average man's a coward. In the north he lets anybody walk over him that wants to, and goes home and prays for a humble spirit to bear it. In the south one man, all by himself, has stopped a stage full of men, in the daytime, and robbed the lot. Your newspapers call you a brave people so much that you think you *are* braver than any other people—whereas you're just *as* brave, and no braver." Coming from the South and the North and even the West and the East, Sam Clemens did "know the average all around." His reconstruction was thus not a desouthernization; rather, it was based on an intimate connection to the South as a *point d'appui*. In many works, Clemens's southernness provided the crucial kernel of his criticism. In *Following the Equator* (1897), he attacked American and European imperialism and "the white man's notion that he is less savage than the other savages." Clemens supported his many criticisms of white mistreatment of blacks, Aborigines, and Indians by comparing it to his own childhood. Seeing a German strike an Indian servant, Clemens mused, "I had not seen the like of this for fifty years. It carried me back to my boyhood, and flashed upon me the forgotten fact that this was the *usual* way of explaining one's desires to a slave." Clemens linked the colonial situation to the antebellum world of his "Missourian village" a half century before, and the writer's criticisms of the great powers in 1897 were all the more powerful by virtue of his experiences as a reconstructed southerner. Historian Walter A. Mc-Dougall has argued that "Americans drew such self-confidence from their scientific, industrial, and presumed moral progress that in just twenty more years they would step forth as redemptive crusaders, certain they knew how to do for Cuba, the Philippines, Mexico, China, and the world itself what they were manifestly unable to do for their own conquered South." Clemens understood the connection between the Civil War, Reconstruction, and imperialism. Leslie Butler has noted that the Mugwumps formed the core of the anti-imperialist movement, specifically the reaction against American involvement in the Philippines. "A sense of common purpose and an overlapping set of figures linked the anti-imperialism of the late 1890s to the pro-Cleveland movement of 1884 . . . The roster of Mugwump celebrities was also the same, with Mark Twain and William James heading the list of notable writers and scholars." Distinct from that of most of his Yankee Mugwump associates, Clemens's pronounced anti-imperialism of later years surely owed a great deal to his southern roots and the triumphalism of the conquering North and its attitude toward the defeated South; likely, too, Clemens's anti-imperialist writings owed a great deal to the failures of Reconstruction, specifically the failure of the country to adhere to is loftiest, one might say its "right, righteous, sacred," ideals. If, with all its military might, America could not reconstruct itself, then how could it reconstruct the rest of the world, from China to Cuba and the Philippines? During the war, Sam's southern identity was a liability, as it left him open to charges of disloyalty and even treason. As discussed in previous chapters, he had good reason to fear such charges. After the war, however, the southern identity became more valuable, providing him with the bona fides, the warrant, to criticize both North and South, the entire country, and even the world.[12]

With the conviction that his own ideals, however confused they had been in 1861, were misplaced, Sam Clemens developed the persona of Mark Twain, a persona that had all the fire of the true believer. He embraced the ideals of Radical Republicanism, and often in later years invoked Lincoln to call America to greatness, to embrace its "better angels." Because of Clemens's southern identity, these calls to his society had all the greater power. Sam Clemens's heart was clearly still in—though not with—Dixie, especially in his satires that grounded criticism of American society on the identity of the reconstructed rebel. Truly, as historian Reinhart Koselleck has mordantly observed, "history is made by the victors in the short run." The defeated, because their investment in the framing of history is greater, often determine how the story is written in the long term. Koselleck has cited the example of the historian Polybius, who, "taken to Rome as a hostage, had to first experience the absolute estrangement of the vanquished before he learned to identify himself with the victor." Even then, however, his insight differed from what a Roman would have seen in Rome's rise to power, for Polybius, one might say, was a reconstructed Roman; his perspective "was both internal and external." Clemens's reconstruction was wrenching, for it exacerbated the sense of alienation he had experienced as a border-stater, betwixt and between, neither here nor entirely there, a foreshadowing of the Mugwump he later became. Clemens's writing did not champion the South at the expense of the North, but provided, rather, the ground for criticism of all sides. Radical Republican Carpetbagger Albion Tourgée had predicted early in Reconstruction that "within thirty years after the close of the rebellion, popular sympathy will be with those who upheld the Confederate cause rather than with those by whom it was overthrown; our popular heroes will be Confederate leaders; our fiction will be Southern in its prevailing types and distinctively Southern in its character." Tourgée's comment was prescient, but it did not fit with Sam Clemens's writing, at least not entirely. Clemens's writing was "distinctively Southern in its character" in the sense that it most often featured, to a greater or lesser degree, the persona of the reconstructed southerner. But Clemens used that persona to criticize the entire country, often invoking the figure of Lincoln as part of the argument.[13]

In a July 4, 1907 speech, "The Day We Celebrate," Clemens joked about American traditions of holiday fireworks, relating the anecdote of an uncle "who was blown up that way, and really it trimmed him as it would a tree. He had hardly a limb left on him anywhere." Clemens then waxed serious, moving from a discussion of the Declaration of Independence to the Emancipation Proclamation. "Lincoln's proclamation . . . not only set the black slaves free, but set the white man free also," he maintained. The Great Emancipator figured as well in his "To the Person Sitting in Darkness" (1901), an anti-imperialist piece patterned after Isaiah 42:1, 7 (see also Matthew 4:36 and Micah 7:8). Clemens cast himself again in the role of prophet, building his jeremiad around the two verses, "I have put my spirit upon him: he shall bring forth judgment to the Gentiles" and "To open the blind eyes, to bring out the prisoners from the prison, *and* them that sit in darkness out of the prison house." Outraged at the imperialist ventures by America, Great Britain, France, Germany, and Russia, Clemens indicted "Christian" civilization as based upon sham and hypocrisy. From Cuba to China to South Africa and the Philippines, countries around the globe suffered from America's post–Civil War nationalism. "[W]e have debauched America's honor and blackened her face before the world," Clemens lamented. In lacerating language, he labeled America's ventures abroad a re-institution of slavery. Alongside of "Lincoln, the Slave's Broken Chains" we have placed the "Master, the Chains Repaired." He concluded by proposing that our national flag should be changed, "with the white stripes painted black and the stars replaced by the skull and cross-bones."[14]

In a speech delivered in 1907, Clemens demonstrated his Mugwump and border mentality by referring to America as a "republican monarchy" suffering from a "hereditary monarchy under a permanent political party." Clemens fumed that this state of affairs seemed intractable. Using language recalling his "Petrified Man" hoax, Clemens argued that "you couldn't dislodge ours with dynamite." "There is a President of the Republican party, but there has been only one President of the United States since the country lost Mr. Lincoln forty-two years ago. The highest duty of the President of the Republican party is to watch diligently over his party's interest, urgently promoting all measures, good or bad, which may procure votes for it, and as urgently obstructing all, good or bad, which might bring its rule into disfavor." Clemens's invective illustrated that his conversion was neither to Unionism nor to the Republican Party, but to the highest ideals behind those political concepts. Likewise, his reconstruction was hardly a desouthernization; the rant was evidence that Twain's reconstruction owed a great deal to his original construction. A Mugwump from a southern border state, Clemens defined patriotism in terms of skepticism and disloyalty, invoking the assassination of President Lincoln not as party hacks did, to win votes by "waving the bloody shirt," but to provoke citizens to rise above party and seize justice.[15]

Most notably, in "The Stupendous Procession" (1901), Clemens wrote a burlesque news item describing a parade procession. Following a banner emblazoned, "THE TWENTIETH CENTURY" with its motto, *"Get what you can, keep what you get"* marched all the dominant powers. While the major imperialist countries were represented (England, Spain, Russia, France, and Germany), America occupied about half of the procession. Clemens invoked Lincoln repeatedly, suggesting that the American Eagle once held in the "hand of Lincoln" had been reduced to being "policeman over this carrion!" America had followed European examples even with the emancipated slaves, for Clemens lamented that "in the Civil War" the slaves were used as soldiers but then did not receive the civil liberties for which they had fought. The *"Spectre of Jefferson Davis"* even materialized in the article: "The North said that as I manufactured the Civil War, I was personally responsible for every man that was killed in it." Who, then, was responsible for all the later wars, inquired the shade of Jefferson Davis. Clemens criticized the failure of Reconstruction by putting words in the mouth of the president of the Confederacy, again targeting northern hypocrisy that failed to live up to the idealistic rhetoric it had used to defeat the South. Later, he took similar liberties with President Lincoln's most famous words. "THE GETTYSBURG SPEECH—a noble figure, and mournful. Broken sentences, embroidered upon its robe, are vaguely legible: 'Our fathers brought forth a new nation, conceived in liberty and dedicated to the proposition that all men are created equal . . . Now we are . . . testing whether this nation, or any nation, so conceived and so dedicated can long endure'" (ellipses in original). The reconstructed Mark Twain waved the "bloody shirt," invoking Lincoln's powerful figure as the martyred president who gave his life to preserve the Union and end slavery. Here, Clemens altered the lines of the famous "Battle Hymn of the Republic" in his sketch, writing "'Christ died to make men holy, *He* died to make white men free.' (Battle Hymn of the Republic. 'He' is Abraham Lincoln.)" The parenthetical notation is in the original, and here the writer savaged the American government for not living up to the ideals that Sam Clemens had embraced, perhaps only after Lincoln's assassination. He concluded "The Stupendous Procession" with the "SHADE OF LINCOLN, towering vast and dim toward the sky, brooding with pained aspect over the far-reaching pageant."[16]

In 1831, President Abraham Lincoln found his true identity as an opponent of slavery by traveling South. Samuel Langhorne Clemens's enlightenment, his reconstruction as Mark Twain, was a longer pilgrimage. The journey began in the border state of Missouri, but ranged north to New York City; west to the Nevada Territory and California; around the world; and even into the "political stink-pots" of Washington, D.C. Mark Twain's emergence as the "Lincoln of our literature" occurred not in a single revelation. Responding as a person who could see all sides, who was put on the defensive by a seemingly high-minded but hypocritical government that failed to live up to its espoused ideals, he became an ardent champion of African American rights; a proponent of Radical Reconstruction; the friend and publisher of General Grant; and a writer who often used himself as an example of a southerner who retained cultural identity even while passionately attacking the racist elements of the larger American culture. Indeed, the persona of Mark Twain, the reconstructed southerner, served as a platform to criticize American culture, often specifically northern culture. Clemens used the dynamic pattern in some of his greatest works, and in many speeches he delivered on the Civil War and Reconstruction—including his addresses at West Point, at a dinner honoring General William Tecumseh Sherman, and at a gathering to honor former President Ulysses S. Grant, who had led the troops Sam Clemens had nearly skirmished with before his desertion in 1861. Most telling was Clemens's service in 1901 as chairman of an event in honor of President Lincoln. Remarkably, this supposedly "desouthernized southerner" embraced the Lost Cause, at least in its sentimental version, for the purpose of heightening how far he had come during his own private reconstruction. After leading the audience at Carnegie Hall in singing "The Battle Hymn of the Republic," Clemens spoke in his most heartfelt way about the Civil War:

> We of the South were not ashamed of the part we took. We believed in those days we were fighting for the right—and it was a noble fight, for we were fighting for our sweethearts, our homes, and our lives. Today we no longer regret the result, today we are glad that it came out as it did, but we of the South are not ashamed that we made an endeavor. And you, too, are proud of the record we made.
>
> We are here to honor the noblest and the best man after Washington that this land, or any other land, has yet produced. When the great conflict began the soldiers from the North and South swung into line to the tune of that same old melody, "We are coming, Father Abraham, three hundred thousand strong." The choicest of the young and brave went forth to fight and shed their blood under the flag and for what they thought was right. They endured hardships equivalent to circumnavigating the globe four or five times in the olden days. They suffered untold hardships and fought battles night and day.

The old wounds are healed, and you of the North and we of the South are brothers yet. We consider it to be an honor to be of the soldiers who fought for the Lost Cause, and now we consider it a high privilege to be here tonight and assist in laying our humble homage at the feet of Abraham Lincoln. And we do not forget that you of the North and we of the South, one-time enemies, can now unite in singing that great hymn, "America."

Sam's "part" in the conflict had been minimal, but its part in him was crucial. One sees here the rush to reunion, to reinforce a national identity. Clemens's performance did not follow the Lost Cause image in the way that others used it, however. Invoking, and helping to create, the Lost Cause mythos in his 1868 book with that title, Edward Pollard asserted that "The war has left the South its own memories, its own heroes, its own tears, its own dead." Glorification of the Confederate dead incensed Frederick Douglass, who felt they did not deserve the honor. "We are sometimes asked, in the name of patriotism, to forget the merits of this fearful struggle," he declaimed in his 1871 address at Arlington National Cemetery, "and to remember with equal admiration those who struck at the nation's life, and those who struck to save it—those who fought for slavery, and those who fought for liberty and justice." Douglass rejected the servants of the Lost Cause. Only the soldier who fought "in a noble cause" was worthy of devotion. But Clemens emphasized his devotion to the Confederate cause in his speech precisely to accentuate his southernness for the purpose of advancing the "liberty and justice" Union soldiers had fought for. Clemens stressed what his devotion to the Confederacy in 1861 may have been precisely to elevate the significance of his devotion to the values of Lincoln in 1901. As scholar Harold Bush has contended, "confessing former ties with the Lost Cause mythos serves the rhetorical purpose of positioning himself as a convert." Embracing the Confederacy in 1901 allowed Clemens to convincingly embrace President Lincoln as a symbol of what was best in Unionist politics. Whatever the reality, Clemens created a unique position for himself as a southerner who grew up with slaves and joined the Confederacy. He fashioned a privileged position that authorized him to tell the story in the first person while invoking a sense of guilt because he was late realizing that slaves were fully human. As Howells eulogized him, "Out of a nature rich and fertile beyond any I have known, the material given him by the Mystery that makes a man and then leaves him to make himself over, he wrought a character of high nobility." Sam Clemens did "make himself over," and the reconstruction of Mark Twain testified to the nobility of the result.[17]

As surprising as the assertion by William Dean Howells and others that Twain is the "Lincoln of our literature," much connected the two men, and Clemens himself recognized it. In 1907, nearing the end of his own life, he wrote a plea in support of setting aside Abraham Lincoln's birthplace as a national park. Clemens commented on the fact that Lincoln's birthplace might seem a bit out of the way, a bit inconsequential.

> But it was no accident that planted Lincoln on a Kentucky farm, half way between the lakes and the Gulf. The association there had substance in it. Lincoln belonged just where he was put. If the Union was to be saved, it had to be a man of such an origin that should save it . . . It needed a man of the border, where civil war meant the grapple of brother and brother and disunion a raw and gaping wound. It needed one who knew slavery not from books only, but as a living thing, knew the good that was mixed with its evil, and knew the evil not merely as it affected the negroes, but in its hardly less baneful influence upon the poor whites. It needed one who knew how human all the parties to the quarrel were, how much alike they were at bottom, who saw them all reflected in himself, and felt their dissensions like the tearing apart of his own soul.

A man of the border state, Lincoln could see all sides, could feel the Civil War and all of its issues founded on race and place in his very bones. Every statement Clemens made about Lincoln was true of himself, too. The Civil War had been, in many respects, "like the tearing apart of his own soul." The reconstruction of that soul was protracted, wrenching, and at times raucously humorous. Mark Twain learned the truth of Lincoln's assertion that "we cannot escape history," and his reconstruction testified powerfully and profoundly to the human ability to learn from history even while living it.[18]

NOTES

PREFACE

EPIGRAPHS: Abraham Lincoln, "'A House Divided': Speech at Springfield, Illinois" [speech at the Republican State Convention], in *The Collected Works of Abraham Lincoln*, vol. 2, ed. Roy Basler, Marion Pratt, and Lloyd Dunlap (New Brunswick, N.J.: Rutgers University Press, 1953), 461; Mark Twain, "The Private History of a Campaign That Failed," in *Mark Twain: Collected Tales, Sketches, Speeches, and Essays, 1852–1890* (New York: Library of America, 1992), 863.

1. Thomas Jefferson, *Memoirs, Correspondence, and Private Papers of Thomas Jefferson*, ed. Thomas Jefferson Randolph, vol. 4 (London: Henry Colburn and Richard Bentley, 1829), 332; Chief Justice Roger Taney, "Dred Scott, Plaintiff in Error, v. John F. A. Sanford," in *Readings in American Constitutional History, 1776–1876*, ed. Allen Johnson (New York: Houghton Mifflin Company, 1912), 440.

2. Mark Twain, "Dinner Speech" (March 17, 1909), in *Mark Twain Speaking*, ed. Paul Fatout (Iowa City: University of Iowa Press, 1976), 637; Twain, "The Private History of a Campaign That Failed," 863; Mark Twain, *The Autobiography of Mark Twain*, ed. Charles Neider (New York: HarperPerennial, 1990), 102; William Dean Howells, "My Mark Twain," in *Literary Friends and Acquaintance*, ed. David F. Hiatt and Edwin Cady (Bloomington: Indiana University Press, 1968), 277–78.

3. Mark Twain, *Life on the Mississippi*, in *Mark Twain: Mississippi Writings* (New York: Library of America, 1982), 491.

CHAPTER ONE

EPIGRAPHS: Mark Twain, "The Private History of a Campaign That Failed," in *Mark Twain: Collected Tales, Sketches, Speeches, and Essays, 1852–1890* (New York: Library of America, 1992), 880; Mark Twain, *Tom Sawyer's Conspiracy*, in *Hannibal, Huck & Tom*, ed. Walter Blair (Berkeley: University of California Press, 1969), 165–66; William Dean Howells, "My Mark Twain," in *Literary Friends and Acquaintance*, ed. David F. Hiatt and Edwin Cady (Bloomington: Indiana University Press, 1968), 277.

1. Lincoln had made the trip once before, but had apparently not seen the slave auctions. For whatever reason, it was this trip in 1831 that "run its iron in him" and confirmed his antislavery views. John G. Nicolay and John Hay, *Abraham Lincoln: A History*, vol. 1 (New York: The Century Company, 1914), 72–74. Lincoln discussed the trip in his campaign biography, "Autobiography Written for John L. Scripps," in *The Collected Works of Abraham Lincoln*, vol. 4, ed. Roy P. Basler, Marion D. Pratt, and Lloyd A. Dunlap (New Brunswick, N.J.: Rutgers University Press, 1953), 62–64.

2. Charles Miner Thompson, "Mark Twain as an Interpreter of American Character," *The*

Atlantic Monthly 79 (April 1897): 447–48; T. M. Parrott, "Mark Twain: Made in America," reprinted in *Mark Twain: The Critical Heritage,* ed. Frederick Anderson and Kenneth Sanderson (New York: Barnes & Noble, 1971), 253; George Ade, "Mark Twain as Our Emissary," in *Critical Essays on Mark Twain, 1867–1910,* ed. Louis J. Budd (Boston: G. K. Hall and Company, 1982), 241; William Dean Howells, "Mark Twain: An Inquiry," in *W. D. Howells as Critic* ed. Edwin H. Cady (Boston: Routledge & Kegan Paul, 1973), 340, 351; Howells, "My Mark Twain," 277–78; Orville Vernon Burton, *The Age of Lincoln* (New York: Hill and Wang, 2007), 106.

3. Mark Twain, *The Autobiography of Mark Twain,* ed. Charles Neider (New York: HarperPerennial, 1990), 94; Mark Twain, *Mark Twain's Letters,* vol. 1, *1853–1866,* ed. Edgar M. Branch, Michael B. Frank, and Kenneth M. Sanderson (Berkeley: University of California Press, 1988), 13, 10.

4. Twain, *The Autobiography of Mark Twain,* 2; Mark Twain, "Jane Lampton Clemens," in *Hannibal, Huck & Tom,* ed. Walter Blair (Berkeley: University of California Press, 1969), 46–49. Information about Clemens's father selling the slave for barrels of tar and about the Quarles farm is from Dixon Wecter, *Sam Clemens of Hannibal* (Boston: Houghton Mifflin, 1961), 75, 99.

5. Harold K. Bush Jr., *Mark Twain and the Spiritual Crisis of his Age* (Tuscaloosa: University of Alabama Press, 2007), 152; Twain, *The Autobiography of Mark Twain,* 6; Reinhart Koselleck, *The Practice of Conceptual History: Timing History, Spacing Concepts,* trans. Todd Samuel Presner et al. (Stanford: Stanford University Press, 2002), 80.

6. Twain, *Mark Twain's Letters,* vol. 1, *1853–1866,* 4.

7. Justice Joseph Story, "Prigg v. Pennsylvania," in *Readings in American Constitutional History, 1776–1876,* ed. Allen Johnson (New York: Houghton Mifflin Company, 1912), 419; Frederick Douglass, "An Inspiration to High and Virtuous Endeavor: An Address Delivered in Syracuse, New York, on 1 October 1884," in *The Frederick Douglass Papers, Speeches, Debaters, and Interviews.* vol. 5, *1881–95,* ed. John W. Blassingame and John R. McKivigan (New Haven: Yale University Press, 1992), 161; Ulysses S. Grant, *Personal Memoirs of U. S. Grant* (New York: Library of America, 1990), 773; Ralph Waldo Emerson, "The Fugitive Slave Law," in *The Complete Works of Ralph Waldo Emerson,* vol. 1 (Boston: Riverside Press, 1904), 179, 212; Walter A. McDougall, *Throes of Democracy: The American Civil War Era: 1829–1877* (New York: HarperCollins, 2008), 319.

8. Terrell Dempsey, *Searching for Jim: Slavery in Sam Clemens's World* (Columbia: University of Missouri Press, 2003), 8; "Negro Stealing," *Missouri Courier* (Hannibal), November 10, 1853, 2; "Abolitionist Incendiaries," *Missouri Courier* (Hannibal), September 22, 1853, 1; Mark Twain, "Villagers of 1840–3," in *Hannibal, Huck & Tom,* ed. Walter Blair (Berkeley: University of California Press, 1969), 36, 368; Wecter, *Sam Clemens of Hannibal,* 215; "Burning a Negro for Murder," *Missouri Courier* (Hannibal) July 28, 1853, 1. Italics in original.

9. Twain, *Tom Sawyer's Conspiracy,* 172; Wecter, *Sam Clemens of Hannibal,* 72–73; Mark Twain, *Adventures of Huckleberry Finn,* ed. Victor Fischer, Lin Salamo, and Walter Blair (Berkeley: University of California Press, 2003), 52; "Another Abolition Riot—Rights of a Missourian Outraged," *Missouri Courier* (Hannibal), October 16, 1851, 2; "Mob at Syracuse," *Hannibal Journal,* October 16, 1851, 2; "The Syracuse Outrage," *Hannibal Journal,* October 23, 1851, 2; Douglass, "An Inspiration to High and Virtuous Endeavor," 162.

10. Twain, *Mark Twain's Letters,* vol. 1, *1853–1866,* 41; Edgar Branch, *Mark Twain's Letters,*

vol. 1, *1853–1866*, 6 n. 6. For information about Calhoun, Clay, and Webster, see Richard B. Morris, *Encyclopedia of American History* (New York: Harper & Row, 1976), 250–53, 996, 1002, 1179; Emerson, "The Fugitive Slave Law," 203; Mark Twain, "The Sex in New York," in *Mark Twain's Travels with Mr. Brown*, ed. Franklin Walker and G. Ezra Dane (New York: Russell & Russell, 1971), 227; Edwin M. Stanton, "Contraband of War," in *Readings in American Constitutional History, 1776–1876*, ed. Allen Johnson (New York: Houghton Mifflin Company, 1912), 501. For Clemens's further comments on "contrabands," see his 1869 speech at Delmonico's, "The Reliable Contraband," in *Mark Twain Speaking*, ed. Paul Fatout (Iowa City: University of Iowa Press, 1976), 38–41.

11. According to Twain scholar Louis J. Budd, Clemens even "watched some nativist riots in St. Louis without disapproval." *Mark Twain: Social Philosopher* (Bloomington: Indiana University Press, 1962), 4.

12. William E. Parrish, *Turbulent Partnership: Missouri and the Union, 1861–1865* (Columbia: University of Missouri Press, 1963), 17, 29; Michael Fellman, *Inside War: The Guerrilla Conflict in Missouri During the American Civil War* (New York: Oxford University Press, 1989), 3; John C. Frémont, "In Command in Missouri," in *Battles and Leaders of the Civil War*, ed. Robert Johnson and Clarence Buel (New York: Castle Books, 1956), vol. 1, 278; Mark Twain, Unpublished Notebook 48 (Old 38) 1905–1908, Mark Twain Papers TS, University of California at Berkeley, 9; Twain, *Mark Twain's Letters*, vol. 1, *1853–1866*, 121; Mark Twain, *Mark Twain's Notebooks and Journals*, vol. 2, *1877–1883*, ed. Frederic Anderson, Lin Salamo, and Bernard Stein (Berkeley: University of California Press, 1975), 530 n. 21; Twain, *Mark Twain's Letters*, vol. 1, *1853–1866*, 121. Will Bowen's unpublished December 10, 1889 letter to Mark Twain is quoted by courtesy of the Mark Twain Project at the University of California at Berkeley.

13. Report No. 420, *Report of Committees of the Senate of the United States for the First Session of the Forty-Fourth Congress, 1875–76*, 3 vols. (Washington: Government Printing Office, 1876), vol. 2, 1–3; Harry P. Owens, *Steamboats and the Cotton Economy: River Trade in the Yazoo–Mississippi Delta* (Jackson: University Press of Mississippi, 1990), 40–41, 50; Mark Twain, "The Facts in the Case of the Great Beef Contract," in *Mark Twain: Collected Tales, Sketches, Speeches, and Essays, 1852–1890* (New York: Library of America, 1992), 367, 373.

14. Mark Twain, *Life on the Mississippi*, ed. Guy Cardwell (New York: Library of America, 1982), 409.

15. Samuel Charles Webster, ed., *Mark Twain, Businessman* (Boston: Little, Brown and Company, 1946), 60; Colonel Thomas L. Snead, "The First Year of the War in Missouri," in *Battles and Leaders of the Civil War* ed. Robert Johnson and Clarence Buel (New York: Castle Books, 1956), vol. 1, 268; Parrish, *Turbulent Partnership*, 26.

16. Snead, "The First Year of the War in Missouri," 268. See Fellman's useful chart showing the slave populations in Missouri counties in *Inside War*, 6.

17. Absalom Grimes, *Absalom Grimes, Confederate Mail Runner*, ed. M. M. Quaife (New Haven: Yale University Press, 1926), 3–5. John Gerber, for example, has claimed that Grimes's discussion "sounds more like old Southwestern yarn-spinning than history" in "Mark Twain's 'Private Campaign,'" *Civil War History* 1 (1955): 38 n. 6. Records from the Steamboat Inspection Service of the Department of Commerce record that Clemens renewed his license on March 21, 1860, and again on March, 20, 1861. See George H. Brownell, "License Mystery

Nears Solution," *Twainian* 2, no. 1 (January 1940): 2–3. The information does, perhaps, cast further doubt on Grimes's account, but Grimes claimed only that he was renewing his license, not that Clemens was there to renew his.

18. Twain, *Autobiography*, 102; Fred W. Lorch, "Mark Twain and the 'Campaign that Failed,'" *American Literature* 12 (January 1941): 466; Frederick H. Dyer, *A Compendium of the War of the Rebellion*, vol. 3, *Regimental Histories* (New York: Thomas Yoseloff, 1959), 1340–42; Budd, *Mark Twain: Social Philosopher*, 3; Mark Twain, Unpublished Notebook 48 (Old 38) 1905–1908, Mark Twain Papers TS, University of California at Berkeley, 8; J. Stanley Mattson, "Mark Twain on War and Peace: The Missouri Rebel and 'The Campaign that Failed,'" *American Quarterly* 20 (Winter 1968): 790; Edwin C. McReynolds, *Missouri: A History of the Crossroads State* (Norman: University of Oklahoma Press, 1962), 248.

19. Twain, "The Private History of a Campaign That Failed," 863, 864, 866; Mark Twain, *Mark Twain's Notebooks and Journals*, vol. 3, *1883–1891*, ed. Robert Pack Browning, Michael Frank, and Lin Salamo (Berkeley: University of California Press, 1979), 153; James Cox, *Mark Twain: The Fate of Humor* (Princeton, N.J.: Princeton University Press, 1966), 190; Gerber, "Mark Twain's 'Private Campaign,'" 60. Gerber's timetable is quite useful, but contains errors, most notably those based on the spurious Quintus Curtius Snodgrass letters, once mistakenly ascribed to Clemens by Ernest Leisy in *The Letters of Quintus Curtius Snodgrass* (Dallas: Southern Methodist University Press, 1946). The writer of those letters had published them in the *Daily Crescent* while serving in the Louisiana Guard in early 1861. For arguments against Clemens's authorship, see Allan Bates, "The Quintus Curtius Snodgrass Letters: A Clarification of the Mark Twain Canon," *American Literature* 36, no. 1 (1964): 31–37, and Claude S. Brinegar, "Mark Twain and the Quintus Curtius Snodgrass Letters: A Statistical Test of Authorship," *Journal of the American Statistical Association* 58, no. 301 (1963): 85–96.

20. Robert Johnson and Clarence Buel, "Preface," in *Battles and Leaders of the Civil War*, ed. Robert Johnson and Clarence Buel (New York: Castle Books, 1956), ix; Roy F. Nichols, "Introduction," in *Battles and Leaders of the Civil War* ed. Robert Johnson and Clarence Buel (New York: Castle Books, 1956), iii; Snead, "The First Year of the War in Missouri," 262. See, for example, the letter of James F. Huntington, "In Reply to General Pleasonton," that enumerated six points of disagreement with a previous article about the Battle of Chancellorsville, and also H. M. M. Richards's letter, "Citizens of Gettysburg in the Battle," that took exception to the notion that "the people of Gettysburg were lacking in patriotism because they did not spring to arms *en masse*, and assist in repelling the invaders." Both letters typified letters seeking to clarify some point. See the letters in James F. Huntington, "In Reply to General Pleasonton," *Century* 33 (January 1887): 471–72, and H. M. M. Richards, "Citizens of Gettysburg in Battle," *Century* 33 (January 1887): 472–73; Timothy P. Caron, "'How Changeable Are the Events of War': National Reconciliation in the *Century Magazine*'s 'Battles and Leaders of the Civil War," *American Periodicals* 16 (2006): 169; Gaines M. Foster, *Ghosts of the Confederacy: Defeat, the Lost Cause, and the Emergence of the New South, 1865 to 1913* (New York: Oxford University Press, 1987), 69.

21. Mark Twain, *Following the Equator* (Hartford: American Publishing Company, 1897), 679–81. Dan Beard's comments appeared in "Gossip," *Twainian* 2 (June 1940): 4; Tom Z. Parrish, "Civil War," in *The Mark Twain Encyclopedia*, ed. J. R. LeMaster and James D. Wilson (New York: Garland Publishing, Inc., 1993), 148.

22. Neil Schmitz, "Mark Twain's Civil War: Humor's Reconstructive Writing," in *The Cambridge Companion to Mark Twain*, ed. Forrest G. Robinson (Cambridge: Cambridge University Press, 1995), 74–78. Johnson's unpublished July 16, 1885 letter to Mark Twain is quoted by courtesy of the Mark Twain Project at the University of California at Berkeley. Clemens hoped to get the *Century* series for his own publishing house and advised Charles Webster in a March 16, 1885 letter to "[k]eep on good terms with the *Century* people. We will presently prove to them that they can't *afford* to publish their war book themselves—we must have it." *Mark Twain's Letters to his Publishers, 1867–1894*, ed. Hamlin Hill (Berkeley: University of California Press, 1967), 184. Likewise, Johnson exploited Clemens's connection to General Grant to assist him in getting the "General's name on our Copyright list," as he wrote in the July 16 letter, requesting that the humorist "could find time to put the question clearly to the General."

23. Johnson's unpublished May 11, 1885 letter to Mark Twain is quoted by courtesy of the Mark Twain Project at the University of California at Berkeley. Mark Twain, *Mark Twain's Notebooks and Journals*, vol. 1, *1855–1873*, ed. Frederick Anderson, Michael Frank, and Kenneth Sanderson (Berkeley: University of California Press, 1975), 84–89; Twain, *Autobiography*, 300; Mark Twain, "Map of Paris," in *Mark Twain: Collected Tales, Sketches, Speeches, and Essays, 1852–1890* (New York: Library of America, 1992), 471–76.

24. One can read the details of Grant's final days in Mark Perry, *Grant and Twain: The Story of an American Friendship* (New York: Random House, 2004), 219–27; Twain, *Autobiography*, 253.

25. See Grant, *Personal Memoirs of U. S. Grant*, 849; John Y. Simon, "Introduction," in *General Grant by Mathew Arnold with a Rejoinder by Mark Twain* (Kent, Ohio: Kent State University Press, 1995), 3; Twain, *Autobiography*, 251; *Century*, "The 'Century' War Series," 29 (March 1885): 78.

26. Twain, "The Private History of a Campaign That Failed," 872–73; Peter Messent, *The Short Works of Mark Twain: A Critical Study* (Philadelphia: University of Pennsylvania Press, 2001), 144; Bruce Michelson, *Mark Twain on the Loose: A Comic Writer and the American Self* (Amherst: University of Massachusetts Press, 1995), 11; David W. Blight, *Race and Reunion: The Civil War in American Memory* (Cambridge, Mass.: Harvard University Press, 2001), 175; John Bird, *Mark Twain and Metaphor* (Columbia: University of Missouri Press, 2007), 98.

27. Twain, "The Private History of a Campaign That Failed," 867–68; Twain, *Life on the Mississippi*, 500–501; Mark Twain, "My Military History," in *Mark Twain: Collected Tales, Sketches, Speeches, and Essays, 1852–1890* (New York: Library of America, 1992), 679. Will Bowen's unpublished December 10, 1889 letter to Mark Twain is quoted by courtesy of the Mark Twain Project at the University of California at Berkeley.

28. Twain, *Mark Twain's Letters*, vol. 1, *1853–1866*, 165.

29. Edgar M. Branch, "Introduction," in *Mark Twain's Letters*, vol. 1, *1853–1866*, xxi; Paul Fatout, *Mark Twain in Virginia City* (Bloomington: Indiana University Press, 1964), 63; Twain, "The Private History of a Campaign That Failed," 868–69, 878.

30. Twain, "The Private History of a Campaign That Failed," 874–75.

31. Edgar M. Branch, *Mark Twain and the Starchy Boys* (Elmira, N.Y.: Elmira College Center for Mark Twain Studies, 1992), 39; Wecter, *Sam Clemens of Hannibal*, 182–83; McReynolds, *Missouri*, 232. The quotation from Bates and information about confiscation is from

Fellman, *Inside War*, 86, 92, 94. Mark Twain, letter to unidentified person, 1891, in *Mark Twain's Letters*, ed. Albert Bigelow Paine (New York: Gabriel Wells, 1923), vol. 2, 541.

32. Twain, "The Private History of a Campaign That Failed," 877; Richard Taylor, *Destruction and Reconstruction: Personal Experiences of the Late War* (New York: D. Appleton and Company, 1879), 126; Alan Gribben, *Mark Twain's Library: A Reconstruction*, 2 vols. (Boston: G. K. Hall, 1980), vol. 1, 689; Twain, "My Military History," 680; Grant, *Personal Memoirs of U. S. Grant*, 969, 970.

33. Considerable confusion surrounds the several soldiers named Thomas Harris. Some sources list a Thomas A. Harris as a Confederate soldier who was born in Virginia and served primarily in Virginia. Other sources give that soldier's name as "Thomas H. Harris." At the same time, Lieutenant Colonel Thomas H. Harris served as assistant adjutant-general in the Union Army. Another Thomas Harris, a true bushwhacker, rode in Missouri and Kansas with Frank and Jesse James and William Quantrill; see John McCorkle, *Three Years with Quantrill* (Norman: University of Oklahoma Press, 1992). Neither of these was Twain's Thomas Harris, whose obituaries all give "A" as his middle initial for "Alexander." Twain, "The Private History of a Campaign That Failed," 877; Twain, *Autobiography*, 56–57; Elmo Howell, "Mark Twain and the Civil War," *Ball State University Forum* 13, no. 4 (1972): 54.

34. The masthead of the *Missouri Courier* for February 23, 1854, listed Thomas A. Harris as editor. For Twain's service as an apprentice on the *Courier*, see Edgar M. Branch, "Introduction," in *Early Tales and Sketches*, vol. 1, *1851–1864*, ed. Edgar M. Branch (Berkeley: University of California Press, 1979), 5; "Gen. T. A. Harris Dead," *Daily Globe-Democrat* (St. Louis), April 10, 1895, 2, column 4; "Gen. Thos. A. Harris," *Palmyra Spectator* (Missouri), April 11, 1895, 1. column 6; Bruce Allardice, *More Generals in Gray* (Baton Rouge: Louisiana State University Press, 1995), 121; Ezra Warner and W. Buck Yearns, *Biographical Register of the Confederate Congress* (Baton Rouge: Louisiana State University Press, 1975), 109–10.

35. *Journal of the Congress of the Confederate States of America, 1861–1865* (Washington: Government Printing Office, 1904), vol. 1, 544. For Harris's actions against summary executions, see *The War of the Rebellion: A Compilation of the Official Records of the Union and Confederate Armies*, series 2, vol. 4 (Washington: Government Printing Office, 1899), 784–85, 793–94, 807–8; *Journal of the Congress of the Confederate States of America, 1861–1865* (Washington: Government Printing Office, 1905), vol. 5, 122, 364, 524–25; *Journal of the Congress of the Confederate States of America, 1861–1865* (Washington: Government Printing Office, 1905), vol. 6, 182; Richard N. Current, ed., *Encyclopedia of the Confederacy* (New York: Simon and Schuster, 1993), vol. 2, 747; Jon L. Wakelyn, "Thomas Harris," in *Biographical Dictionary of the Confederacy*, ed. Frank E. Vandiver (Westport, Conn.: Greenwood Press, 1977), 218.

36. Grant, *Memoirs*, 164, 763; Twain, "The Private History of a Campaign That Failed," 878–79; Philip W. Leon, *Mark Twain and West Point: America's Favorite Storyteller at the United States Military Academy* (Toronto: ECW Press, 1996), 72; Gerber, "Mark Twain's 'Private Campaign,'" 42–43; Twain, *Mark Twain's Notebooks and Journals*, vol. 3, *1883–1891*, 105; Albert Bigelow Paine, *Mark Twain: A Biography*, 2 vols. (New York: Harper & Brothers, 1912), vol. 1, 163; Twain, "Villagers of 1840–3," 28; Twain, *Autobiography*, 72; Frémont, "In Command in Missouri," 287; David M. Potter, *The Impending Crisis, 1848–1861* (New York: Harper Torchbooks, 1976), 200; James M. McPherson, *Ordeal by Fire: The Civil War and Reconstruction* (New York: Alfred A. Knopf, 1982), 154.

37. Frémont, "In Command in Missouri," 288.

38. Johnson's unpublished May 11, 1885 letter to Mark Twain is quoted by courtesy of the Mark Twain Project at the University of California at Berkeley. Twain, "Private History of a Campaign That Failed," 881–82; Twain, *Autobiography*, 102.

39. Twain, "Private History of a Campaign That Failed," 880. Johnson's unpublished May 11, 1885 letter to Mark Twain is quoted by courtesy of the Mark Twain Project at the University of California at Berkeley. Gaines M. Foster, *Ghosts of the Confederacy: Defeat, the Lost Cause, and the Emergence of the New South, 1865 to 1913* (New York: Oxford University Press, 1987), 196; John Warwick Daniel, "Conquered Nations," in *Speeches and Orations of John Warwick Daniel*, ed. Edward M. Daniel (Lynchburg: J. P. Bell Co., 1911), 127–28; Koselleck, *The Practice of Conceptual History*, 83; Twain, *Tom Sawyer's Conspiracy*, 165–66.

40. Abraham Lincoln, "Fourth Annual Message," December 6, 1864, in *A Compilation of the Messages and Papers of the Presidents*, vol. 8, ed. James D. Richardson (New York: Bureau of National Literature, 1897), 3452–53; McReynolds, *Missouri*, 260. The loyalty oath is printed in *A Compilation of the Messages and Papers of the Presidents*, vol. 8, ed. James D. Richardson (New York: Bureau of National Literature, 1897), 3508–9.

41. James Russell Lowell, *The Poetical Works of James Russell Lowell* (Boston: Houghton Mifflin and Company, 1890), 297; John W. De Forest, *A Union Officer in the Reconstruction*, ed. James H. Croushore and David Morris Potter (New Haven: Yale University Press, 1948), 5.

42. Albion W. Tourgée, *A Fool's Errand* (Cambridge, Mass.: Harvard University Press, 1961), 109; Edward Alfred Pollard, *The Lost Cause: A New Southern History of the War of the Confederates* (New York: E. B. Treat, 1868), 750.

43. Bush, *Mark Twain and the Spiritual Crisis of his Age*, 176; Arthur G. Pettit, *Mark Twain and the South* (Lexington: University Press of Kentucky, 1974), 9, 33, 30; Roy Blount Jr., "Mark Twain's Reconstruction," *The Atlantic Monthly* 288 (July–August 2001): 81; Howells, "My Mark Twain," 277.

44. Forrest G. Robinson, "Afterword," in *Merry Tales by Mark Twain* (New York: Oxford University Press, 1996), 9; Hamlin Hill, "Mark Twain Goes to War," *The Dial* (April 1981): 43; Koselleck, *The Practice of Conceptual History*, 76–77; Twain, *Life on the Mississippi*, 409; Paine, *Mark Twain*, vol. 1, 161.

45. Twain, *Life on the Mississippi*, 491, 472, 538, 540; Koselleck, *The Practice of Conceptual History*, 80; Daniel, "Conquered Nations," 119.

46. Twain, *Life on the Mississippi*, 500–501, 489, 375; Twain, *Mark Twain's Notebooks and Journals*, vol. 2, *1877–1883*, 553–54. Clemens removed significant material from *Life on the Mississippi* in which, it is sometimes claimed, his criticism of the South was more pronounced. Guy Cardwell's refutation of that argument is convincing. "Mark Twain, James R. Osgood, and Those 'Suppressed' Passages," *New England Quarterly* 46, no. 2 (1973): 163–88.

47. Mark Twain, "Blue and Gray Pay Tribute to Lincoln," *The New York Times*, February 12, 1901, 1. Allison Ensor has noted that several versions of the speech exist and favors the Paine text over the *Times* version "on the assumption that he had access to a copy of the speech." "Lincoln, Mark Twain, and Lincoln Memorial University," *Lincoln Herald* 78 (Summer 1976): 51 n. 18. Regrettably, given Paine's frequent editorial malpractice, one might make a strong argument in favor of the *Times* version. For a critique of Paine's editorial practices, see Joe Fulton, "The Lost Manuscript Conclusion to Mark Twain's 'Corn-Pone Opinions': An

Editorial History and an Edition of the Restored Text," *American Literary Realism* 37 (2005): 238–58; Blight, *Race and Reunion*, 357, 205.

48. Louis J. Budd, "Hiding Out in Public: Mark Twain as a Speaker," *Studies in American Fiction* 13 (1985): 135; Mark Twain, "Plymouth Rock and the Pilgrims," in *Mark Twain: Collected Tales, Sketches, Speeches, and Essays, 1891–1910* (New York: Library of America, 1992), 782–85; Neil Schmitz, "Mark Twain, Traitor," *Arizona Quarterly* 63 (2007): 36.

49. Mark Twain and Charles Dudley Warner, *The Gilded Age: A Tale of Today* (New York: Gabriel Wells, 1922), vol. 2, 176–77; Mark Twain, "Battle Hymn of the Republic (Brought Down to Date)," in *Mark Twain: Collected Tales, Sketches, Speeches, and Essays, 1891–1910* (New York: Library of America, 1992), 475; Mark Twain, "To the Person Sitting in Darkness," in *Mark Twain: Collected Tales, Sketches, Speeches, and Essays, 1891–1910* (New York: Library of America, 1992), 471–72; Mark Twain, "As Regards Patriotism," in *Mark Twain: Collected Tales, Sketches, Speeches, and Essays, 1891–1910* (New York: Library of America, 1992), 477.

50. Mark Twain, "The United States of Lyncherdom," in *Mark Twain: Collected Tales, Sketches, Speeches, and Essays, 1891–1910* (New York: Library of America, 1992), 479.

51. Twain, "The United States of Lyncherdom," 479, 480, 481, 482. Clemens viewed lynching as unjust and evil. In at least one instance, however, he advocated it, privately, when two scions of wealthy families murdered a young female servant after her seduction and pregnancy. "They ought to be taken from Court & lynched—if I were kin to the girl I would kill them on the threshold of the court." See Twain, *Mark Twain's Notebooks and Journals*, vol. 2, *1877–1883*, 482–83.

52. Twain, "The United States of Lyncherdom," 485; Schmitz, "Mark Twain's Civil War: Humor's Reconstructive Writing," 81; Blight, *Race and Reunion*, 357.

53. Mark Twain, "The War Prayer," in *Mark Twain: Collected Tales, Sketches, Speeches, and Essays, 1891–1910* (New York: Library of America, 1992), 654–55.

CHAPTER TWO

EPIGRAPHS: Abraham Lincoln, "Second Annual Message," December 1, 1862, in *A Compilation of the Messages and Papers of the Presidents*, vol. 7, ed. James D. Richardson (New York: Bureau of National Literature, 1897), 3343; Mark Twain, *Mark Twain's Letters*, vol. 1, *1853–1866*, ed. Edgar Marquess Branc, Michael B. Frank, and Kenneth M. Sanderson (Berkeley: University of California Press, 1988), 171.

1. Mark Twain, "Roughing It Lecture," in *Mark Twain Speaking*, ed. Paul Fatout (Iowa City: University of Iowa Press, 1976), 49.

2. Twain, *Mark Twain's Letters*, vol. 1, *1853–1866*, 132; Kenneth Owens, "Pattern and Structure in Western Territorial Politics," *The Western Historical Quarterly* 1 (1970): 377; Gunther Peck, "Manly Gambles: The Politics of Risk on the Comstock Lode, 1860–1880," *Journal of Social History* 26 (1993): 714; Joseph Goodman, "Virginia City," in *The History of Nevada*, ed. Sam Davis, vol. 1 (Las Vegas: Nevada Publications, 1913), 472; Wells Drury, "Journalism," in *The History of Nevada*, ed. Sam Davis, vol. 1 (Las Vegas: Nevada Publications, 1913), 485; see also Myron Angel, *History of Nevada* (Oakland: Thompson & West, 1881), 291–332.

3. Mark Twain, *The Autobiography of Mark Twain*, ed. Charles Neider (New York: Harp-

erPerennial, 1959), 103; Senator William M. Stewart, *Reminiscences of Senator William M. Stewart of Nevada,* ed. George Rothwell Brown (New York: The Neale Publishing Company, 1908), 220; Mark Twain, "Letter from Mark Twain" (May 16, 1863), in *Early Tales and Sketches,* vol. 1, *1851–1864,* ed. Edgar M. Branch (Berkeley: University of California Press, 1979), 250–51; Mark Twain, *Roughing It,* ed. Harriet Elinor Smith and Edgar M. Branch (Berkeley: University of California Press, 1993), 58.

4. Mark Twain, "A Bloody Massacre Near Carson," in *Early Tales and Sketches,* vol. 1, *1851–1864,* ed. Edgar M. Branch (Berkeley: University of California Press, 1979), 324–25; Richard G. Lillard, "Contemporary Reaction to 'The Empire City Massacre,'" *American Literature* 16 (November 1944): 198; Mark Twain, "A Couple of Sad Experiences," in *Mark Twain: Collected Tales, Sketches, Speeches, and Essays, 1852–1890* (New York: Library of America, 1992), 392–94, 389. Twain described the landscape as a singed cat in "Washoe.—'Information Wanted,'" in *Early Tales and Sketches,* vol. 1, *1851–1864,* ed. Edgar M. Branch (Berkeley: University of California Press, 1979), 368.

5. Twain, "Petrified Man," in *Early Tales and Sketches,* vol. 1, *1851–1864,* ed. Edgar M. Branch (Berkeley: University of California Press, 1979), 159. See the discussion of judicial appointments in Hon. Frank H. Norcross, "The Bench and the Bar," in *The History of Nevada,* ed. Sam Davis (Las Vegas: Nevada Publications, 1913), 273–314; Jennifer L. Weber, *Copperheads: The Rise and Fall of Lincoln's Opponents in the North* (New York: Oxford University Press, 2006), 2–3; Twain, *Mark Twain's Letters,* vol. 1, *1853–1866,* 242, 170; Louis J. Budd, "Notes," in *Mark Twain: Collected Tales, Sketches, Speeches, and Essays, 1852–1890* (New York: Library of America, 1992), 1027 n. 19.16; Mark Twain, "'Mark Twain's' Letter. (July 12, 1863)," *Twainian* 11 (January–February, 1952): 2; Twain, "A Couple of Sad Experiences," 391–92.

6. Paul J. Carter, "The Influence of the Nevada Frontier on Mark Twain," *Western Humanities Review* 13 (Winter 1959): 68; Twain, "A Couple of Sad Experiences," 389, 392; "Horrible," *Daily News* (Gold Hill), October 28, 1863, 3; "Still Harping On," *Daily News* (Gold Hill), October 30, 1863, 3; "An Asylum Needed," *Daily News* (Gold Hill), November 11, 1863, 2.

7. Carter, "The Influence of the Nevada Frontier on Mark Twain," 68; Henry Nash Smith, *Mark Twain of the Enterprise: Newspaper Articles and Other Documents 1862–1864* (Berkeley: University of California Press, 1957), 19; Mark Twain, "Bigler vs. Tahoe," in *Early Tales and Sketches,* vol. 1, *1851–1864,* ed. Edgar M. Branch (Berkeley: University of California Press, 1979), 290; Joseph Coulombe, *Mark Twain and the American West* (Columbia: University of Missouri Press, 2003), 99; Paul Fatout, *Mark Twain in Virginia City* (Bloomington: Indiana University Press, 1964), 79; "Tahoe vs. Bigler," *Daily News* (Gold Hill), November 5, 1863, 1.

8. Mark Twain, "Unfortunate Blunder," in *Early Tales and Sketches,* vol. 1, *1851–1864,* ed. Edgar M. Branch (Berkeley: University of California Press, 1979), 287; Walter McDougall, *Throes of Democracy: The American Civil War Era: 1829–1877* (New York: HarperCollins, 2008), 474; Patricia L. Faust, ed., *Historical Times Illustrated Encyclopedia of the Civil War* (New York: Harper & Row, 1986), 63; Frank L. Klement, "Catholics as Copperheads During the Civil War," *The Catholic Historical Review* 80 (1994): 37.

9. Lucius Beebe, *Comstock Commotion, The Story of the Territorial Enterprise and Virginia City News* (Stanford: Stanford University Press, 1954), 7–8; John W. DeForest, *Miss Ravenel's Conversion from Secession to Loyalty* (New York: Penguin, 2000), 147; Twain, *Mark Twain's Letters,* vol. 1, *1853–1866,* 144–45.

10. Twain, *Mark Twain's Letters*, vol. 1, *1853–1866*, 165, 171–72 n. 4; Edwin C. McReynolds, *Missouri: A History of the Crossroads State* (Norman: University of Oklahoma Press, 1962), 239–43; Smith, *Mark Twain of the Enterprise*, 19, 17. A notable exception to commentary on the letter is Kenneth Lynn's assessment that "the point of view, as betrayed by the use of 'they' and 'our,' is clearly Confederate." *Mark Twain and Southwestern Humor* (Westport, Conn.: Greenwood Press, 1959), 144; "Questionable Taste," *Daily Union* (Virginia City), July 6, 1864, 2; Charles G. Halpine [Miles O'Reilly], *The Poetical Works of Charles G. Halpine*, ed. Robert B. Roosevelt (New York, 1869), 289; W. W. Dixon, "Sketch of the Life and Character of William H. Clagett," in *Contributions to the Historical Society of Montana*, vol. 4 (Boston: J. S. Canner and Company, Inc., 1996), 249–50, 256; "W. H. Clagett," *Daily Union* (Virginia City), October 9, 1864, 2; Honorable W. H. Clagett, *Money, Banks, Panics, and Prosperity* (Washington, D.C.: Cromwell Brothers, 1898), 27.

11. Twain, *Mark Twain's Letters*, vol. 1, *1853–1866*, 171–72, 275; Smith, *Mark Twain of the Enterprise*, 17.

12. Mark Twain, "The Great Prize Fight," in *Mark Twain's San Francisco*, ed. Bernard Taper (New York: McGraw-Hill, 1963), 16, 20, 23, 22; Winfield J. Davis, *History of Political Conventions in California, 1849–1892* (Sacramento: California State Library, 1893), 192–96; Sylvia S. Larsen, "Low, Frederick Ferdinand," in *American National Biography Online* (New York: Oxford University Press, 2000), access date, June 10, 2009; Twain, "A Couple of Sad Experiences," 388–89.

13. Twain, *Mark Twain's Letters*, vol. 1, *1853–1866*, 275.

14. Mark Twain, "Nevada State Constitutional Convention; Third House, Carson City, December 13, 1863," in *Mark Twain of the Enterprise*, ed. Henry Nash Smith (Berkeley: University of California Press, 1957), 102–3; Twain, *Roughing It*, 376; Mark Twain, "The Facts in the Case of the Great Beef Contract," in *Mark Twain: Collected Tales, Sketches, Speeches, and Essays, 1852–1890* (New York: Library of America, 1992), 373.

15. Mark Twain, "Letter from Mark Twain, Carson City, December 12, 1863," in *Mark Twain of the Enterprise*, ed. Henry Nash Smith (Berkeley: University of California Press, 1957), 100–105; Beebe, *Comstock Commotion*, 40.

16. Twain, "Letter from Mark Twain, Carson City, December 12, 1863," 108; quoted in Fatout, *Mark Twain in Virginia City*, 148.

17. Twain, "Letter from Mark Twain, Carson City, December 12, 1863," 109.

18. Smith, *Mark Twain of the Enterprise*, 101; Claude M. Simpson, "Captain Jim and the 'Third House,'" *Western Folklore* 9, no. 2 (1950): 105, 109. The *Leader* is quoted in Fatout, *Mark Twain in Virginia City*, 61. Mark Twain, "Mark Twain's Letter, (August 2, 1863)," *Twainian* 11 (March–April, 1952): 2.

19. Frank Fuller quotes Nye's comment in "Letters from Frank Fuller," *Twainian* 15 (July–August, 1956), 1. "The Virginia Press," *Aurora Daily Times*, December 1, 1863, 2; Sam Davis, "Political History," in *The History of Nevada*, vol. 1, ed. Sam Davis (Las Vegas: Nevada Publications, 1913), 420.

20. Twain, *Autobiography*, 128, 113; Edgar M. Branch, *The Literary Apprenticeship of Mark Twain* (Urbana: University of Illinois Press, 1950), 78–79; Mark Twain, "A Duel Prevented," in *Early Tales and Sketches*, vol. 1, *1851–1864*. ed. Edgar M. Branch et al. (Berkeley: University of California Press, 1979), 265–66; Mark Twain, "Another Traitor—Hang Him!" in Paul Fatout,

Mark Twain in Virginia City (Bloomington: Indiana University Press, 1964), 180; John Denton Carter, "Abraham Lincoln and the California Patronage," *The American Historical Review* 48 (1943): 497, 499–500; Fatout, *Mark Twain in Virginia City,* 180.

21. Charles J. Stillé, *History of the United States Sanitary Commission. Being the General Report of its Work During the War of the Rebellion* (Philadelphia: J. B. Lippincott & Co., 1866), 63, 547, 201; Mark Twain, *Mark Twain's Notebooks and Journals,* vol. 1, *1855–1873,* ed. Frederick Anderson, Michael B. Frank, and Kenneth M. Sanderson (Berkeley: University of California Press, 1975), 477.

22. Mark Twain, "Letter from Mark Twain, Carson City, January 14, 1864," [Miss Clapp's School], in *Early Tales and Sketches,* vol. 1, *1851–1864,* ed. Edgar M. Branch (Berkeley: University of California Press, 1979), 334–38.

23. Mark Twain, "The Sanitary Ball," in *Early Tales and Sketches,* vol. 1, *1851–1864,* ed. Edgar M. Branch (Berkeley: University of California Press, 1979), 185, 187; Mark Twain, "Those Blasted Children," in *Early Tales and Sketches,* vol. 1, *1851–1864,* ed. Edgar M. Branch (Berkeley: University of California Press, 1979), 352; Mark Twain, "The Lick House Ball," in *Early Tales and Sketches,* vol. 1, *1851–1864,* ed. Edgar M. Branch (Berkeley: University of California Press, 1979), 319; Ulysses S. Grant, *Memoirs and Selected Letters, Personal Memoirs of U. S. Grant, Selected Letters 1839–1865* (New York: Library of America, 1990), 208.

24. Mark Twain, "Letter from Mark Twain, Carson City, April 25, 1864," in *Mark Twain of the Enterprise,* ed. Henry Nash Smith (Berkeley: University of California Press, 1957), 181.

25. Quoted in Ivan Benson, *Mark Twain's Western Years* (Stanford: Stanford University Press, 1938), 106.

26. Twain, *Autobiography,* 76; Twain, *Roughing It,* 294; Mark Twain, "History of the Gold and Silver Bars—How They Do Things in Washoe," in *Mark Twain of the Enterprise,* ed. Henry Nash Smith (Berkeley: University of California Press, 1957), 187. Historian Effie Mona Mack clarifies some of Clemens's details in the story in *Mark Twain in Nevada* (New York: Charles Scribner's Sons, 1947), 308–12.

27. Mark Twain, "The Famous Sanitary Flour Sack," *New York Tribune,* December 13, 1870, 5; Twain, "History of the Gold and Silver Bars—How They Do Things in Washoe," 186, 188; Stillé, *History of the United States Sanitary Commission,* 208–9, 239–40, 546. Stillé notes that the chapter on California and Nevada, quoted in this paragraph, was written by the "Rev. Dr. Bellows, President of the Commission," iv. Clemens and Bellows later met in San Francisco and became friends.

28. Lawrence Berkove, *The Sagebrush Anthology* (Columbia: University of Missouri Press, 2006), 5–7; Mark Twain, "How Is It?—How It Is," [Fragment], in *Mark Twain's Letters,* vol. 1, *1853–1866,* ed. Edgar Marquess Branc, Michael B. Frank, and Kenneth M. Sanderson (Berkeley: University of California Press, 1988), 289; Stewart, *Reminiscences of Senator William M. Stewart of Nevada,* 220.

29. "Rogues," *Sacramento Daily Union,* May 23, 1864, 3; "The Gridley Sack of Flour and the Sacramento Star," *Reese River Reveille,* May 31, 1864, 2.

30. Hubert Howe Bancroft, *History of Nevada, 1540–1888* (San Francisco: The History Company, 1890), 162; David Goodman Croly, *Miscegenation: The Theory of the Blending of the Races, Applied to the American White Man and Negro* (New York: H. Dexter, Hamilton & Co., 1864), ii; "Political Miscegenation," *The Liberator,* April 8, 1864, 1; Noah Webster,

An American Dictionary of the English Language, Thoroughly Revised, and Greatly Enlarged and Improved, by Chauncey A. Goodrich and Noah Porter (Springfield: G. C. Merriam, 1864).

31. See Sidney Kaplan's exemplary discussion of the pamphlet and its importance to the 1864 election in "The Miscegenation Issue in the Election of 1864," *The Journal of Negro History* 34 (1949): 274–343; Croly, *Miscegenation,* 50, 61, 19; "Miscegenation Sent Home," *Sacramento Daily Union,* June 1, 1864, 2.

32. P. T. Barnum, *The Humbugs of the World, An Account of Humbugs, Delusions, Impositions, Quackeries, Deceits and Deceivers Generally, In All Ages* (New York: Carleton Publisher, 1865), 277; Theodore Tilton, "The Union of Races," *The Independent,* February 25, 1864, 4; "Pamphlets," *The Methodist Quarterly Review* 16 (April 1864): 354; McDougall, *Throes of Democracy,* 358; "Miscegenation," *Sacramento Daily Union,* May 21, 1864, 2; "Civilization in the Free and 'Slave' States," *The Old Guard* 2 (May 1864): 8; Croly, *Miscegenation,* 49; D.W.B., "Our Washington Correspondence," *The Independent,* March 3, 1864, 1.

33. James E. Caron, *Mark Twain: Unsanctified Newspaper Reporter* (Columbia: University of Missouri Press, 2008), 151; Major G. W. Ingalls, "Washoe County," in *The History of Nevada,* ed. Sam Davis, vol. 2 (Las Vegas: Nevada Publications, 1913), 1022–23; "The Slander on the Teachers," *The Liberator,* April 8, 1864, 1.

34. Twain, *Mark Twain's Letters,* vol. 1, *1853–1866,* 289; Campaign Document, No. 11, "Miscegenation Indorsed by the Republican Party" ("Sold at 13 Park Row, New York, and at all Democratic Newspaper Offices, at $1 per 1,000 pages," New York: n.d.), 8.

35. Twain, *Mark Twain's Letters,* vol. 1: *1853–1866,* 287–88, 296; Mark Twain, "Miscegenation," in *Mark Twain of the Enterprise,* ed. Henry Nash Smith (Berkeley: University of California Press, 1957), 197; Stillé, *History of the United States Sanitary Commission* 541; Twain, *Mark Twain's Letters,* vol. 1, *1853–1866,* 291. The unsigned articles "How It Is" and "The 'How Is It' Issue" are reprinted in Twain, *Mark Twain's Letters,* vol. 1, *1853–1866,* 290–91.

36. Twain, *Mark Twain's Letters,* vol. 1, *1853–1866,* 294, 301, 288.

37. Caron, *Mark Twain,* 151 n. 7; James Cox, *Mark Twain: The Fate of Humor* (Princeton, N.J.: Princeton University Press, 1966), 17; Fred Lorch, "Review of *Mark Twain of the Enterprise,*" *American Literature* 30 (1958): 127; Fatout, *Mark Twain in Virginia City,* 212; Stephen Fender, "'The Prodigal in a Far Country Chawing of Husks': Mark Twain's Search for Style in the West," *Modern Language Review* 71 (1976): 751; Arthur G. Pettit, "Mark Twain's Attitude Toward the Negro in the West, 1861–1867," *The Western Historical Quarterly* 1 (1970): 55; Christopher Wienandt, "Mark Twain, Nevada Frontier Journalism, and the Territorial Enterprise: Crisis in Credibility" (Ph.D. diss., University of North Texas, 1995), 157.

38. "Hoity! Toity!!" *Daily News* (Gold Hill), May 24, 1864, 2. The editorial from the Virginia City *Evening Bulletin* for October 28, 1863, is quoted in Fender, "'The Prodigal in a Far Country Chawing of Husks,'" 750. One assumes that Paine was being disingenuous when he wrote that "the original grievance, whatever it was, was lost sight of in the fireworks and vitriol-throwing of personal recrimination" between Twain and Laird. Albert B. Paine, *Mark Twain: A Biography,* 2 vols. (New York: Harper & Brothers, 1912), vol. 1, 249; Coulombe, *Mark Twain and the American West,* 38.

39. Quoted in Lawrence J. Berkove, "Ethical Records of Twain and his Circle of Sagebrush Journalists," *Quarry Farm Papers,* no. 5 (Elmira: Elmira College Center for Mark Twain Studies, 1994), 6.

40. "Mark Twain," *Humboldt Register,* June 11, 1864, 3. The article from the *Daily Old Piute* was reprinted in the latter portion of the article in the *Humboldt Register.*

41. Twain, *Autobiography,* 118; "An Exile," *Daily News* (Gold Hill), May 30, 1864, 2; William Dwight Whitney, *Century Dictionary,* 6 vols. (New York: The Century Company, 1889); "What's the News?" *Daily News* (Gold Hill), June 8, 1864, 2; Twain, *Mark Twain's Letters,* vol. 1, *1853–1866,* 297–98.

42. Mark Twain, "How I Escaped Being Killed in a Duel," in *Mark Twain: Collected Tales, Sketches, Speeches, and Essays, 1852–1890* (New York: Library of America, 1992), 543, 544. Twain, *Autobiography,* 115; "Mark Twain," *Humboldt Register,* June 11, 1864, 3.

CHAPTER THREE

EPIGRAPHS: James Ryder Randall, "Maryland," in *Poets of the Civil War,* ed. J. D. McClatchy (New York: Library of America, 2005), 180; Mark Twain, *Mark Twain's Letters,* vol. 1, *1853–1866,* ed. Edgar Marquess Branc, Michael B. Frank, and Kenneth M. Sanderson (Berkeley: University of California Press, 1988), 322.

1. Mark Twain, *Mark Twain's Notebooks and Journals,* vol. 1, *1855–1873,* ed. Frederick Anderson, Michael Frank, and Kenneth Sanderson (Berkeley: University of California Press, 1975),75, 75 n. 21.

2. Mark Twain, *The Autobiography of Mark Twain,* ed. Charles Neider (New York: HarperPerennial, 1959), 120, 122; Twain, *Mark Twain's Letters,* vol. 1, *1853–1866,* 312, 322, 328, 323; William Dean Howells, "Mark Twain: An Inquiry," in *William Dean Howells as Critic,* ed. Edwin H. Cady (Boson: Routledge, 1973), 351.

3. Twain, *Mark Twain's Letters,* vol. 1, *1853–1866,* 368; Mark Twain, "A Philanthropic Nation," in *Clemens of the Call,* ed. Edgar M. Branch (Berkeley: University of California Press, 1969), 110; Mark Twain, "Fourth of July" (July 6, 1864), in *Clemens of the Call,* ed. Edgar M. Branch (Berkeley: University of California Press, 1969), 89.

4. Mark Twain, "Lucretia Smith's Soldier," in *Early Tales and Sketches,* vol. 2, *1864–1865,* ed. Edgar M. Branch (Berkeley: University of California Press, 1981), 128.

5. Mark Twain, "A Couple of Sad Experiences," in *Mark Twain: Collected Tales, Sketches, Speeches, and Essays, 1852–1890* (New York: Library of America, 1992), 389; "Camp Fun," *Alta California,* April 3, 1863, 1. For the original southern version by "Hard Cracker," see "Foot Cavalry Chronicle," *Southern Illustrated News,* October 18, 1862, 3; "Untitled (Shiloh Dutchman Joke)," *Sacramento Daily Union,* May 28, 1864, 3; Daniel Aaron, *The Unwritten War* (New York: Knopf, 1973), 134.

6. For information on "Bluemass Pills," see the entries for "Bluemass," "Blue Pills," and "Mercury" in the Goodrich and Porter 1864 revision of Noah Webster's *An American Dictionary of the English Language* and the 1889 edition of the *Century Dictionary,* 6 vols., ed. William Dwight Whitney (New York: The Century Company, 1889).

7. Edgar M. Branch, "Samuel Clemens and the Copperheads of 1864," *Mad River Review* 2 (1967): 6; Mark Twain, "Calaboose Theatricals," in *Clemens of the Call,* ed. Edgar M. Branch (Berkeley: University of California Press, 1969), 141; Mark Twain, "Enlisted for the War," in *Clemens of the Call,* ed. Edgar M. Branch (Berkeley: University of California Press, 1969),

145; Mark Twain, "Lucretia Smith's Soldier," in *Early Tales and Sketches*, vol. 2, *1864–1865*, ed. Edgar M. Branch et al. (Berkeley: University of California Press, 1981), 130; William Dean Howells, "Editha," in *The American Tradition in Literature*, 8th ed., vol. 2, ed. George and Barbara Perkins (New York: McGraw-Hill, 1994), 408.

8. Twain, "Lucretia Smith's Soldier," 131.

9. Twain, "Lucretia Smith's Soldier," 131–32.

10. Twain, "Lucretia Smith's Soldier," 132–33.

11. Mark Twain, "Blue and Gray Pay Tribute to Lincoln," *The New York Times*, February 12, 1901, 1.

12. Edgar M. Branch, *The Literary Apprenticeship of Mark Twain* (Urbana: University of Illinois Press, 1950), 118; Twain, "Lucretia Smith's Soldier," 131; Abraham Lincoln, "Second Inaugural Address," in *A Compilation of the Messages and Papers of the Presidents*, vol. 8, ed. James D. Richardson (New York: Bureau of National Literature, 1897), 3478; Drew Gilpin Faust, *This Republic of Suffering: Death and the American Civil War* (New York: Alfred A. Knopf, 2008), 194.

13. Ivan Benson, *Mark Twain's Western Years* (Stanford: Stanford University Press, 1938), 115.

14. Barbara Cloud, *The Business of Newspapers on the Western Frontier* (Reno: University of Nevada Press, 1992), 160; "A French Secession Organ," *Alta California*, April 5, 1865, 1; see also, "Is There no Punishment for Newspaper Treason?" *Alta California*, November 8, 1863, 2. Franklin Walker lists several such examples from Stockton, San Jose, Tulare, and Visalia in *San Francisco's Literary Frontier* (New York: Alfred A. Knopf, 1939), 111; George F. Root, "Just Before the Battle, Mother," in *The American Civil War: An Anthology of Essential Writings*, ed. Ian Frederick Finseth (New York: Routledge, 2006), 353.

15. "An Expression of Anger—A Word of Caution," *Daily Evening Bulletin*, April 18, 1865, 3; "The Effect in San Francisco," *Alta California*, April 16, 1865, 1; "Irregular Justice," *Dramatic Chronicle*, April 17, 1865, 3; "Treason Mills Under Repair," *Dramatic Chronicle*, April 26, 1865, 2.

16. Mark Twain's comment about Lincoln is from a letter written to Bayard Taylor and is reproduced in John Schultz, "New Letters of Mark Twain," *American Literature* 8 (1936): 49. "A Good 'Goak,'" *Daily Appeal*, (Marysville, Calif.), March 15, 1865, 2; Walker, *San Francisco's Literary Frontier*, 183–84.

17. Mark Twain, "Answers to Correspondents" (June 10, 1865), in *Early Tales and Sketches*, vol. 2, *1864–1865*, ed. Edgar M. Branch (Berkeley: University of California Press, 1981), 182–86; Mark Twain, "Answers to Correspondents" (June 3, 1865), in *Early Tales and Sketches*, vol. 2, *1864–1865*, ed. Edgar M. Branch (Berkeley: University of California Press, 1981), 178. See Albert Furtwangler, *Assassin on Stage: Brutus, Hamlet, and the Death of Lincoln* (Urbana: University of Illinois Press, 1991), 107–8. For the entire variety of exclamations the eyewitnesses claim to have heard, see Timothy S. Good, *We Saw Lincoln Shot: One Hundred Eyewitness Accounts* (Jackson: University Press of Mississippi, 1995), esp. 18–73.

18. Twain, "Answers to Correspondents" (June 10, 1865), 185; John Rhodehamel and Louise Taper, "Introduction," in *"Right or Wrong, God Judge Me": The Writings of John Wilkes Booth* (Urbana: University of Illinois Press, 1997), 1.

19. Twain, "Answers to Correspondents" (June 10, 1865), 185; Rhodehamel and Taper, "Introduction," 6–7; "J. Wilkes Booth—A Modern Erostratus," *Territorial Enterprise* (Virginia City), April 18, 1865, 4; "John Wilkes Booth, the Infamous Assassin," *Daily Evening Bulletin*, April 18, 1865, 3; "THE ASSASSINATION," *Territorial Enterprise* (Virginia City), April 18, 1865, 8.

20. "President Lincoln's Obsequies in New York City," *Alta California*, May 25, 1865, 1; "The Assassin," *Dramatic Chronicle*, April 17, 1865, 2; John Wilkes Booth, *"Right or Wrong, God Judge Me": The Writings of John Wilkes Booth* (Urbana: University of Illinois Press, 1997), 154; John Wilkes Booth, "To the Editors of the National Intelligencer, Washington, D.C., 14 April 1865," in *"Right or Wrong, God Judge Me": The Writings of John Wilkes Booth*, ed. John Rhodehamel and Louise Taper (Urbana: University of Illinois Press, 1997), 147–53.

21. See *A Compilation of the Messages and Papers of the Presidents*, vol. 8, ed. James D. Richardson (New York: Bureau of National Literature, 1897), 3488–89, 3491, 3492, 3493; Andrew Johnson, "Proclamations," in *A Compilation of the Messages and Papers of the Presidents*, vol. 8, ed. James D. Richardson (New York: Bureau of National Literature, 1897), 3504, 3537.

22. "A Completed Life," *Dramatic Chronicle*, April 17, 1865, 2; "Abraham Lincoln," *Territorial Enterprise* (Virginia City), April 18, 1865, 4; "Our Great National Calamity," *Alta California*, April 16, 1865, 2; Reverend L. Hamilton, "Remarks of Rev. L. Hamilton at Oakland, on the Death of President Lincoln," *Alta California*, April 19, 1865, 1; "The Popular Feeling," *Daily Evening Bulletin*, April 19, 1865, 3; Emilie Lawson, "Abraham Lincoln," *Daily Evening Bulletin*, April 19, 1865, 3; "The Last of Earth. The Greatest Demonstration Ever Made on the Pacific Coast," *Alta California*, April 20, 1865, 1; "The Funeral of President Lincoln," *Daily Evening Bulletin*, April 19, 1865, 3.

23. Judge Mason is quoted in Furtwangler, *Assassin on Stage*, 99; Mark Twain, "Answers to Correspondents" (June 24, 1865), in *Early Tales and Sketches*, vol. 2, *1864–1865*, ed. Edgar M. Branch (Berkeley: University of California Press, 1981), 200–202; Edgar M. Branch, ed., *Early Tales and Sketches*, vol. 2, *1864–1865* (Berkeley: University of California Press, 1981), 197–98.

24. Twain, "Answers to Correspondents" (June 24, 1865), 202.

25. Mark Twain, "Answers to Correspondents" (July 8, 1865), in *Early Tales and Sketches*, vol. 2, *1864–1865*, ed. Edgar M. Branch (Berkeley: University of California Press, 1981), 221–23; Mark Twain, *Adventures of Huckleberry Finn*, ed. Victor Fischer, Lin Salamo, and Walter Blair (Berkeley: University of California Press, 2003), 190; Twain, "Fourth of July" (July 6, 1864), 88; Branch, ed., *Early Tales and Sketches*, vol. 2, *1864–1865*, 219; Howells, "Mark Twain," 351.

26. Mark Twain, "Mark Twain on the Colored Man," in *Early Tales and Sketches*, vol. 2, *1864–1865*, ed. Edgar M. Branch (Berkeley: University of California Press, 1981), 248–49.

27. Evans's comment is quoted in Franklin Rogers, *Mark Twain's Burlesque Patterns, as Seen in the Novels and Narratives, 1855–1885* (Dallas: Southern Methodist University Press, 1960), 18–19; Franklin Walker, ed., *The Washoe Giant in San Francisco* (San Francisco: George Fields, 1938), 95. The phrase "editorial manifesto" is Paine's, and the item is reprinted in his *Mark Twain: A Biography*, vol. 1, 228. Twain's derision of Evans continued. In 1870, he refused to endorse publication of one of Evans's manuscripts to his own publisher Elisha Bliss, saying, "I want you to do just as you please with that Evans. I wash my hands of him." Letter to Elisha Bliss, January 28, 1870, in Mark Twain, *Mark Twain's Letters to his Publishers, 1867–1894*, ed. Hamlin Hill (Berkeley: University of California Press, 1967), 30.

28. Patrick D. Morrow, "Bret Harte, Mark Twain, and the San Francisco Circle," in *A Literary History of the American West*, ed. J. Golden Taylor (Fort Worth: Texas Christian University Press, 1987), 341–42.

29. Twain, *Autobiography*, 125; Mark Twain, "Caustic," in *Mark Twain's San Francisco*, ed.

Bernard Taper (New York: McGraw-Hill, 1963), 159–60; Albert S. Evans, "In Memoriam," *Alta California,* April 17, 1865, 1; Paine, *Mark Twain: A Biography,* vol. 1, 275.

30. Mark Twain, "The Righteous Shall Not Be Forgotten," *Bancroftiana* 115 (Fall 1999): 10, 12.

31. Edmund Wilson, *Patriotic Gore: Studies in the Literature of the American Civil War* (New York: Oxford University Press, 1962), 115; Andrew Johnson, "First Annual Message," in *A Compilation of the Messages and Papers of the Presidents,* vol. 8, ed. James D. Richardson (New York: Bureau of National Literature, 1897), 3551.

32. Albert S. Evans, "Our San Francisco Correspondence," *Daily News* (Gold Hill), July 22, 1864, 2; Mark Twain, quoted in Gary Scharnhorst, "Mark Twain's Imbroglio with the San Francisco Police: Three Lost Texts," *American Literature* 62 (1990): 687–88.

33. Albert S. Evans, "A Chapter in the History of the San Francisco Police," *Alta California,* January 12, 1866, 1; Mark Twain, "Gorgeous New Romance, By Fitz Smythe!" in *Mark Twain: San Francisco Correspondent* (San Francisco: Book Club of California, 1957), 25; see also "Another Romance," in *Mark Twain: San Francisco Correspondent* (San Francisco: Book Club of California, 1957), 29–32.

34. Twain, "Gorgeous New Romance, By Fitz Smythe!" 25–28; Walker, *The Washoe Giant in San Francisco,* 95; Twain, "Another Romance," 32.

35. James M. McPherson, *Ordeal by Fire: The Civil War and Reconstruction* (New York: Alfred A. Knopf, 1982), 557; Albion W. Tourgée, *A Fool's Errand* (Cambridge, Mass.: Harvard University Press, 1961), 142; Mark Twain, "Take the Stand, Fitz Smythe," in *Early Tales and Sketches,* vol. 2, *1864–1865,* ed. Edgar M. Branch (Berkeley: University of California Press, 1981), 350–52; Mark Twain (attrib.), "How Dare You?" in *Early Tales and Sketches,* vol. 2, *1864–1865,* ed. Edgar M. Branch (Berkeley: University of California Press, 1981), 512.

36. Mark Twain, "Fitz Smythe's Horse," in *Early Tales and Sketches,* vol. 2, *1864–1865,* ed. Edgar M. Branch (Berkeley: University of California Press, 1981), 346; Mark Twain, "What Have the Police Been Doing?" in *Mark Twain's San Francisco,* ed. Bernard Taper (New York: McGraw-Hill Book Company, Inc., 1963), 189–90; Mark Twain, "Miscegenation," in *Clemens of the Call,* ed. Edgar M. Branch (Berkeley: University of California Press, 1969), 187; Mark Twain, "Disgraceful Persecution of a Boy," in *Mark Twain: Collected Tales, Sketches, Speeches, and Essays, 1852–1890* (New York: Library of America, 1992), 380; Chief Justice Roger Taney, "Dred Scott, Plaintiff in Error, v. John F. A. Sanford," in *Readings in American Constitutional History, 1776–1876,* ed. Allen Johnson (New York: Houghton Mifflin Company, 1912), 439; Branch, *The Literary Apprenticeship of Mark Twain,* 133–34.

37. Mark Twain, "Remarkable Dream," in *Early Tales and Sketches,* vol. 2, *1864–1865,* ed. Edgar M. Branch (Berkeley: University of California Press, 1981), 355, 358.

38. Twain, *Mark Twain's Notebooks and Journals,* vol. 1, *1855–1873,* 143.

CHAPTER FOUR

EPIGRAPHS: "The Returning Sisters," *Daily Evening Bulletin* (San Francisco), April 20, 1865, 2; Mark Twain, "Mark Twain's Letters from Washington, March 2, 1868," *Territorial Enterprise,* April 7, 1868, 1.

1. Generals Robert E. Lee and Joseph E. Johnston surrendered their armies in April, with Generals Richard Taylor and Edmund Kirby-Smith surrendering in May. Abraham Lincoln,

"Fourth Annual Message," in *A Compilation of the Messages and Papers of the Presidents*, vol. 8, ed. James D. Richardson (New York: Bureau of National Literature, 1897), 3452–53; Edwin C. McReynolds, *Missouri: A History of the Crossroads State* (Norman: University of Oklahoma Press, 1962), 256–57; Wiley Britton, "Résumé of Military Operations in Missouri and Arkansas, 1864–65," in *Battles and Leaders of the Civil War* (New York: Castle Books, 1956), vol. 4, 374–77; Eric Foner, *Reconstruction: America's Unfinished Revolution, 1863–1877* (New York: Harper & Row, 1988), 41.

2. Frederick Douglass, "Black Freedom is the Prerequisite of Victory: An Address Delivered in New York, New York, on 13 January 1865," in *The Frederick Douglass Papers, Series One: Speeches, Debates, and Interviews*, vol. 4, ed. John W. Blassingame and John R. McKivigan (New Haven, Conn.: Yale University Press, 1991), 52–53; Robert Manson Myers, ed., *The Children of Pride: A True Story of Georgia and the Civil War* (New Haven: Yale University Press, 1972), 1294, 1268.

3. David W. Blight, *Race and Reunion* (Cambridge, Mass.: Harvard University Press, 2001), 45; Mark Twain, Letter to Frank Fuller, November 24, 1867, in *Mark Twain's Letters*, vol. 2, *1867–68*, ed. Harriet Elinor Smith, Richard Bucci, and Lin Salamo (Berkeley: University of California Press, 1990), 112; Mark Twain, *Mark Twain's Travels with Mr. Brown*, ed. Franklin Walker and G. Ezra Dane (New York: Alfred A. Knopf, 1940), 142–43, 163–64, 219.

4. "The Returning Sisters," *Daily Evening Bulletin* (San Francisco), April 20, 1865, 2; Lt. Col. Marvin A. Kreidberg and First Lt. Merton G. Henry, *History of the Military Mobilization in the United States Army, 1775–1945* (Washington, D.C.: Department of the Army, 1955), 95, 141. Total casualty figures for the Battle of Antietam are usually given at approximately 23,000. Twain, *Mark Twain's Travels with Mr. Brown*, 163, 167.

5. Twain, *Mark Twain's Travels with Mr. Brown*, 106; Mark Twain and Charles Dudley Warner, *The Gilded Age. A Tale of Today* (New York: Gabriel Wells, 1922), vol. 2, 176–77; Mark Twain, *A Connecticut Yankee in King Arthur's Court*, ed. Bernard L. Stein (Berkeley: University of California Press, 1979), 50, 343.

6. Twain, *Mark Twain's Travels with Mr. Brown*, 106; Twain, *Mark Twain's Letters*, vol. 1, *1853–1866*, 10.

7. Mark Twain, *Mark Twain's Letters from Hawaii*, ed. A. Grove Day (Honolulu: University of Hawaii Press, 1975), 219; Fred W. Lorch, *The Trouble Begins at Eight: Mark Twain's Lecture Tours* (Ames: Iowa State University Press, 1966), 277.

8. A. H. Saxon, *P. T. Barnum: The Legend and the Man* (New York: Columbia University Press, 1989), 220, 223. Settle is quoted in Sidney Andrews, *The South Since the War* (Boston: Ticknor & Fields, 1866), 154. "The Two Hundred Thousand and First Curiosity in Congress," *The Nation*, March 7, 1867, 190; "Two Barnums in the Field," *New York Herald*, February 21, 1867, 6; "Barnum at His Tricks Again—A New Political Feejee Mermaid," *New York Herald*, February 27, 1867, 6.

9. Mark Twain, "Barnum's First Speech in Congress (By Spiritual Telegraph)," in *Mark Twain: Collected Tales, Sketches, Speeches, and Essays, 1852–1890* (New York: Library of America, 1992), 211, 212–13.

10. P. T. Barnum, *Struggles and Triumph: Or, Forty Years' Recollections of P. T. Barnum* (Hartford: J. B. Burr & Company, 1869), 626–27. For a discussion of Barnum's speech and his unsuccessful run for Congress, see Barnum's work and also Saxon, *P. T. Barnum*, 217–25.

11. Twain, "Barnum's First Speech in Congress," 212; Barnum, *Struggles and Triumphs*, 631–32.

12. David E. E. Sloane, *Mark Twain as a Literary Comedian* (Baton Rouge: Louisiana State University Press, 1979), 89; Twain, "Barnum's First Speech in Congress," 211–13; Twain, *Mark Twain's Travels with Mr. Brown*, 117.

13. Andrew Johnson, Veto Messages, in *A Compilation of the Messages and Papers of the Presidents*, vol. 8, ed. James D. Richardson (New York: Bureau of National Literature, 1897), 3696–3709, 3732. For a discussion of the first impeachment effort, see James M. McPherson, *Ordeal by Fire: The Civil War and Reconstruction* (New York: Alfred A. Knopf, 1982), 525–26; Twain, "Barnum's First Speech in Congress," 211–13.

14. Joseph L. Coulombe, *Mark Twain and the American West* (Columbia: University of Missouri Press, 2003), 12; Mark Twain, *The Innocents Abroad* (Hartford: The American Publishing Company, 1869), 382.

15. Twain, *The Innocents Abroad*, 56–57, 195, 336; Mark Twain, "Letter from Carson City," in *Early Tales and Sketches*, vol. 1, *1851–1864*, ed. Edgar M. Branch (Berkeley: University of California Press, 1979), 197; Mark Twain, "Is Shakespeare Dead?" in *The Complete Essays of Mark Twain*, ed. Charles Neider (New York: Da Capo, 1991), 440; Mark Twain, "An Important Question Settled," *Cincinnati Evening Chronicle*, March 9, 1868, 3.

16. Elizabeth Akers Allen, "Rock Me to Sleep," in *American Poetry: The Nineteenth Century, Volume Two* (New York: Library of America, 1993), 321; Mark Twain, "No. 44, The Mysterious Stranger," in *Mark Twain's Mysterious Stranger Manuscripts*, ed. William M. Gibson (Berkeley: University of California Press, 1969), 395, 397, 400.

17. Mark Twain, "Letter from Washington," *Territorial Enterprise*, January 11, 1868, 2; Ulysses S. Grant, *Memoirs and Selected Letters, Personal Memoirs of U. S. Grant, Selected Letters 1839–1865* (New York: Library of America, 1990), 752; Foner, *Reconstruction: America's Unfinished Revolution*, 245, 249, 250–51; Blight, *Race and Reunion*, 45; W. E. B. Du Bois, *Black Reconstruction: An Essay Toward a History of the Part which Black Folk Played in the Attempt to Reconstruct Democracy in America, 1860–1880* (New York: Harcourt, Brace and Company, 1935), 317.

18. Paine, *Mark Twain: A Biography*, vol. 1, 346; Senator William M. Stewart, *Reminiscences of Senator William M. Stewart of Nevada*, ed. George Rothwell Brown (New York: The Neale Publishing Company, 1908), 219–23; Eric Foner, *Forever Free: The Story of Emancipation and Reconstruction* (New York: Alfred A. Knopf, 2006), 148; C. C. Goodwin, *As I Remember Them* (Salt Lake City: Special Committee of the Salt Lake Commercial Club, 1913), 143. Goodwin was a former editor of the Virginia City *Enterprise*.

19. William R. Gillis, *Gold Rush Days with Mark Twain* (New York: Albert & Charles Boni, 1930), 156; Twain, *Roughing It*, 288–89. This according to Frank Fuller. See "Letters from Frank Fuller," *Twainian* (July–August 1956): 1; Twain, *Mark Twain's Letters*, vol. 2, *1867–1868*, 116–17; Vincent L. Eaton, "Mark Twain, Washington Correspondent," *Manuscripts* 11 (1959): 19; Mark Twain, "The Facts Concerning the Recent Resignation," in *Mark Twain: Collected Tales, Sketches, Speeches, and Essays, 1852–1890* (New York: Library of America, 1992), 243; Mark Twain, "My Late Senatorial Secretaryship," in *Mark Twain: Collected Tales, Sketches, Speeches, and Essays, 1852–1890* (New York: Library of America, 1992), 257, 261; Goodwin, *As I Remember Them*, 153.

20. Twain, *Mark Twain's Letters*, vol. 2, *1867–1868*, 165–66.

21. Mark Twain, "Mark Twain's Letters from Washington, (December 4, 1867)," *Territorial*

Enterprise (Virginia City), December 22, 1867, 2; Andrew Johnson, "Third Annual Message," in *A Compilation of the Messages and Papers of the Presidents*, vol. 8, ed. James D. Richardson (New York: Bureau of National Literature, 1897), 3761–62.

22. Mark Twain, "The Facts in the Case of the Senate Doorkeeper," *Twainian* 6, no. 6 (November–December 1947): 3–4; Foner, *Forever Free*, 129.

23. Twain, *Mark Twain's Letters*, vol. 2, *1867–1868*, 197; Mark Twain, "Mark Twain's Letters from Washington, (December 16, 1867)," *Territorial Enterprise* (Virginia City), January 7, 1868, 2; Mark Twain, "Mark Twain's Letters from Washington, December 20, 1867," *Territorial Enterprise* (Virginia City), January 11, 1868, 2; Mark Twain, "Mark Twain's Letters from Washington, (January 10, 1868)," *Territorial Enterprise* (Virginia City), January 30, 1868, 2; Mark Twain, "Letter from Washington, (January 31, 1868)," *Chicago Republican*, February 8, 1868, 2.

24. Mark Twain, "Female Suffrage," in *Mark Twain: Collected Tales, Sketches, Speeches, and Essays, 1852–1890* (New York: Library of America, 1992), 226–27; Mark Twain, "At Home Again," in *Mark Twain's Travels with Mr. Brown*, ed. Franklin Walker and G. Ezra Dane (New York: Russell & Russell, 1971), 134; Mark Twain, "Mark Twain's Letter (February 21, 1868)," *Chicago Republican*, March 1, 1868, 2.

25. Mark Twain, "Gossip at the National Capital, (February 1, 1868)," *New York Herald*, February 3, 1868, 5. Louis J. Budd has attributed this letter to Clemens. "Did Mark Twain Write 'Impersonally' for the *New York Herald*?" *Library Notes* 43 (November 1972): 5–9. Mark Twain, "Mark Twain's Letter (February 21, 1868)," *Chicago Republican*, March 1, 1868, 2.

26. Mark Twain, "Letter from Washington, January 11, 1868," *Territorial Enterprise* (Virginia City), February 18, 1868, 2; Foner, *Reconstruction: America's Unfinished Revolution*, 272, 336.

27. Twain, "Mark Twain's Letters from Washington, (January 11, 1868)," 2; Mark Twain, "Mark Twain in Washington, (January 12, 1868)," *Alta California*, February 19, 1868; Johnson, "Third Annual Message," 3757.

28. Twain, *Mark Twain's Notebooks and Journals*, vol. 1, *1855–1873*, 487–93; Mark Twain, "The Facts Concerning the Recent Important Resignation," *Twainian* 5, no. 3 (May–June 1946): 1–3.

29. Twain, *Mark Twain's Notebooks and Journals*, vol. 1, *1855–1873*, 492–94; Mark Twain, "Mark Twain's Letters from Washington, (January 30, 1868)," *Territorial Enterprise* (Virginia City), February 27, 1868, 2; Mark Twain, "Mark Twain's Letters from Washington, (January 10, 1868)," *Territorial Enterprise* (Virginia City), January 30, 1868, 2.

30. Mark Twain, "Mark Twain's Letter (February 14, 1868)," *Chicago Republican*, February 19, 1868, 2; Mark Twain, "Mark Twain's Letters from Washington, (February, 1868)," *Territorial Enterprise* (Virginia City), March 7, 1868, 1.

31. Mark Twain, "Mark Twain's Letter (February 21, 1868)," *Chicago Republican*, March 1, 1868, 2; Samuel Eliot Morison, Henry Steele Commager, and William E. Leuchtenburg, *The Growth of the American Republic*, vol. 1 (New York: Oxford University Press, 1980), 750; Mark Twain, "Mark Twain's Letters from Washington, (February 22, 1868)," *Territorial Enterprise* (Virginia City), March 13, 1868, 1.

32. Mark Twain, "Mark Twain's Letters from Washington, (February 22, 1868)," *Territorial Enterprise* (Virginia City), March 13, 1868, 1.

33. Mark Twain, "Mark Twain's Letters from Washington, (February 22, 1868)," *Territorial Enterprise* (Virginia City), March 13, 1868, 1; Mark Twain, "Mark Twain's Letter, (February 21, 1868)," *Chicago Republican*, March 1, 1868, 2.

34. Mark Twain, "Mark Twain's Letter (February 21, 1868)," *Chicago Republican*, March 1, 1868, 2.

35. For Twain's commentary on the *Alta California's* plans, see his letters to Mary (Mollie) Clemens, Jane Clemens, and Mary Mason ("Mother") Fairbanks, in *Mark Twain's Letters*, vol. 2, *1867–1868*, 198–203; Morison, Commager, and Leuchtenburg, *The Growth of the American Republic*, vol. 1, 752.

36. Mark Twain, "Riley-Newspaper Correspondent," in *Mark Twain: Collected Tales, Sketches, Speeches, and Essays, 1852–1890* (New York: Library of America, 1992), 477; Mark Twain, "'Mark Twain' in the Metropolis," in *Early Tales and Sketches*, vol. 2, *1864–1865*, ed. Edgar M. Branch (Berkeley: University of California Press, 1981), 10; Twain, *Mark Twain's Letters*, vol. 2, *1867–1868*, 195; Mark Twain, "The Story of Mamie Grant, the Child Missionary," in *Mark Twain: Collected Tales, Sketches, Speeches, and Essays, 1852–1890* (New York: Library of America, 1992), 264 ; Mark Twain, "Cannibalism in the Cars," in *Mark Twain: Collected Tales, Sketches, Speeches, and Essays, 1852–1890* (New York: Library of America, 1992), 272–74, 277.

37. Mark Twain, "Concerning Gen. Grant's Intentions," in *Mark Twain: Collected Tales, Sketches, Speeches, and Essays, 1852–1890* (New York: Library of America, 1992), 283–84; Twain, *Autobiography*, 241.

38. Walter A. McDougall, *Throes of Democracy: The American Civil War Era: 1829–1877* (New York: HarperCollins, 2008), 527.

39. Twain, "Concerning Gen. Grant's Intentions," 282–83.

40. Gaines M. Foster, *Ghosts of the Confederacy: Defeat, the Lost Cause, and the Emergence of the New South, 1865 to 1913* (New York: Oxford University Press, 1987), 19; Mark Twain, "L'Homme Qui Rit," in *Mark Twain's Satires & Burlesques*, ed. Franklin R. Rogers (Berkeley: University of California Press, 1967), 41–43, 45, 47–48; Franklin R. Rogers, "Clemens' Political Affiliations in Bearing on 'L'Homme Qui Rit,'" in *Mark Twain's Satires & Burlesques*, ed. Franklin R. Rogers (Berkeley: University of California Press, 1967), 460. Rogers's is the most extended commentary on the piece and is very helpful in understanding the allegory.

41. Mark Twain, "The White House Funeral," in *Mark Twain's Letters*, vol. 3, *1869*, ed. Victor Fischer and Michael B. Frank (Berkeley: University of California Press, 1992), 463, 465 n. 20, 464–65, 459; Budd, *Mark Twain: Social Philosopher*, 35–36.

42. Twain, *Mark Twain's Letters*, vol. 3, *1869*, 151 n. 1, 298.

CHAPTER FIVE

EPIGRAPH: Mark Twain, "Monarchical and Republican Patriotism," in *Mark Twain's Weapons of Satire: Anti-Imperialist Writings on the Philippine-American War*, ed. Jim Zwick (Syracuse, N.Y.: Syracuse University Press, 1992), 190.

1. Mark Twain, "Disgraceful Persecution of a Boy," in *Mark Twain: Collected Tales, Sketches, Speeches, and Essays, 1852–1890* (New York: Library of America, 1992), 380; Mark Twain,

"Goldsmith's Friend Abroad Again," in *Mark Twain: Collected Tales, Sketches, Speeches, and Essays, 1852–1890* (New York: Library of America, 1992), 456; Mark Twain, "Fourth of July Speech in London," in *Mark Twain: Collected Tales, Sketches, Speeches, and Essays, 1852–1890* (New York: Library of America, 1992), 556–57.

2. Mark Twain, "The Revised Catechism," in *Mark Twain: Collected Tales, Sketches, Speeches, and Essays, 1852–1890* (New York: Library of America, 1992), 539; Mark Twain, "The Secret of Dr. Livingstone's Continued Voluntary Exile," in *Mark Twain: Collected Tales, Sketches, Speeches, and Essays, 1852–1890* (New York: Library of America, 1992), 541–42; Eric Foner, *Forever Free: The Story of Emancipation and Reconstruction* (New York: Alfred A. Knopf, 2006), 179–80; Quoted in Edward J. Blum, *Reforging the White Republic: Race, Religion, and American Nationalism, 1865–1898* (Baton Rouge: Louisiana State University Press, 2005), 11. Clemens may have written some even more acerbic, unsigned articles in the *Buffalo Express* while editor. See *Mark Twain at the Buffalo Express: Articles and Sketches by America's Favorite Humorist,* ed. Joseph B. McCullough and Janice McIntire-Strasburg (DeKalb: Northern Illinois University Press, 1999).

3. "A Connecticut Carpet-bag," in *Mark Twain: The Complete Interviews,* ed. Gary Scharnhorst (Tuscaloosa: University of Alabama Press, 2006), 7–8; *Mark Twain–Howells Letters: The Correspondence of Samuel Langhorne Clemens and William D. Howells,* ed. Henry Nash Smith (Cambridge, Mass.: Harvard University Press, 1960), vol. 1, 145, 149, 151; Mark Twain, "Political Speech" (September 30, 1876), in *Mark Twain Speaking,* ed. Paul Fatout (Iowa City: University of Iowa Press, 1976), 97–98. For details of the context surrounding the speech, see Howard G. Baetzhold, "Mark Twain Stumps for Hayes," *Hayes Historical Journal* 1, no. 2 (1976): 111–14; Keith Ian Polakoff, *The Politics of Inertia: The Election of 1876 and the End of Reconstruction* (Baton Rouge: Louisiana State University Press, 1973), 181; Ulysses S. Grant, "Message to the Senate," July 31, 1876, in *A Compilation of the Messages and Papers of the Presidents,* vol. 9, ed. James D. Richardson (New York: Bureau of National Literature, 1897), 4330; Foner, *Forever Free,* 173.

4. Mark Twain, *Autobiography,* ed. Charles Neider (New York: HarperPerennial, 1990), 303; Shelley Fisher Fishkin, "Which Twain do we Claim?" keynote address, Texas American Studies Association, Baylor University, November 17, 2006, 7–8.

5. Blum, *Reforging the White Republic,* 149; Rutherford B. Hayes, "Second Annual Message," in *A Compilation of the Messages and Papers of the Presidents,* vol. 9, ed. James D. Richardson (New York: Bureau of National Literature, 1897), 4445.

6. Mark Twain, "Political Speech" (October 26, 1880), in *Mark Twain Speaking.* ed. Paul Fatout (Iowa City: University of Iowa Press, 1976), 139–43; Mark Twain, "Funeral Oration over the Grave of the Democratic Party," in *Mark Twain Speaking,* ed. Paul Fatout (Iowa City: University of Iowa Press, 1976), 146–47.

7. Mark Twain, in *Mark Twain–Howells Letters,* vol. 2, 571; Leslie Butler, *Critical Americans: Victorian Intellectuals and Transatlantic Liberal Reform* (Chapel Hill: University of North Carolina Press, 2007), 200, 202; Twain, *Mark Twain's Notebooks and Journals,* vol. 2, *1877–1883,* 503. Quoted in Joe B. Fulton, *Mark Twain in the Margins: The Quarry Farm Marginalia and* A Connecticut Yankee in King Arthur's Court (Tuscaloosa: University of Alabama Press, 2000), 108. Eric Foner, *Reconstruction: America's Unfinished Revolution, 1863–1877* (New York: Harper & Row, 1988), 566; Henry L. Stoddard, *As I Knew Them: Presidents and Politics from Grant to*

Coolidge (New York: Harper & Row, 1927), 94; Mark Twain, "Turncoats," in *Mark Twain: Collected Tales, Sketches, Speeches, and Essays, 1852–1890* (New York: Library of America, 1992), 850; Gaines M. Foster, *Ghosts of the Confederacy: Defeat, the Lost Cause, and the Emergence of the New South, 1865 to 1913* (New York: Oxford University Press, 1987), 66.

8. Mark Twain, "The Character of Man," in *Mark Twain: Collected Tales, Sketches, Speeches, and Essays, 1852–1890* (New York: Library of America, 1992), 856; Foster, *Ghosts of the Confederacy*, 196; Mark Twain, "Mock Oration on the Dead Partisan," in *Mark Twain: Collected Tales, Sketches, Speeches, and Essays, 1852–1890* (New York: Library of America, 1992), 852; Twain, *Mark Twain's Notebooks and Journals*, vol. 3, *1883–1891*, 425–26; Mark Twain, "Lotos Club Dinner Speech" (November 11, 1893), in *Mark Twain Speaking*, ed. Paul Fatout (Iowa City: University of Iowa Press, 1976), 267.

9. Twain, "Jane Lampton Clemens," 46–47; Mark Twain, "Man's Place in the Animal World," in *What Is Man? And Other Philosophical Writings*, ed. Paul Baender (Berkeley: University of California Press, 1973), 80, 84–85.

10. Mark Twain, "As Regards Patriotism," in *Mark Twain: Collected Tales, Sketches, Speeches, and Essays, 1891–1910* (New York: Library of America, 1992), 477; Twain, "Monarchical and Republican Patriotism," 190.

11. Mark Twain, *Mark Twain's Letters*, vol. 6, *1874–1875*, ed. Michael B. Frank and Harriet Elinor Smith (Berkeley: University of California Press, 2002), 217; Mark Twain, "A True Story," in *Mark Twain: Collected Tales, Sketches, Speeches, and Essays, 1852–1890* (New York: Library of America, 1992), 578–82; William Dean Howells, "Review of Mark Twain's Sketches, New and Old," in *Mark Twain's Letters*, vol. 6, *1874–1875*, ed. Michael B. Frank and Harriet Elinor Smith (Berkeley: University of California Press, 2002), 657–58.

12. Mark Twain, *Adventures of Huckleberry Finn*, ed. Victor Fischer, Lin Salamo, and Walter Blair (Berkeley: University of California Press, 2003), 190; Twain, "The Private History of a Campaign That Failed," 881–82; Mark Twain, *Following the Equator: A Journey Around the World* (Hartford, Conn.: American Publishing Company, 1897), 213, 351–52; Walter A. McDougall, *Throes of Democracy: The American Civil War Era: 1829–1877* (New York: HarperCollins, 2008), 583; Butler, *Critical Americans*, 249.

13. Reinhart Koselleck, *The Practice of Conceptual History: Timing History, Spacing Concepts*, trans Todd Samuel Presner et al. (Stanford: Stanford University Press, 2002), 76, 78; Albion Tourgée, "The South as a Field for Fiction," in *The American Civil War: An Anthology of Essential Writings*, ed. Ian Frederick Finseth (New York: Routledge, 2006), 534. Tourgée made the claim in 1865, but the quotation is from the article published in 1888.

14. Mark Twain, "The Day We Celebrate," in *Mark Twain: Collected Tales, Sketches, Speeches, and Essays, 1891–1910* (New York: Library of America, 1992), 820–21; Mark Twain, "To the Person Sitting in Darkness," in *Mark Twain: Collected Tales, Sketches, Speeches, and Essays, 1891–1910* (New York: Library of America, 1992), 471–73. For a masterful discussion of Clemens's later anti-imperialist writings, see Jim Zwick's introduction to *Mark Twain's Weapons of Satire*, xvii–xlii. Zwick, too, connects Clemens' anti-imperialism with his attitudes toward the American Civil War (see xxx).

15. Mark Twain, "Bishop Speech" (October, 1907), in *Mark Twain Speaking*, ed. Paul Fatout (Iowa City: University of Iowa Press, 1976), 591.

16. Mark Twain, "The Stupendous Procession," in *Mark Twain's Fables of Man*, ed. John S. Tuckey (Berkeley: University of California Press, 1972), 405, 409, 412–13, 418–19.

17. Twain, "Blue and Gray Pay Tribute to Lincoln," 1; Edward Alfred Pollard, *The Lost Cause: A New Southern History of the War of the Confederates* (New York: E. B. Treat, 1868), 751; Frederick Douglass, "Address at the Graves of the Unknown Dead," in *The American Civil War: An Anthology of Essential Writings,* ed. Ian Frederick Finseth (New York: Routledge, 2006), 520–21; Harold K. Bush, *Mark Twain and the Spiritual Crisis of his Age* (Tuscaloosa: University of Alabama Press, 2007), 198; Howells, "My Mark Twain," 277.

18. Mark Twain, "A Lincoln Memorial," *The New York Times,* January 13, 1907, 1.

WORKS CITED

Aaron, Daniel. *The Unwritten War*. New York: Knopf, 1973.

Ade, George. "Mark Twain as Our Emissary." In *Critical Essays on Mark Twain, 1867–1910*. Ed. Louis J. Budd. Boston: G. K. Hall and Company, 1982. 241–44.

Allardice, Bruce. *More Generals in Gray*. Baton Rouge: Louisiana State University Press, 1995.

Allen, Elizabeth Akers. "Rock Me to Sleep." In *American Poetry: The Nineteenth Century, Volume Two*. New York: Library of America, 1993. 321–22.

Alta California (San Francisco). "Camp Fun." April 3, 1863, 1.

———. "The Effect in San Francisco." April 16, 1865, 1.

———. "A French Secession Organ." April 5, 1865, 1.

———. "Is There No Punishment for Newspaper Treason?" November 8, 1863, 2.

———. "The Last of Earth. The Greatest Demonstration Ever Made on the Pacific Coast." April 20, 1865, 1.

———. "Our Great National Calamity." April 16, 1865, 2.

———. "President Lincoln's Obsequies in New York City." May 25, 1865, 1.

Andrews, Sidney. *The South Since the War*. Boston: Ticknor & Fields, 1866.

Andrews, Wayne, ed. *Concise Dictionary of American History*. New York: Charles Scribner's Sons, 1962.

Angel, Myron. *History of Nevada, with Illustrations and Biographical Sketches of its Prominent Men and Pioneers*. Oakland: Thompson & West, 1881.

Aurora Daily Times (Nevada). "The Virginia Press." December 1, 1863, 2.

Baetzhold, Howard G. "Mark Twain Stumps for Hayes." *Hayes Historical Journal* 1, no. 2 (1976): 111–14.

Bancroft, Hubert Howe. *History of Nevada, 1540–1888*. San Francisco: The History Company, 1890.

Barnum, P. T. *The Humbugs of the World, An Account of Humbugs, Delusions, Impositions, Quackeries, Deceits and Deceivers Generally, In All Ages*. New York: Carleton Publisher, 1865.

———. *Struggles and Triumph: Or, Forty Years' Recollections of P. T. Barnum*. Hartford: J. B. Burr & Company, 1869.

Bates, Allan. "The Quintus Curtius Snodgrass Letters: A Clarification of the Mark Twain Canon." *American Literature* 36, no. 1 (1964): 31–37.

Beebe, Lucius. *Comstock Commotion, The Story of the Territorial Enterprise and Virginia City News*. Stanford: Stanford University Press, 1954.

Benson, Ivan. *Mark Twain's Western Years*. Stanford: Stanford University Press, 1938.

Berkove, Lawrence. "Ethical Records of Twain and His Circle of Sagebrush Journalists." *Quarry Farm Papers*. No. 5. Elmira, N.Y.: Elmira College Center for Mark Twain Studies, 1994.

——. *The Sagebrush Anthology: Literature from the Silver Age of the Old West*. Columbia: University of Missouri Press, 2006.

Bird, John. *Mark Twain and Metaphor*. Columbia: University of Missouri Press, 2007.

Blight, David W. *Race and Reunion: The Civil War in American Memory*. Cambridge, Mass.: Harvard University Press, 2001.

Blount, Roy, Jr. "Mark Twain's Reconstruction." *Atlantic Monthly* 288 (July–August, 2001): 67–81.

Blum, Edward J. *Reforging the White Republic: Race, Religion, and American Nationalism, 1865–1898*. Baton Rouge: Louisiana State University Press, 2005.

Booth, John Wilkes. *"Right or Wrong, God Judge Me": The Writings of John Wilkes Booth, ed. John Rhodehamel and Louise Taper*. Urbana: University of Illinois Press, 1997.

——. "To the Editors of the National Intelligencer, Washington, D.C., April 14, 1865." In *"Right or Wrong, God Judge Me": The Writings of John Wilkes Booth*. Ed. John Rhodehamel and Louise Taper (Urbana: University of Illinois Press, 1997). 14–53.

Bowen, William. Unpublished correspondence to Mark Twain, Mark Twain Project, University of California at Berkeley.

Branch, Edgar Marquess. "Introduction." In *Early Tales and Sketches*. Vol. 1, *1851–1864*. Ed. Edgar M. Branch. Berkeley: University of California Press, 1979. 1–57.

——. "Introduction." In *Mark Twain's Letters*. Vol. 1, *1853–1866*. Ed. Edgar Marquess Branch, Michael B. Frank, and Kenneth M. Sanderson. Berkeley: University of California Press, 1988. xxi–xxiii.

——. *The Literary Apprenticeship of Mark Twain*. Urbana: University of Illinois Press, 1950.

——. *Mark Twain and the Starchy Boys*. Elmira, N.Y.: Elmira College Center for Mark Twain Studies, 1992.

——. "Samuel Clemens and the Copperheads of 1864." *Mad River Review* 2, no. 1 (1967): 3–20.

Branch, Edgar Marquess, ed. *Early Tales and Sketches*. Vol. 1, *1851–1864*. Berkeley: University of California Press, 1979.

——. *Early Tales and Sketches*. Vol. 2, *1864–1865*. Berkeley: University of California Press, 1981.

Brinegar, Claude S. "Mark Twain and the Quintus Curtius Snodgrass Letters: A Statistical Test of Authorship." *Journal of the American Statistical Association* 58 (1963): 85–96.

Britton, Wiley. "Résumé of Military Operations in Missouri and Arkansas, 1864–65." In *Battles and Leaders of the Civil War*. Vol. 4. New York: Castle Books, 1956. 374–77.

Brownell, George H. "License Mystery Nears Solution." *Twainian* 2 (January 1940): 2–3.

Budd, Louis J. "Did Mark Twain Write 'Impersonally' for the *New York Herald*?" *Library Notes* 43 (November 1972): 5–9.

———. "Hiding Out in Public: Mark Twain as a Speaker." *Studies in American Fiction* 13 (1985): 129–41.

———. *Mark Twain: Social Philosopher*. Columbia: University of Missouri Press, 2001. (1962).

———. "Notes." In *Mark Twain: Collected Tales, Sketches, Speeches, and Essays, 1852–1890* New York: Library of America, 1992. 1025–71.

Burton, Orville Vernon. *The Age of Lincoln*. New York: Hill and Wang, 2007.

Bush, Harold K. *Mark Twain and the Spiritual Crisis of his Age*. Tuscaloosa: University of Alabama Press, 2007.

Butler, Leslie. *Critical Americans: Victorian Intellectuals and Transatlantic Liberal Reform*. Chapel Hill: University of North Carolina Press, 2007.

Cardwell, Guy. "Mark Twain, James R. Osgood, and Those 'Suppressed' Passages." *New England Quarterly* 46, no. 2 (1973): 163–88.

Caron, James E. *Mark Twain: Unsanctified Newspaper Reporter*. Columbia: University of Missouri Press, 2008.

Caron, Timothy P. "'How Changeable Are the Events of War': National Reconciliation in the *Century Magazine*'s 'Battles and Leaders of the Civil War.'" *American Periodicals* 16 (2006): 151–71.

Carter, John Denton. "Abraham Lincoln and the California Patronage." *The American Historical Review* 48 (1943): 495–506.

Carter, Paul J. "The Influence of the Nevada Frontier on Mark Twain." *Western Humanities Review* 13 (1959): 61–70.

The Century. "The 'Century' War Series." 29 (1885): 78.

The Century Dictionary. 6 vols. Ed. William Dwight Whitney. New York: The Century Company, 1889.

Clagett, Honorable W. H. *Money, Banks, Panics, and Prosperity*. Washington, D.C.: Cromwell Brothers, 1898.

Clemens, Samuel Langhorne. *See* Mark Twain.

Cloud, Barbara. *The Business of Newspapers on the Western Frontier*. Reno: University of Nevada Press, 1992.

A Compilation of the Messages and Papers of the Presidents. 20 vols. Ed. James D. Richardson. New York: Bureau of National Literature, 1897.

"A Connecticut Carpet-bag." In *Mark Twain: The Complete Interviews*. Ed. Gary Scharnhorst. Tuscaloosa: University of Alabama Press, 2006. 7–8.

Coulombe, Joseph L. *Mark Twain and the American West*. Columbia: University of Missouri Press, 2003.

Cox, James. *Mark Twain: The Fate of Humor*. Princeton, N.J.: Princeton University Press, 1966.

Croly, David Goodman. *Miscegenation: The Theory of the Blending of the Races, Applied to the American White Man and Negro*. New York: H. Dexter, Hamilton & Co., 1864.

Current, Richard N., ed. *Encyclopedia of the Confederacy*. 4 vols. New York: Simon and Schuster, 1993.

Daily Appeal (Marysville, California). "A Good 'Goak.'" March 15, 1865, 2.

Daily Evening Bulletin (San Francisco). "An Expression of Anger—A Word of Caution." April 18, 1865, 3.

———. "The Funeral of President Lincoln." April 19, 1865, 3.

———. "JOHN WILKES BOOTH, THE INFAMOUS ASSASSIN." April 18, 1865, 3.

———. "The Popular Feeling." April 19, 1865, 3.

———. "The Returning Sisters." April 20, 1865, 2.

Daily Globe-Democrat (St. Louis). "Gen. T. A. Harris Dead." April 10, 1895, 2.

Daily News (Gold Hill). "An Asylum Needed." November 11, 1863, 2.

———. "An Exile." May 30, 1864, 2.

———. "Hoity! Toity!!" May 24, 1864, 2.

———. "Horrible." October 28, 1863, 3.

———. "Still Harping On." October 30, 1863, 3.

———. "Tahoe vs. Bigler." November 5, 1863, 1.

———. "What's the News?" June 8, 1864, 2.

Daily Union (Virginia City, Nevada). "Questionable Taste." July 6, 1864, 2.

———. "W. H. Clagett." October 9, 1864, 2.

Daniel, John Warwick. "Conquered Nations." In *Speeches and Orations of John Warwick Daniel*. Ed. Edward M. Daniel. Lynchburg: J. P. Bell Co., 1911. 105–58.

Davis, Sam P., ed. *The History of Nevada*. 2 vols. Las Vegas: Nevada Publications, 1913.

———. "Political History." In *The History of Nevada*. Vol. 1. Las Vegas: Nevada Publications, 1913. 420–58.

Davis, Winfield J. *History of Political Conventions in California, 1849–1892*. Sacramento: California State Library, 1893.

De Forest, John W. *Miss Ravenel's Conversion from Secession to Loyalty*. New York: Penguin, 2000.

———. *A Union Officer in the Reconstruction*. Ed. James H. Croushore and David Morris Potter. New Haven: Yale University Press, 1948.

Dempsey, Terrell. *Searching for Jim: Slavery in Sam Clemens's World*. Columbia: University of Missouri Press, 2003.

Dixon, W. W. "Sketch of the Life and Character of William H. Clagett." In *Contributions to the Historical Society of Montana*. Vol. 4. Boston: J. S. Canner and Company, Inc., 1996. 249–57.

Douglass, Frederick. "Address at the Graves of the Unknown Dead." In *The American Civil War: An Anthology of Essential Writings*. Ed. Ian Frederick Finseth. New York: Routledge, 2006. 520–21.

———. "Black Freedom is the Prerequisite of Victory: An Address Delivered in New York, New York, on 13 January 1865." In *Speeches, Debates, and Interviews*. Vol. 4. Ed. John W. Blassingame and John R. McKivigan. New Haven, Conn.: Yale University Press, 1991. 51–59.

———. "An Inspiration to High and Virtuous Endeavor: An Address Delivered in Syracuse, New York, on 1 October 1884." In *Speeches, Debates, and Interviews*. Vol. 5, *1881–95*. Ed. John W. Blassingame and John R. McKivigan. New Haven: Yale University Press, 1992. 159–66.

Dramatic Chronicle (San Francisco). "THE ASSASSIN." April 17, 1865, 2.

———. "A Completed Life." April 17, 1865, 2.

———. "Irregular Justice." April 17, 1865, 3.

———. "Treason Mills Under Repair." April 26, 1865, 2.

Drury, Wells. "Journalism." In *The History of Nevada*. Ed. Sam P. Davis. Vol. 1. Las Vegas: Nevada Publications, 1913. 459–302.

Du Bois, W. E. B. *Black Reconstruction: An Essay Toward a History of the Part which Black Folk Played in the Attempt to Reconstruct Democracy in America, 1860–1880*. New York: Harcourt, Brace and Company, 1935.

Duckett, Margaret. *Mark Twain and Bret Harte*. Norman: University of Oklahoma Press, 1964.

D.W.B. "Our Washington Correspondence." *The Independent*, March 3, 1864, 1.

Dyer, Frederick H. *A Compendium of the War of the Rebellion*. Vol. 3, *Regimental Histories*. New York: Thomas Yoseloff, 1959.

Eaton, Vincent L. "Mark Twain, Washington Correspondent." *Manuscripts* 11 (1959): 16–26.

Emerson, Ralph Waldo. "The Fugitive Slave Law." In *The Complete Works of Ralph Waldo Emerson*. Vol. 11. Boston: Riverside Press, 1904. 177–214.

Encyclopedia of the Confederacy. Ed. Richard N. Current. 4 vols. new York: Simon and Schuster, 1993.

Ensor, Allison. "Lincoln, Mark Twain, and Lincoln Memorial University." *Lincoln Herald* 78 (1976): 43–51.

Evans, Albert S. (Fitz Smythe). "A Chapter in the History of the San Francisco Police." *Alta California*, January 12, 1866, 1.

———. "In Memoriam." *Alta California*, April 17, 1865, 1.

———. "Our San Francisco Correspondence." Gold Hill *Daily News*, July 22, 1864, 2.

Fatout, Paul. *Mark Twain in Virginia City*. Bloomington: Indiana University Press, 1964.

———. *Mark Twain Speaking*. Iowa City: University of Iowa Press, 1976.

Faust, Drew Gilpin. *This Republic of Suffering: Death and the American Civil War*. New York: Alfred A. Knopf, 2008.

Faust, Patricia L., ed. *Historical Times Illustrated Encyclopedia of the Civil War*. New York: Harper & Row, 1986.

Fellman, Michael. *Inside War: The Guerrilla Conflict in Missouri During the American Civil War*. New York: Oxford University Press, 1989.

Fender, Stephen. "'The Prodigal in a Far Country Chawing of Husks': Mark Twain's Search for Style in the West." *Modern Language Review* 71 (1976): 737–56.

Finseth, Ian Frederick, ed. *The American Civil War: An Anthology of Essential Writings*. New York: Routledge, 2006.

Fishkin, Shelley Fisher. "Which Twain do we Claim?" Keynote address, Texas American Studies Association, November 17, 2006, 1–18.

Fitz Smythe. *See* Albert Evans.

Foner, Eric. *Forever Free: The Story of Emancipation and Reconstruction*. New York: Alfred A. Knopf, 2006.

———. *Reconstruction: America's Unfinished Revolution, 1863–1877*. New York: Harper & Row, 1988.

Foster, Gaines M. *Ghosts of the Confederacy: Defeat, the Lost Cause, and the Emergence of the New South, 1865 to 1913*. New York: Oxford University Press, 1987.

Frémont, John C. "In Command in Missouri." In *Battles and Leaders of the Civil War*. Vol. 1. Ed. Robert Johnson and Clarence Buel. New York: Castle Books, 1956. 278–88.

Fuller, Frank. "Letters of Frank Fuller." *Twainian* 15 (July–August 1956): 1.

Fulton, Joe B. "The Lost Manuscript Conclusion to Mark Twain's 'Corn-Pone Opinions': An Editorial History and an Edition of the Restored Text." *American Literary Realism* 37 (2005): 238–58.

———. *Mark Twain in the Margins: The Quarry Farm Marginalia and A Connecticut Yankee in King Arthur's Court*. Tuscaloosa: University of Alabama Press, 2000.

Furtwangler, Albert. *Assassin on Stage: Brutus, Hamlet, and the Death of Lincoln*. Urbana: University of Illinois Press, 1991.

Gerber, John C. "Mark Twain's 'Private Campaign.'" *Civil War History* 1 (1955): 37–60.

Gillis, William R. *Gold Rush Days with Mark Twain*. New York: Albert & Charles Boni, 1930.

Good, Timothy S. *We Saw Lincoln Shot: One Hundred Eyewitness Accounts*. Jackson: University Press of Mississippi, 1995.

Goodman, Joseph. "Virginia City." In *The History of Nevada*. Ed. Sam P. Davis. Vol. 1. Las Vegas: Nevada Publications, 1913. 472.

Goodwin, C. C. *As I Remember Them*. Salt Lake City: Special Committee of the Salt Lake Commercial Club, 1913.

Grant, Ulysses S. *Memoirs and Selected Letters, Personal Memoirs of U. S. Grant, Selected Letters 1839–1865*. New York: Library of America, 1990.

———. "Message to the Senate," July 31, 1876. In *A Compilation of the Messages and Papers of the President*. Vol. 9. Ed. James D. Richardson. New York: Bureau of National Literature, 1897. 4329–30.

Gribben, Alan. *Mark Twain's Library: A Reconstruction*. 2 vols. Boston: G. K. Hall, 1980.

Grimes, Absalom. *Absalom Grimes, Confederate Mail Runner*. Ed. M. M. Quaife. New Haven: Yale University Press, 1926.

Halpine, Charles G. [Miles O'Reilly]. *The Poetical Works of Charles G. Halpine*. Ed. Robert B. Roosevelt. New York, 1869.

Hamilton, Reverend L. "Remarks of Rev. L. Hamilton at Oakland, on the Death of President Lincoln." *Alta California*, April 19, 1865, 1.

Hannibal Journal. "Mob at Syracuse." October 16, 1851, 2.

———. "The Syracuse Outrage." October 23, 1851, 2.

Hard Cracker. "Foot Cavalry Chronicle." *Southern Illustrated News*, October 18, 1862, 3.

Hayes, Rutherford B. "Second Annual Message." In *A Compilation of the Messages and Papers of the Presidents*. Vol. 9. Ed. James D. Richardson. New York: Bureau of National Literature, 1897. 4444–59.

Hill, Hamlin. "Mark Twain Goes to War." *The Dial* (April 1981): 42–44.

"The 'How Is It' Issue." In *Mark Twain's Letters*. Vol. 1, *1853–1866*. Ed. Edgar Marquess Branch, Michael B. Frank, and Kenneth M. Sanderson. Berkeley: University of California Press, 1988. 291.

"How It Is." In *Mark Twain's Letters*. Vol. 1, *1853–1866*. Ed. Edgar Marquess Branch, Michael B. Frank, and Kenneth M. Sanderson. Berkeley: University of California Press, 1988. 290–91.

Howell, Elmo. "Mark Twain and the Civil War." *Ball State University Forum* 13 (1972): 53–61.

Howells, William Dean. "Editha." In *The American Tradition in Literature*. Vol. 2. 8th ed. Ed. George and Barbara Perkins. New York: McGraw-Hill, 1994. 404–13.

———. "Mark Twain: An Inquiry." In *William Dean Howells as Critic*. Ed. Edwin H. Cady. Boston: Routledge, 1973. 337–51.

———. "My Mark Twain." In *Literary Friends and Acquaintance*. Ed. David F. Hiatt and Edwin Cady. Bloomington: Indiana University Press, 1968. 256–322.

———. "Review of Mark Twain's Sketches, New and Old." In *Mark Twain's Letters*.

Vol. 6, *1874–1875*. Ed. Michael B. Frank and Harriet Elinor Smith. Berkeley: University of California Press, 2002. 655–58.

Humboldt Register (Nevada). "Mark Twain." June 11, 1864, 3.

Huntington, James F. "In Reply to General Pleasonton." *Century* 33 (January 1887): 471–72.

Ingalls, Major G. W. "Washoe County." In *The History of Nevada*. Ed. Sam P. Davis. Vol. 2. Las Vegas: Nevada Publications, 1913. 1004–41.

Jefferson, Thomas. *Memoirs, Correspondences, and Private Papers of Thomas Jefferson*. Ed. Thomas Jefferson Randolph. 4 vols. London: Henry Colburn and Richard Bentley, 1829.

Johnson, Andrew. "First Annual Message." In *A Compilation of the Messages and Papers of the Presidents*. Vol. 8. Ed. James D. Richardson. New York: Bureau of National Literature, 1897. 3551–69.

———. "Proclamations." In *A Compilation of the Messages and Papers of the Presidents*. Vol. 8. Ed. James D. Richardson. New York: Bureau of National Literature, 1897. 3504–31.

———. "Third Annual Message." In *A Compilation of the Messages and Papers of the Presidents*. Vol. 8. Ed. James D. Richardson. New York: Bureau of National Literature, 1897. 3756–79.

———. Veto Messages. In *A Compilation of the Messages and Papers of the Presidents*. Vol. 8. Ed. James D. Richardson. New York: Bureau of National Literature, 1897. 3729–33.

Johnson, Robert Underwood. Unpublished correspondence to Mark Twain, Mark Twain Project, University of California at Berkeley.

Johnson, Robert Underwood, and Clarence Buel. "Preface." In *Battles and Leaders of the Civil War*. Ed. Robert Johnson and Clarence Buel. New York: Castle Books, 1956. ix–xi.

Journal of the Congress of the Confederate States of America, 1861–1865. 7 vols. Washington: Government Printing Office, 1904.

Kaplan, Sidney. "The Miscegenation Issue in the Election of 1864." *The Journal of Negro History* 34 (1949): 274–343.

Klement, Frank L. "Catholics as Copperheads During the Civil War." *The Catholic Historical Review* 80 (1994): 36–57.

Koselleck, Reinhart. *The Practice of Conceptual History: Timing History, Spacing Concepts*. Trans. Todd Samuel Presner et al. Stanford: Stanford University Press, 2002.

Kreidberg, Lt. Col. Marvin A., and First Lt. Merton G. Henry. *History of the Military Mobilization in the United States Army, 1775–1945*. Washington, D.C.: Department of the Army, 1955.

Larsen, Sylvia S. "Low, Frederick Ferdinand." In *American National Biography Online*.

New York: Oxford University Press, 2000. Access date June 10, 2009.

Lawson, Emilie. "Abraham Lincoln." San Francisco *Daily Evening Bulletin,* April 19, 1865, 3.

Leisy, Ernest, ed. *The Letters of Quintus Curtius Snodgrass.* Dallas: Southern Methodist University Press, 1946.

Leon, Phillip. *Mark Twain and West Point: America's Favorite Storyteller at the United States Military Academy.* Toronto: ECW Press, 1996.

The Liberator. "Political Miscegenation." April 8, 1864, 1.

———. "The Slander on the Teachers." April 8, 1864, 1.

Lillard, Richard G. "Contemporary Reaction to 'The Empire City Massacre.'" *American Literature* 16 (1944): 198–203.

Lincoln, Abraham. "Autobiography Written for John L. Scripps." In *The Collected Works of Abraham Lincoln.* Vol. 4. Ed. Roy P. Basler, Marion D. Pratt, and Lloyd A. Dunlap. New Brunswick, N.J.: Rutgers University Press, 1953. 60–67.

———. "Fourth Annual Message," December 6, 1864. In *A Compilation of the Messages and Papers of the Presidents.* Vol. 8. New York: Bureau of National Literature, 1897. 3444–56.

———. "'A House Divided': Speech at Springfield, Illinois" [speech at the Republican State Convention]. In *The Collected Works of Abraham Lincoln.* Vol. 2. Ed. Roy P. Basler, Marion Pratt, and Lloyd Dunlap. New Brunswick, N.J.: Rutgers University Press, 1953. 461–69.

———. "Second Annual Message." December 1, 1862. In *A Compilation of the Messages and Papers of the Presidents.* Vol. 7. New York: Bureau of National Literature, 1897. 3327–43.

———. "Second Inaugural Address," March 4, 1865. In *A Compilation of the Messages and Papers of the Presidents.* Vol. 8. New York: Bureau of National Literature, 1897. 3477–78.

Lorch, Fred W. "Mark Twain and the 'Campaign that Failed.'" *American Literature* 12 (1941): 454–70.

———. "Review of *Mark Twain of the Enterprise.*" *American Literature* 30 (1958): 125–27.

———. *The Trouble Begins at Eight: Mark Twain's Lecture Tours.* Ames: Iowa State University Press, 1966.

Lowell, James Russell. *The Poetical Works of James Russell Lowell.* Boston: Houghton Mifflin and Company, 1890.

Lynn, Kenneth. *Mark Twain and Southwestern Humor.* Westport, Conn.: Greenwood, 1959.

Mack, Effie Mona. *Mark Twain in Nevada.* New York: Charles Scribner's Sons, 1947.

Mattson, J. Stanley. "Mark Twain on War and Peace: The Missouri Rebel and 'The Campaign that Failed.'" *American Quarterly* 20 (1968): 783–94.

McCorkle, John. *Three Years with Quantrill*. Norman: University of Oklahoma Press, 1992.

McDougall, Walter A. *Throes of Democracy: The American Civil War Era: 1829–1877.* New York: HarperCollins, 2008.

McPherson, James M. *Ordeal by Fire: The Civil War and Reconstruction.* New York: Alfred A. Knopf, 1982.

McReynolds, Edwin C. *Missouri: A History of the Crossroads State.* Norman: University of Oklahoma Press, 1962.

Messent, Peter. *The Short Works of Mark Twain: A Critical Study.* Philadelphia: University of Pennsylvania Press, 2001.

Methodist Quarterly Review. "Pamphlets." 16 (April 1864): 354.

Michelson, Bruce. *Mark Twain on the Loose: A Comic Writer and the American Self.* Amherst: University of Massachusetts Press, 1995.

"Miscegenation Indorsed by the Republican Party." Campaign Document, No. 11. "Sold at 13 Park Row, New York, and at all Democratic Newspaper Offices, at $1 per 1,000 pages." New York: n.d.

Missouri Courier (Hannibal). "Abolitionist Incendiaries." September 22, 1853, 1.

———. "Another Abolition Riot—Rights of a Missourian Outraged." October 16, 1851, 2.

———. "Burning a Negro for Murder." July 28, 1853, 1.

———. "Negro Stealing." November 10, 1853, 2.

Morison, Samuel Eliot, Henry Steele Commager, and William E. Leuchtenburg. *The Growth of the American Republic.* 2 vols. New York: Oxford University Press, 1980.

Morris. Richard B. *Encyclopedia of American History.* New York: Harper & Row, 1976.

Morrow, Patrick D. "Bret Harte, Mark Twain, and the San Francisco Circle." In *A Literary History of the American West.* Ed. J. Golden Taylor. Fort Worth: Texas Christian University Press, 1987. 339–58.

Myers, Robert Manson, ed. *The Children of Pride: A True Story of Georgia and the Civil War.* New Haven: Yale University Press, 1972.

The Nation. "The Two Hundred Thousand and First Curiosity in Congress." March 7, 1867, 190.

New York Herald, "Barnum at His Tricks Again—A New Political Feejee Mermaid." February 27, 1867, 6.

———. "Two Barnums in the Field." February 21, 1867, 6.

Nicolay, John G., and John Hay. *Abraham Lincoln: A History.* Vol. 1. New York: The Century Company, 1914.

Nichols, Roy F. "Introduction." In *Battles and Leaders of the Civil War.* Ed. Robert Johnson and Clarence Buel. New York: Castle Books, 1956. iii–vii.

Norcross, Hon. Frank H. "The Bench and the Bar." In *The History of Nevada*. Ed. Sam P. Davis. Las Vegas: Nevada Publications, 1913. 273–314.

The Old Guard. "Civilization in the Free and 'Slave' States." 2 (May 1864): 2–10.

Owens, Harry P. *Steamboats and the Cotton Economy: River Trade in the Yazoo–Mississippi Delta*. Jackson: University Press of Mississippi, 1990.

Owens, Kenneth. "Pattern and Structure in Western Territorial Politics." *The Western Historical Quarterly* 1 (1970): 373–92.

Paine, Albert Bigelow. *Mark Twain: A Biography*. 2 vols. New York: Harper & Brothers, 1912.

Palmyra Spectator (Missouri). "Gen. Thos. A. Harris." April 11, 1895, 1.

Parrish, Tom Z. "Civil War." In *The Mark Twain Encyclopedia*. Ed. J. R. LeMaster and James D. Wilson. New York: Garland Publishing, Inc., 1993. 146–49.

Parrish, William E. *Turbulent Partnership: Missouri and the Union, 1861–1865*. Columbia: University of Missouri Press, 1963.

Parrott, T. M. "Mark Twain: Made in America." Reprinted in *Mark Twain: The Critical Heritage*. Ed. Frederick Anderson and Kenneth Sanderson. New York: Barnes & Noble, 1971. 243–53.

Peck, Gunther. "Manly Gambles: The Politics of Risk on the Comstock Lode, 1860–1880." *Journal of Social History* 26 (1993): 701–23.

Perry, Mark. *Grant and Twain: The Story of an American Friendship*. New York: Random House, 2005.

Pettit, Arthur G. "Mark Twain and the Negro, 1867–1869." *The Journal of Negro History* 56 (1971): 88–96.

———. *Mark Twain & the South*. Lexington: University Press of Kentucky, 1974.

———. "Mark Twain's Attitude Toward the Negro in the West, 1861–1867." *The Western Historical Quarterly* 1 (1970): 51–62.

Polakoff, Keith Ian. *The Politics of Inertia: The Election of 1876 and the End of Reconstruction*. Baton Rouge: Louisiana State University Press, 1973.

Pollard, Edward Alfred. *The Lost Cause: A New Southern History of the War of the Confederates*. New York: E. B. Treat, 1868.

Potter, David M. *The Impending Crisis, 1848–1861*. New York: Harper Torchbooks, 1976.

Randall, James Ryder. "Maryland." In *Poets of the Civil War*. Ed. J. D. McClatchy. New York: Library of America, 2005. 179–81.

Reese River Reveille (Austin, Nevada). "The Gridley Sack of Flour and the Sacramento Star." May 31, 1864, 2.

Report No. 420. *Report of Committees of the Senate of the United States for the First Session of the Forty-Fourth Congress, 1875–76*. 3 vols. Washington: Government Printing Office, 1876. Vol. 2, 1–3.

Rhodehamel, John, and Louise Taper. "Introduction." In "*Right or Wrong, God Judge*

Me": The Writings of John Wilkes Booth. Ed. John Rhodehamel and Louise Taper. Urbana: University of Illinois Press, 1997. 1–21.

Richards, H. M. M. "Citizens of Gettysburg in Battle." *Century* 33 (January 1887): 472–73.

Richardson, James D., ed. *A Compilation of the Messages and Papers of the Presidents.* 20 vols. New York: Bureau of National Literature, 1897.

Robinson, Forrest G. "Afterword." In *Merry Tales,* by Mark Twain. New York: Oxford University Press, 1996. 1–13.

Rogers, Franklin. "Clemens' Political Affiliations Bearing on "L'Homme Qui Rit." In *Mark Twain's Satires & Burlesques.* Ed. Franklin Rogers. Berkeley: University of California Press, 1967. 460–64.

———. *Mark Twain's Burlesque Patterns, as Seen in the Novels and Narratives, 1855–1885.* Dallas: Southern Methodist University Press, 1960.

Root, George F. "Just Before the Battle, Mother." In *The American Civil War: An Anthology of Essential Writings.* Ed. Ian Frederick Finseth. New York: Routledge, 2006. 353.

Sacramento Daily Union. "Miscegenation." May 21, 1864, 2.

———. "Miscegenation Sent Home." June 1, 1864, 2.

———. "Rogues." May 23, 1864, 3.

———. "Untitled (Shiloh Dutchman Joke)." May 28, 1864, 3.

Saxon, A. H. *P. T. Barnum: The Legend and the Man.* New York: Columbia University Press, 1989.

Scharnhorst, Gary. "Mark Twain's Imbroglio with the San Francisco Police: Three Lost Texts." *American Literature* 62 (1990): 686–91.

Schultz, John. "New Letters of Mark Twain." *American Literature* 8 (1936): 47–51.

Schmitz, Neil. "Mark Twain, Traitor." *Arizona Quarterly* 63 (2007): 25–37.

———. "Mark Twain's Civil War: Humor's Reconstructive Writing." In *The Cambridge Companion to Mark Twain.* Ed. Forrest G. Robinson. Cambridge: Cambridge University Press, 1995. 74–92.

Simon, John Y. "Introduction." In *General Grant by Mathew Arnold with a Rejoinder by Mark Twain.* Ed. John Y. Simon. Kent, Ohio: Kent State University Press, 1995.

Simpson, Claude M. "Captain Jim and the 'Third House.'" *Western Folklore* 9, no. 2 (1950): 101–10.

Sloane, David E. E. *Mark Twain as a Literary Comedian.* Baton Rouge: Louisiana State University Press, 1979.

Smith, Henry Nash. *Mark Twain of the Enterprise: Newspaper Articles and Other Documents 1862–1864.* Ed. Henry Nash Smith with the Assistance of Frederick Anderson. Berkeley: University of California Press, 1957.

Snead, Colonel Thomas L. "The First Year of the War in Missouri." In *Battles and*

Leaders of the Civil War. Vol. 1. Ed. Robert Johnson and Clarence Buel. New York: Castle Books, 1956. 262–77.

Stanton, Edwin M. "Contraband of War." In *Readings in American Constitutional History, 1776–1876.* Ed. Allen Johnson. New York: Houghton Mifflin Company, 1912. 500–502.

Stewart, Senator William M. *Reminiscences of Senator William M. Stewart of Nevada.* Ed. George Rothwell Brown. New York: The Neale Publishing Company, 1908.

Stillé, Charles J. *History of the United States Sanitary Commission. Being the General Report of its Work During the War of the Rebellion.* Philadelphia: J. B. Lippincott & Co, 1866.

Stoddard, Henry L. *As I Knew Them: Presidents and Politics from Grant to Coolidge.* New York: Harper & Row, 1927.

Story, Justice Joseph. "Prigg v. Pennsylvania." In *Readings in American Constitutional History, 1776–1876.* Ed. Allen Johnson. New York: Houghton Mifflin Company, 1912. 416–21.

Taney, Chief Justice Roger. "Dred Scott, Plaintiff in Error, v. John F. A. Sanford." In *Readings in American Constitutional History, 1776–1876.* Ed. Allen Johnson. New York: Houghton Mifflin Company, 1912. 436–43.

Taylor, Richard. *Destruction and Reconstruction: Personal Experiences of the Late War.* New York: D. Appleton and Company, 1879.

Territorial Enterprise (Virginia City, Nevada). "Abraham Lincoln." April 18, 1865, 4.

———. "THE ASSASSINATION." April 18, 1865, 8.

———. "J. Wilkes Booth—A Modern Erostratus." April 18, 1865, 4.

Thompson, Charles Miner. "Mark Twain as an Interpreter of American Character." *The Atlantic Monthly* 79 (1897): 443–50.

Tilton, Theodore. "The Union of Races." *The Independent*, February 25, 1864, 4.

Tourgée, Albion W. *A Fool's Errand.* Cambridge, Mass.: Harvard University Press, 1961.

———. "The South as a Field for Fiction." In *The American Civil War: An Anthology of Essential Writings.* Ed. Ian Frederick Finseth. New York: Routledge, 2006. 533–38.

Twain, Mark. *Adventures of Huckleberry Finn.* Ed. Victor Fischer, Lin Salamo, and Walter Blair. Berkeley: University of California Press, 2003.

———. "An Important Question Settled." *Cincinnati Evening Chronicle*, March 9, 1868, 3.

———. "Another Romance." In *Mark Twain: San Francisco Correspondent.* Book Club of California, 1957. 29–32.

———. "Another Traitor—Hang Him!" [Fragment]. In *Mark Twain in Virginia City.* Ed. Paul Fatout. Bloomington: Indiana University Press, 1964. 180.

——. "Answers to Correspondents" (June 3, 1865). In *Early Tales and Sketches.* Vol. 2,*1864–1865.* Ed. Edgar M. Branch et al. Berkeley: University of California Press, 1981. 174–80.

——. "Answers to Correspondents" (June 10, 1865). In *Early Tales and Sketches.* Vol. 2, *1864–1865.* Ed. Edgar M. Branch et al. Berkeley: University of California Press, 1981. 181–86.

——. "Answers to Correspondents" (June 24, 1865). In *Early Tales and Sketches.* Vol. 2, *1864–1865.* Ed. Edgar M. Branch et al. Berkeley: University of California Press, 1981. 197–207.

——. "Answers to Correspondents" (July 8, 1865). In *Early Tales and Sketches.* Vol. 2, *1864–1865.* Ed. Edgar M. Branch et al. Berkeley: University of California Press, 1981. 219–32.

——. "As Regards Patriotism." In *Mark Twain: Collected Tales, Sketches, Speeches, and Essays, 1891–1910.* New York: Library of America, 1992. 476–78.

——. "At Home Again." In *Mark Twain's Travels with Mr. Brown.* Ed. Franklin Walker and G. Ezra Dane. New York: Russell & Russell, 1971. 131–40.

——. *The Autobiography of Mark Twain.* Ed. Charles Neider. New York: HarperPerennial, 1990. (1959).

——. "The Ballad Affliction." In *Mark Twain's San Francisco.* Ed. Bernard Taper. New York: McGraw-Hill Book Company, Inc., 1963. 128–30.

——. "Barnum's First Speech in Congress (By Spiritual Telegraph)." In *Mark Twain: Collected Tales, Sketches, Speeches, and Essays, 1852–1890.* New York: Library of America, 1992. 210–13.

——. "Battle Hymn of the Republic (Brought Down to Date)." In *Mark Twain: Collected Tales, Sketches, Speeches, and Essays, 1891–1910.* New York: Library of America, 1992. 474–75.

——. "Bigler vs. Tahoe." In *Early Tales and Sketches.* Vol. 1, *1851–1864.* Ed. Edgar M. Branch et al. Berkeley: University of California Press, 1979. 290.

——. "Bishop Speech" (October, 1907). In *Mark Twain Speaking.* Ed. Paul Fatout. Iowa City: University of Iowa Press, 1976. 590–95.

——. "A Bloody Massacre Near Carson." In *Early Tales and Sketches.* Vol. 1, *1851–1864.* Ed. Edgar M. Branch et al. Berkeley: University of California Press, 1979. 324–26.

——. "Blue and Gray Pay Tribute to Lincoln." *The New York Times,* February 12, 1901, 1.

——. "Calaboose Theatricals." In *Clemens of the Call.* Ed. Edgar M. Branch. Berkeley: University of California Press, 1969. 141–42.

——. "Cannibalism in the Cars." In *Mark Twain: Collected Tales, Sketches, Speeches, and Essays, 1852–1890.* New York: Library of America, 1992. 269–77.

——. "Caustic." [Burlesque poem on the Lincoln assassination]. In *Mark Twain's*

San Francisco. Ed. Bernard Taper. New York: McGraw-Hill Book Company, Inc., 1963. 159–60.

———. "The Character of Man." In *Mark Twain: Collected Tales, Sketches, Speeches, and Essays, 1852–1890*. New York: Library of America, 1992. 854–58.

———. *Clemens of the "Call": Mark Twain in San Francisco*. Ed. Edgar Marquess Branch. Berkeley: University of California Press, 1969.

———. "Concerning Gen. Grant's Intentions." In *Mark Twain: Collected Tales, Sketches, Speeches, and Essays, 1852–1890*. New York: Library of America, 1992. 282–84.

———. *A Connecticut Yankee in King Arthur's Court*. Ed. Bernard L. Stein. Berkeley: University of California Press, 1979.

———. "A Couple of Sad Experiences." In *Mark Twain: Collected Tales, Sketches, Speeches, and Essays, 1852–1890*. New York: Library of America, 1992. 388–95.

———. "The Day We Celebrate." In *Mark Twain: Collected Tales, Sketches, Speeches, and Essays, 1891–1910*. New York: Library of America, 1992. 820–21.

———. "Dinner Speech" (March 17, 1909). In *Mark Twain Speaking*. Ed. Paul Fatout. Iowa City: University of Iowa Press, 1976. 637–39.

———. "Disgraceful Persecution of a Boy." In *Mark Twain: Collected Tales, Sketches, Speeches, and Essays, 1852–1890*. New York: Library of America, 1992. 379–82.

———. "A Duel Prevented." In *Early Tales and Sketches*. Vol. 1, *1851–1864*. Ed. Edgar M. Branch et al. Berkeley: University of California Press, 1979. 265–66.

———. "Editorial Puffing." In *Early Tales and Sketches*. Vol. 2, *1864–1865*. Ed. Edgar M. Branch et al. Berkeley: University of California Press, 1981. 331.

———. "Enlisted for the War." In *Clemens of the Call*. Ed. Edgar M. Branch. Berkeley: University of California Press, 1969. 145.

———. "The Facts in the Case of the Great Beef Contract." In *Mark Twain: Collected Tales, Sketches, Speeches, and Essays, 1852–1890*. New York: Library of America, 1992. 367–73.

———. "The Facts in the Case of the Senate Doorkeeper." *Twainian* 6 (1947): 3–4.

———. "The Facts Concerning the Recent Important Resignation." *Twainian* 5 (May–June 1946): 1–3.

———. "The Facts Concerning the Recent Resignation." In *Mark Twain: Collected Tales, Sketches, Speeches, and Essays, 1852–1890*. New York: Library of America, 1992. 240–46.

———. "The Famous Sanitary Flour Sack." *New York Tribune*, December 13, 1870, 5.

———. "Female Suffrage." In *Mark Twain: Collected Tales, Sketches, Speeches, and Essays, 1852–1890*. New York: Library of America, 1992. 224–27.

———. "Fitz Smythe's Horse." In *Early Tales and Sketches*. Vol. 2, *1864–1865*. Ed. Edgar M. Branch et al. Berkeley: University of California Press, 1981. 345–46.

———. *Following the Equator: A Journey Around the World*. Hartford, Conn.: American Publishing Company, 1897.

———. "Fourth of July." In *Clemens of the Call*. Ed. Edgar M. Branch. Berkeley: University of California Press, 1969. 87–90.

———. "Fourth of July Speech in London." In *Mark Twain: Collected Tales, Sketches, Speeches, and Essays, 1852–1890*. New York: Library of America, 1992. 556–58.

———. "Funeral Oration over the Grave of the Democratic Party." In *Mark Twain Speaking*. Ed. Paul Fatout. Iowa City: University of Iowa Press, 1976. 146–48.

———. "Goldsmith's Friend Abroad Again." In *Mark Twain: Collected Tales, Sketches, Speeches, and Essays, 1852–1890*. New York: Library of America, 1992. 455–70.

———. "Gorgeous New Romance, By Fitz Smythe!" In *Mark Twain: San Francisco Correspondent*. Ed. Henry Nash Smith and Frederick Anderson. Book Club of California, 1957. 25–28.

———. "Gossip at the National Capital." (February 1, 1868). *New York Herald*, February 3, 1868, 5.

———. "The Great Prize Fight." In *Mark Twain's San Francisco*. Ed. Bernard Taper. New York: McGraw-Hill, 1963. 15–24.

———. "History of the Gold and Silver Bars—How They Do Things in Washoe." In *Mark Twain of the Enterprise: Newspaper Articles and Other Documents 1862–1864*. Ed. Henry Nash Smith with the Assistance of Frederick Anderson. Berkeley: University of California Press, 1957. 185–89.

———. "L'Homme Qui Rit." In *Mark Twain's Satires & Burlesques*. Ed. Franklin Rogers. Berkeley: University of California Press, 1967. 40–48.

———. "How Dare You." (attrib.). In *Early Tales and Sketches*. Vol. 2, *1864–1865*. Ed. Edgar M. Branch et al. Berkeley: University of California Press, 1981. 512.

———. "How I Escaped Being Killed in a Duel." In *Mark Twain: Collected Tales, Sketches, Speeches, and Essays, 1852–1890*. New York: Library of America, 1992. 543–46.

———. "How Is It?—How It Is." [Fragment]. In *Mark Twain's Letters*. Vol. 1, *1853–1866*. Ed. Edgar Marquess Branch, Michael B. Frank, and Kenneth M. Sanderson. Berkeley: University of California Press, 1988. 289.

———. "An Important Question Settled." *Cincinnati Evening Chronicle*, March 9, 1868, 3.

———. *The Innocents Abroad*. Hartford, Conn.: The American Publishing Company, 1869.

———. "Jane Lampton Clemens." In *Mark Twain's Hannibal, Huck & Tom*. Ed. Walter Blair. Berkeley: University of California Press, 1969. 41–53.

———. "Letter from Carson City." In *Early Tales and Sketches*. Vol. 1, *1851–1864*. Ed. Edgar M. Branch et al. Berkeley: University of California Press, 1979. 192–98.

———. "Letter from Mark Twain" (May 16, 1863). In *Early Tales and Sketches*. Vol. 1, *1851–1864*. Ed. Edgar M. Branch et al. Berkeley: University of California Press, 1979. 250–53.

———. "Letter from Mark Twain, Carson City, November 7, 1863." In *Mark Twain of the Enterprise: Newspaper Articles and Other Documents 1862–1864*. Ed. Henry Nash Smith with the assistance of Frederick Anderson. Berkeley: University of California Press, 1957. 86–89.

———. "Letter from Mark Twain, Carson City, December 5, 1863." In *Mark Twain of the Enterprise: Newspaper Articles and Other Documents 1862–1864*. Ed. Henry Nash Smith with the assistance of Frederick Anderson. Berkeley: University of California Press, 1957. 92–95.

———. "Letter from Mark Twain, Carson City, December 12, 1863." In *Mark Twain of the Enterprise: Newspaper Articles and Other Documents 1862–1864*. Ed. Henry Nash Smith with the assistance of Frederick Anderson. Berkeley: University of California Press, 1957. 95–100.

———. "Letter from Mark Twain, Carson City, January 14, 1864." [Miss Clapp's School]. In *Early Tales and Sketches*. Vol. 1, *1851–1864*. Ed. Edgar M. Branch et al. Berkeley: University of California Press, 1979. 334–38.

———. "Letter from Mark Twain, Carson City, April 25, 1864." In *Mark Twain of the Enterprise: Newspaper Articles and Other Documents 1862–1864*. Ed. Henry Nash Smith with the assistance of Frederick Anderson. Berkeley: University of California Press, 1957. 178–82.

———. "The Lick House Ball." In *Early Tales and Sketches*. Vol. 1, *1851–1864*. Ed. Edgar M. Branch et al. Berkeley: University of California Press, 1979. 314–19.

———. *Life on the Mississippi. Mark Twain: Mississippi Writings*. New York: Library of America, 1982. 217–616.

———. "A Lincoln Memorial." *The New York Times*, January 13, 1907, 1.

———. "Lotos Club Dinner Speech" (November 11, 1893). In *Mark Twain Speaking*. Ed. Paul Fatout. Iowa City: University of Iowa Press, 1976. 265–68.

———. "Lucretia Smith's Soldier." In *Early Tales and Sketches*. Vol. 2, *1864–1865*. Ed. Edgar M. Branch et al. Berkeley: University of California Press, 1981. 128–33.

———. "Man's Place in the Animal World." In *What Is Man? And Other Philosophical Writings*. Ed. Paul Baender. Berkeley: University of California Press, 1973. 80–89.

———. "Map of Paris." In *Mark Twain: Collected Tales, Sketches, Speeches, and Essays, 1852–1890*. New York: Library of America, 1992. 471–76.

———. *Mark Twain at the Buffalo Express: Articles and Sketches by America's Favorite Humorist*. Ed. Joseph B. McCullough and Janice McIntire-Strasburg. DeKalb: Northern Illinois University Press, 1999.

———. "'Mark Twain' in the Metropolis." In *Early Tales and Sketches*. Vol. 2, *1864–1865*. Ed. Edgar M. Branch et al. Berkeley: University of California Press, 1981. 9–12.

———. "Mark Twain in Washington, (January 12, 1868)." *Alta California*, February 19, 1868.

———. *Mark Twain of the Enterprise: Newspaper Articles and Other Documents 1862–1864.* Ed. Henry Nash Smith with the assistance of Frederick Anderson. Berkeley: University of California Press, 1957.

———. "Mark Twain on the Colored Man." In *Early Tales and Sketches.* Vol. 2, *1864–1865.* Ed. Edgar M. Branch et al. Berkeley: University of California Press, 1981. 248–49.

———. *Mark Twain–Howells Letters: The Correspondence of Samuel Langhorne Clemens and William D. Howells.* 2 vols. Ed. Henry Nash Smith. Cambridge, Mass.: Harvard University Press, 1960.

———. "Mark Twain's' Letter. (July 12, 1863)." *Twainian* 11 (January–February 1952): 2–3.

———. "Mark Twain's' Letter. (August 2, 1863)." *Twainian* 11 (March–April 1952): 1–3.

———. "Mark Twain's Letter (February 14, 1868)." *Chicago Republican,* February 19, 1868.

———. "Mark Twain's Letter (February 21, 1868)." *Chicago Republican,* March 1, 1868.

———. *Mark Twain's Letters from Hawaii.* Ed. A. Grove Day. Honolulu: University of Hawaii Press, 1975.

———. *Mark Twain's Letters.* Vol. 1, *1853–1866.* Ed. Edgar Marquess Branch, Michael B. Frank, and Kenneth M. Sanderson. Berkeley: University of California Press, 1988.

———. *Mark Twain's Letters.* Vol. 2, *1867–1868.* Ed. Harriet Elinor Smith and Richard Bucci. Berkeley: University of California Press, 1990.

———. *Mark Twain's Letters.* Vol. 3, *1869.* Ed. Victor Fischer and Michael B. Frank. Berkeley: University of California Press, 1992.

———. *Mark Twain's Letters.* Vol. 4, *1870–1871.* Ed. Victor Fischer and Michael B. Frank. Berkeley: University of California Press, 1995.

———. *Mark Twain's Letters.* Vol. 5, *1872–1873.* Ed. Lin Salamo and Harriet Elinor Smith. Berkeley: University of California Press, 1997.

———. *Mark Twain's Letters.* Vol. 6, *1874–1875.* Ed. Michael B. Frank and Harriet Elinor Smith. Berkeley: University of California Press, 2002.

———. *Mark Twain's Letters.* 2 vols. *The Writings of Mark Twain Definitive Edition.* 35 vols. Ed. Albert Bigelow Paine. New York: Gabriel Wells, 1923.

———. *Mark Twain's Letters from Hawaii.* Ed. A. Grove Day. Honolulu: University of Hawaii Press, 1975.

———. "Mark Twain's Letters from Washington, (December 4, 1867)." Virginia City *Territorial Enterprise,* December 22, 1867, 2.

———. "Mark Twain's Letters from Washington, (December 16, 1867)." Virginia City *Territorial Enterprise,* January 7, 1868, 2.

———. "Mark Twain's Letters from Washington, (December 20, 1867)." Virginia City *Territorial Enterprise,* January 11, 1868, 2.

———. "Mark Twain's Letters from Washington, (January 10, 1868)." Virginia City *Territorial Enterprise,* January 30, 1868, 2.

———. "Mark Twain's Letters from Washington, (January 31, 1868)." Virginia City *Territorial Enterprise,* February 8, 1868, 2.

———. "Mark Twain's Letters from Washington, (January 11, 1868)." Virginia City *Territorial Enterprise,* February 18, 1868, 2.

———. "Mark Twain's Letters from Washington, (January 30, 1868)." Virginia City *Territorial Enterprise,* February 27, 1868, 2.

———. "Mark Twain's Letters from Washington, (February, 1868)." Virginia City *Territorial Enterprise,* March 7, 1868, 2.

———. "Mark Twain's Letters from Washington, (February 22, 1868)." Virginia City *Territorial Enterprise,* March 13, 1868, 2.

———. "Mark Twain's Letters from Washington, (March 2, 1868)." Virginia City *Territorial Enterprise,* April 7, 1868, 2.

———. *Mark Twain's Letters to his Publishers, 1867–1894.* Ed. Hamlin Hill. Berkeley: University of California Press, 1967.

———. *Mark Twain's Notebooks and Journals.* Vol. 1, *1855–1873.* Ed. Frederick Anderson, Michael B. Frank, and Kenneth M. Sanderson. Berkeley: University of California Press, 1975.

———. *Mark Twain's Notebooks and Journals.* Vol. 2, *1877–1883.* Ed. Frederick Anderson, Lin Salamo, and Bernard Stein. Berkeley: University of California Press, 1975.

———. *Mark Twain's Notebooks and Journals.* Vol. 3, *1883–1891.* Ed. Robert Pack Browning, Michael B. Frank, and Lin Salamo. Berkeley: University of California Press, 1975.

———. *Mark Twain's San Francisco.* Ed. Bernard Taper. New York: McGraw-Hill, 1963.

———. *Mark Twain's Travels with Mr. Brown.* Ed. Franklin Walker and G. Ezra Dane. New York: Alfred A. Knopf, 1940.

———. "Miscegenation." In *Clemens of the Call.* Ed. Edgar M. Branch. Berkeley: University of California Press, 1969. 187.

———. "Miscegenation." In *Mark Twain of the Enterprise: Newspaper Articles and Other Documents 1862–1864.* Ed. Henry Nash Smith with the assistance of Frederick Anderson. Berkeley: University of California Press, 1957. 196–98.

———. "Mock Oration on the Dead Partisan." In *Mark Twain: Collected Tales, Sketches, Speeches, and Essays, 1852–1890,* New York: Library of America, 1992, 852–53.

———. "Monarchical and Republican Patriotism." In *Mark Twain's Weapons of*

Satire: Anti-Imperialist Writings on the Philippine-American War. Ed. Jim Zwick. Syracuse: Syracuse University Press, 1992. 190–91.

———. "My Late Senatorial Secretaryship." In *Mark Twain: Collected Tales, Sketches, Speeches, and Essays, 1852–1890*. New York: Library of America, 1992. 257–61.

———. "My Military History." In *Mark Twain: Collected Tales, Sketches, Speeches, and Essays, 1852–1890*. New York: Library of America, 1992. 679–82.

———. "Nevada State Constitutional Convention; Third House, Carson City, December 13, 1863." In *Mark Twain of the Enterprise: Newspaper Articles and Other Documents 1862–1864*. Ed. Henry Nash Smith with the assistance of Frederick Anderson. Berkeley: University of California Press, 1957. 100–110.

———. "No. 44, The Mysterious Stranger." In *Mark Twain's Mysterious Stranger Manuscripts*. Ed. William M. Gibson. Berkeley: University of California Press, 1969. 221–405.

———. "A Notable Conundrum." In *Mark Twain's San Francisco*. Ed. Bernard Taper. New York: McGraw-Hill Book Company, Inc., 1963. 53–57.

———. "The Old Thing." In *Early Tales and Sketches*. Vol. 2, *1864–1865*. Ed. Edgar M. Branch et al. Berkeley: University of California Press, 1981. 334–35.

———. "Petrified Man." In *Early Tales and Sketches*. Vol. 1, *1851–1864*. Ed. Edgar M. Branch et al. Berkeley: University of California Press, 1979. 159.

———. "A Philanthropic Nation." In *Clemens of the Call*. Ed. Edgar M. Branch. Berkeley: University of California Press, 1969. 109–10.

———. "Plymouth Rock and the Pilgrims." In *Mark Twain: Collected Tales, Sketches, Speeches, and Essays, 1891–1910*. New York: Library of America, 1992. 129–41.

———. "Political Speech (September 30, 1876)." In *Mark Twain Speaking*. Ed. Paul Fatout. Iowa City: University of Iowa Press, 1976. 97–99.

———. "Political Speech" (October 26, 1880). In *Mark Twain Speaking*. Ed. Paul Fatout. Iowa City: University of Iowa Press, 1976. 138–45.

———. "The Portraits." In *Mark Twain: San Francisco Correspondent*. Ed. Henry Nash Smith and Frederick Anderson. Book Club of California, 1957. 60–62.

———. "The Private History of a Campaign That Failed." In *Mark Twain: Collected Tales, Sketches, Speeches, and Essays, 1852–1890*. New York: Library of America, 1992. 863–82.

———. "The Reliable Contraband." In *Mark Twain Speaking*. Ed. Paul Fatout. Iowa City: University of Iowa Press, 1976. 38–41.

———. "Remarkable Dream." In *Early Tales and Sketches*. Vol. 2, *1864–1865*. Ed. Edgar M. Branch et al. Berkeley: University of California Press, 1981. 355–58.

———. "The Revised Catechism." In *Mark Twain: Collected Tales, Sketches, Speeches, and Essays, 1852–1890*. New York: Library of America, 1992. 539–40.

———. "The Righteous Shall Not Be Forgotten." *Bancroftiana* 115 (Fall 1999): 10, 12.

———. "Riley-Newspaper Correspondent." In *Mark Twain: Collected Tales, Sketches, Speeches, and Essays, 1852–1890.* New York: Library of America, 1992. 477–80.

———. *Roughing It.* Ed. Harriet Elinor Smith and Edgar Marquess Branch. Berkeley: University of California Press, 1993.

———. "Roughing It Lecture." In *Mark Twain Speaking.* Ed. Paul Fatout. Iowa City: University of Iowa Press, 1976. 48–64.

———. "San Francisco Letter, 24 or 26 December 1865." In *Early Tales and Sketches.* Vol. 2, *1864–1865.* Ed. Edgar M. Branch et al. Berkeley: University of California Press, 1981. 337–42.

———. "The Sanitary Ball." In *Early Tales and Sketches.* Vol. 1, *1851–1864.* Ed. Edgar M. Branch et al. Berkeley: University of California Press, 1979. 185–87.

———. "The Secret of Dr. Livingstone's Continued Voluntary Exile." In *Mark Twain: Collected Tales, Sketches, Speeches, and Essays, 1852–1890.* New York: Library of America, 1992. 541–42.

———. "The Sex in New York." In *Mark Twain's Travels with Mr. Brown.* Ed. Franklin Walker and G. Ezra Dane. New York: Russell & Russell, 1971. 226–28.

———. "Is Shakespeare Dead?" In *The Complete Essays of Mark Twain.* Ed. Charles Neider. New York: Da Capo, 1991. 407–54.

———. "Still Further Concerning That Conundrum." In *Mark Twain's San Francisco.* Ed. Bernard Taper. New York: McGraw-Hill Book Company, Inc., 1963. 58–62.

———. "The Story of Mamie Grant, the Child Missionary." In *Mark Twain's Satires & Burlesques.* Ed. Franklin Rogers. Berkeley: University of California Press, 1967. 31–39.

———. "The Stupendous Procession." In *Mark Twain's Fables of Man.* Ed. John S. Tuckey. Berkeley: University of California Press, 1972. 405–19.

———. "Take the Stand, Fitz Smythe." In *Early Tales and Sketches.* Vol. 2, *1864–1865.* Ed. Edgar M. Branch et al. Berkeley: University of California Press, 1981. 350–52.

———. "Thief-Catching." In *Mark Twain's San Francisco.* Ed. Bernard Taper. New York: McGraw-Hill Book Company, Inc., 1963. 157–58.

———. "Those Blasted Children." In *Early Tales and Sketches.* Vol. 1, *1851–1864.* Ed. Edgar M. Branch et al. Berkeley: University of California Press, 1979. 351–56.

———. "3,000 Years among the Microbes." In *"Which Was the Dream" and Other Symbolic Writings of the Later Years.* Ed. John S. Tuckey. Berkeley: University of California Press, 1967. 430–553.

———. "To the Person Sitting in Darkness." In *Mark Twain: Collected Tales, Sketches, Speeches, and Essays, 1891–1910.* New York: Library of America, 1992. 457–73.

———. "Tom Sawyer's Conspiracy." In *Mark Twain's Hannibal, Huck & Tom.* Ed. Walter Blair. Berkeley: University of California Press, 1969. 152–242.

———. "A True Story." In *Mark Twain: Collected Tales, Sketches, Speeches, and Essays, 1852–1890*. New York: Library of America, 1992. 578–82.

———. "Turncoats." In *Mark Twain: Collected Tales, Sketches, Speeches, and Essays, 1852–1890*. New York: Library of America, 1992. 849–51.

———. "Unfortunate Blunder." In *Early Tales and Sketches*. Vol. 1, *1851–1864*. Ed. Edgar M. Branch et al. Berkeley: University of California Press, 1979. 286–87.

———. "The United States of Lyncherdom." In *Mark Twain: Collected Tales, Sketches, Speeches, and Essays, 1891–1910*. New York: Library of America, 1992. 479–86.

———. Unpublished Notebook 48 (Old 38) 1905–1908, Mark Twain Papers TS, University of California at Berkeley.

———. "Villagers of 1840–3." In *Mark Twain's Hannibal, Huck & Tom*. Ed. Walter Blair. Berkeley: University of California Press, 1969. 23–40.

———. "The War Prayer." In *Mark Twain: Collected Tales, Sketches, Speeches, and Essays, 1891–1910*. New York: Library of America, 1992. 652–55.

———. *The Washoe Giant in San Francisco*. Ed. Franklin Walker. San Francisco: George Fields, 1938.

———. "Washoe.—'Information Wanted.'" In *Early Tales and Sketches*. Vol. 1, *1851–1864*. Ed. Edgar M. Branch et al. Berkeley: University of California Press, 1979. 367–71.

———. "What Have the Police Been Doing?" In *Mark Twain's San Francisco*. Ed. Bernard Taper. New York: McGraw-Hill Book Company, Inc., 1963. 189–91.

———. "The White House Funeral." In *Mark Twain's Letters*. Vol. 3, *1869*. Ed. Victor Fischer and Michael B. Frank. Berkeley: University of California Press, 1992. 458–66.

Twain, Mark, and Charles Dudley Warner. *The Gilded Age. A Tale of Today*. 2 vols. New York: Gabriel Wells, 1922.

Twainian "Gossip." 2 (June, 1940): 4.

Wakelyn, Jon L. "Thomas Harris." In *Biographical Dictionary of the Confederacy*. Ed. Frank E. Vandiver. Westport, Conn.: Greenwood Press, 1977. 218–19.

Walker, Franklin. *San Francisco's Literary Frontier*. New York: Alfred A. Knopf, 1939.

Walker, Franklin, ed. *The Washoe Giant in San Francisco*. San Francisco: George Fields, 1938.

The War of the Rebellion: A Compilation of the Official Records of the Union and Confederate Armies. Series II. 8 vols. Washington: Government Printing Office, 1899.

Warner, Ezra. and W. Buck Yearns. *Biographical Register of the Confederate Congress*. Baton Rouge: Louisiana State University Press, 1975. 109–10.

Weber, Jennifer L. *Copperheads: The Rise and Fall of Lincoln's Opponents in the North*. New York: Oxford University Press, 2006.

Webster, Samuel Charles. *Mark Twain, Businessman*. Ed. Samuel Charles Webster. Boston: Little, Brown and Company, 1946.

Webster, Noah. *An American Dictionary of the English Language, Thoroughly Revised, and Greatly Enlarged and Improved, by Chauncey A. Goodrich and Noah Porter.* Springfield: G. C. Merriam, 1864.

Wecter, Dixon. *Sam Clemens of Hannibal.* Boston: Houghton Mifflin, 1961.

Wienandt, Christopher. "Mark Twain, Nevada Frontier Journalism, and the Territorial Enterprise: Crisis in Credibility." Ph.D. diss. University of North Texas, May 1995.

Wilson, Edmund. *Patriotic Gore: Studies in the Literature of the American Civil War.* New York: Oxford University Press, 1962.

Zwick, Jim, ed. *Mark Twain's Weapons of Satire: Anti-Imperialist Writings on the Philippine-American War.* Syracuse: Syracuse University Press, 1992.

INDEX